KEEPING FAIT.
with
HUMAN RIGHTS

The Moral Traditions Series

Series Editors: David Cloutier, Kristin Heyer, Andrea Vicini, SJ

Founding Editor: James F. Keenan, SJ

SELECTED TITLES

The Acting Person and Christian Moral Life
Darlene Fozard Weaver

Aquinas on the Emotions: A Religious Ethical Inquiry
Diana Fritz Cates

Catholic Moral Theology in the United States: A History
Charles E. Curran

Creative Conformity: The Feminist Politics of US Catholic and Iranian Shi'i Women
Elizabeth M. Bucar

Defending Probabilism: The Moral Theology of Juan Caramuel
Julia Fleming

Family Ethics: Practices for Christians
Julie Hanlon Rubio

Kinship across Borders: A Christian Ethic of Immigration
Kristin E. Heyer

Loyal Dissent: Memoir of a Catholic Theologian
Charles E. Curran

Moral Evil
Andrew Michael Flescher

Overcoming Our Evil: Human Nature and Spiritual Exercises in Xunzi and Augustine
Aaron Stalnaker

Prophetic and Public: The Social Witness of U.S. Catholicism
Kristin E. Heyer

Sex, Violence, and Justice: Contraception and the Catholic Church
Aline H. Kalbian

The Sexual Person: Toward a Renewed Catholic Anthropology
Todd A. Salzman and Michael G. Lawler

The Social Mission of the US Catholic Church: A Theological Perspective
Charles E. Curran

Theological Bioethics: Participation, Justice, and Change
Lisa Sowle Cahill

KEEPING FAITH
with
HUMAN RIGHTS

Linda Hogan

Georgetown University Press / Washington, DC

Library of Congress Cataloging-in-Publication Data

Hogan, Linda, 1964– author.
Keeping faith with human rights / Linda Hogan.
pages   cm
Includes bibliographical references and index.
ISBN 978-1-62616-232-7 (hc : alk. paper) — ISBN 978-1-62616-233-4 (pb : alk. paper) —
ISBN 978-1-62616-234-1 (eb) 1. Human rights. 2. Human rights—Philosophy.
3. Human rights—Religious aspects—Christianity. 4. Human rights—Moral and
ethical aspects. I. Title.
JC571.H595 2015
323—dc23
2014047104

♾ This book is printed on acid-free paper meeting the requirements of the American National Standard for Permanence in Paper for Printed Library Materials.
22 21 20 19 18 17 16 15   9 8 7 6 5 4 3 2 First printing
Printed in the United States of America

Cover by Brad Norr Design.

Contents

Acknowledgments vii

Introduction 1

1. The Crisis of Legitimacy: Political and
Philosophical Perspectives 12

2. The Crisis of Meaning: Theological Perspectives 52

3. Ethical Formations: Constructing the Subject of
Human Rights 70

4. Building Discursive Bridges: Situated Knowledge, Embedded
Universalism, Plural Foundations 101

5. Resisting Culturalist Frameworks: Porous Communities,
Constructed Traditions 136

6. Resisting Gravity's Pull: Constructing Human Rights
through the Arts 172

Conclusion 205

Bibliography 211

Index 229

Acknowledgments

This work has been in gestation for many years, and during that time I have benefited from conversations with colleagues around the world on this critical issue of human rights. In particular I am grateful to my great friend James Keenan (Boston College) who has been a constant source of inspiration and who has led the way in bringing a global perspective to theological ethics. I have learned a great deal about the complexities associated with advancing human rights from colleagues with whom I have had an ongoing conversation for over a decade, especially Antonio Autiero (Germany), Agnes Brazal (Philippines), Lúcás Chan Yiu Sing (Hong Kong), M. T. Davila (Puerto Rico), Kristin Heyer (USA), Elias Omondi Opongo (Kenya), Agbonkhianmeghe E. Orobator (Nigeria), and Andrea Vicini (Italy), as well as from colleagues at the School of Religions, Peace Studies and Theology at Trinity College Dublin.

Thanks are also due to Richard Brown at Georgetown University Press, whose generosity and patience are much appreciated, and to Patti Bower and Glenn Saltzman for their professionalism.

My family and friends continue to be a source of joy and support, as does my friend and mentor Professor Enda McDonagh, to whom this work is dedicated.

Introduction

Human rights represent one of the great civilizing projects of modernity. From the promulgation in Paris in 1948 of the Universal Declaration of Human Rights to the subsequent embrace of this declaration by the newly independent states from Africa, Asia, and the Middle East, human rights have emerged as the primary discourse of global politics and as an increasingly prominent category in international and domestic legal systems. In the theological realm, the concept of human rights has all but replaced its antecedent, that of the natural right, while in the world of Christian social engagement, the language of human rights has become the lingua franca of political action. Indeed, the UN General Assembly's promotion of the Universal Declaration as "a common standard of achievement for all peoples and all nations" has garnered a remarkable degree of support in the six decades since its adoption.[1]

These successes notwithstanding, the category of human rights continues to be both controversial and contested. Philosopher and social reformer Jeremy Bentham's infamous dismissal of rights claims as "nonsense upon stilts" has now been applied to human rights and characterizes the deep skepticism in contemporary political philosophy regarding the concept.[2] Ironically, much of this skepticism has come from groups whose predecessors initially deployed the language of rights to claim their positions within the dominant discourse, that is, citizens of the former colonies, women, racial minorities, and other dispossessed peoples. Today, however, feminist and postcolonial actors are among the most vocal critics of human rights discourse. This philosophical skepticism is reinforced in the sphere of law by a legal positivism that denies credibility to human rights claims on the basis that there are no global mechanisms of enforcement. Theologians, too, have voiced their concern about the category, with the dispute about the theological appropriation of human rights being a particularly fractious version of the debate about the proper posture of Christianity vis-à-vis liberalism. Insofar as it is regarded as "liberalism gone global," human rights discourse is viewed by its theological critics as nothing more than individualism, secularism, and Western political imperialism in disguise. Furthermore, certain theological critics also claim that each time "Christians adopt one of the internationalized languages of modernity, they contribute to the social marginalization of their own narrative tradition."[3] This theological critique transcends traditional denominational lines and continues to flourish despite the widely acknowledged role that Christians played in the development of the idea of human rights and in the articulation of the Universal Declaration itself.

Highlighting the impact of such critiques, philosopher Conor Gearty strikes a serious note when he argues that the relative success that human rights discourse has achieved is now under threat and that the political and philosophical mood of our age presents challenges that may destroy the language of human rights for generations.[4] Gearty's assessment of the precarious nature of the category is confirmed by Johannes Morsink, in his *Inherent Human Rights.* However, whereas Gearty defends politics as the vehicle through which human rights can be rescued, Morsink argues for the need to go beyond the political and places his hope in the rearticulation of a strong metaphysical grounding for human rights.[5] While not endorsing the remedies proposed by either Gearty or Morsink, this work does share their concern about the future of human rights discourse, and seeks to address this by showing that it is both theoretically possible and politically necessary for theologians to keep faith with human rights. In this way this work stands within a long tradition of theological engagement with and defense of human rights norms. Recent works by David Hollenbach, Jack Mahoney, and Eithne Regan exemplify this in the Roman Catholic tradition, while George Newlands, John Nurser, and Esther Reed endorse the discourse from within various reformed perspectives and this work shares a common objective with these defenders of human rights.[6]

Keeping Faith with Human Rights is differently conceived and, although it has important implications for Christian ethics, is not intended to be specifically a work of Christian ethics. Rather it puts the issue of the future of human rights at its core and seeks to demonstrate that the foundations of human rights can be understood to lie in a pluralistic discourse that, although embedded in the politics of power, has nonetheless been productive of enduring values. It makes the case that, in the context of this reconceptualization of human rights discourse, the Christian tradition has an important role to play. Its importance lies both in the manner in which its world view has shaped many of the seminal ethical commitments that are now central to human rights and in its continuing role as a situated tradition alongside other traditions (be they religious or humanistic) in the ongoing constructive ethical project that is human rights. In terms of this project's positioning vis-à-vis Christian visions of ethics, therefore, it is shaped by but does not rely on them. However, it does want to insist that the Christian tradition keep faith with human rights, and seeks to show how, when human rights is conceived as a pluralistic discourse, this is both possible and necessary.

While not accepting the full force of the radical critique of "the Enlightenment project" and its liberal political manifestation (human rights), this work is nonetheless sympathetic to the postcolonial and feminist critics of human rights. Thus, rather than build the case for human rights on a philosophical system that has been so seriously undermined, I seek to recontextualize human rights within a broader frame of reference, thereby enabling it to address its limitations. As a result, I move away from traditional theological approaches that conceptualize human rights in terms of universal values, usually articulated in terms of either natural law or Christian deontology. Instead I draw on the constructivist strand of political philosophy to argue that human rights are best conceived in a threefold manner: as ethical assertions about the critical importance of certain values for human flourishing; as an emerging consensus generated by situated communities that are open to internally and externally generated social criticism; and as emancipatory politics whose modus operandi is ultimately that of persuasion. Each formulation seeks to articulate an essential dimension of human rights—namely, the normative, the dialogical, and the political. No single dimension alone adequately expresses the nature of human rights. Taken together, however, they capture the complexity of a discourse that, I argue, is situated somewhere between foundationalism and pragmatism. From the perspective of Christian social ethics, this threefold understanding of the nature of human rights is significant because it revalorizes the role of historic memory and of communitarian values in the search for a shared moral vision. It also allows for a prominent role for the lived experiences of communities of solidarity in the articulation of what these rights consist in as well as how they can best be secured. Moreover, it reorients human rights education so that it draws upon aesthetic resources as well as the more traditional modes of rational argumentation and in so doing situates it, appropriately, within the work of the moral imagination.

At the core of this book is the conviction that, its many defects notwithstanding, human rights language continues to be worth defending. Globalization has changed the nature of contemporary economic and political life to such an extent that all our debates about equality and justice must be embedded within this context, and human rights discourse provides us with a language that has a global resonance and reach through which such debate and decision can be pursued. That human rights language can keep the local and global simultaneously in view is also important since these spheres are now entangled to an unprecedented degree through the dynamic of globalization. Human rights norms play a dual role, so they allow us to identify the basic goods to which all human beings are entitled by virtue of our humanity, but they also articulate an account of human flourishing in community. Indeed, it is precisely this ability to speak both to those goods that are essential for the material and social well-being of individuals and to a fuller vision of human solidarity that has established its global appeal. Christians come to the language of human rights, I suggest, not as strangers to a modern discourse but rather from within their theological heritage. As Brian Tierney has demonstrated, there has been a long-standing theological language of rights that was generated from within the life of the Christian community and that was articulated in response to questions about how the good of the church could be protected, both in terms of its individual members and of the corporate body.[7] Thus, human rights language can function also within a theological frame and as a language through which the demands of Christian witness can be expressed.

Chapters 1 and 2 consider the crisis of meaning and legitimacy that has surrounded human rights and that has led Conor Gearty to ask if human

rights can survive. In these two chapters I discuss some of the most enduring critiques of human rights categories. Chapter 1 focuses on the political
and philosophical criticisms, while the concern of chapter 2 is with the
limitations of human rights categories from the theological perspective. In
each case I argue that human rights language has the capacity to transcend
these limitations, but only if it is developed in a particular manner. I argue
that, historically, human rights politics has functioned both as a form of
subjugated knowledge and as a dominatory discourse. As a result, I suggest we will need to consider whether and how it can be rearticulated in
such a way as to retain its ethical force while also acknowledging its contingent character.[8] I conclude these chapters by proposing a constructivist
approach to the nature and substance of human rights claims and suggest that human rights politics is best understood as a deliberative process
through which we articulate a set of moral expectations to which we can be
held to account.[9] Moreover, I argue that this constructivist understanding
of human rights has occasionally been evident in the discussions that both
preceded and succeeded the promulgation of the Universal Declaration
and supplements the more traditional historical narrative that conceptualizes human rights politics in terms of the progressive extension of liberal
philosophy to the four corners of the earth.

In the three chapters that follow, I focus on the main "pillars" of human
rights discourse—namely, the nature of personhood, the structure of moral
truth, and the role of community. In the case of each of these conceptualizations, the philosophical assumptions upon which they are built have
been contested. The purpose of these three chapters, therefore, is to reconstruct an account of each that is both philosophically credible and theologically resonant and that can serve as the basis for a revised understanding
of human rights. Although each of the categories discussed here merits
far more attention, my purpose is to suggest a revised approach rather
than to develop a complete theory. Thus, I focus respectively on the nature
of human personhood, the possibilities of attaining moral understanding,
and the role of communities in the mediation of value, and I argue that,
in each case, human rights would be more robust and more convincing if
these categories were recalibrated. I draw on feminist, communitarian, and
virtue theory in order to rearticulate the contours of a human rights ethic
and propose an understanding of human rights that is not grounded in the
universalist philosophy of liberalism but rather is built within a context of

tradition-thick, cross-cultural, multireligious conversations and is secured through emancipatory politics.

Chapter 3 focuses on the human person. Drawing on the critiques discussed in chapter 1, it argues that we must rethink the role that is ascribed to the concept of the human nature and ought not to persist with a human rights discourse that is bound to the remnants of an essentialist anthropology. Foucault has already alerted us to the fact that all conceptualizations of normative humanity are inevitably reflections of the cultural, political, and historical contexts from which they emerge. We see this exemplified, for instance, when we examine a range of theological texts and discover that, although the language of appealing to human nature is consistently present, the substance of what is regarded as natural changes. In this chapter, therefore, I move away from discussions that base human rights claims on what are perceived to be the natural, constant, and universal markers of humanness. Instead, I suggest that we need to develop a different way of thinking about the person as the subject of human rights and to resist the tendency to develop an account of human rights on the basis of a predetermined and fixed definition of "the human." I develop this approach through engagement with philosophers Gayatri Spivak and Judith Butler and theologians Kwok Pui-lan, Mercy Amba Oduyoye, and Agbonkhiameghe Orobator. In this context I focus on the experiences of relationality, of embodiment, and of solidarity in vulnerability, arguing that it is through reflection on the complexity of such challenges rather than through appeals to a reified and idealized concept of human nature that a more durable basis on which to pursue this profoundly ethical project will be established.

Chapter 4 takes up the epistemological assumptions on which human rights discourse is premised and argues that these too must be recalibrated in light of the legitimate distrust of universalist frameworks. In this chapter I develop an understanding of the nature of moral truth that, on the one hand, acknowledges the bounded condition of ethical knowledge while on the other eschews relativism and resists any retreat into parochialism. Traditionally, Christian social ethics has tended either to stress its universalist character while remaining silent about its tradition-dependent nature or to highlight its distinctiveness and ignored charges of relativism. I argue, however, that we do not have to choose between an ahistorical, abstract, and universalist moral framework that is blind to the particularities of its own origins and a communitarian ethic that cannot transcend them. Rather, building on the recognition that all ethical frameworks are ultimately tradition-dependent, I argue for an approach that is capable of recognizing the contingent nature of moral knowledge while distinguishing "authoritative from authoritarian uses of reason."[10] I draw on insights from Kwame Anthony Appiah, Richard Rorty, and Seyla Benhabib as well as from theologians Kwok Pui-lan, Felix Wilfred, and Jeffrey Stout to develop this line of thought. I argue that human rights discourse can be redescribed as a form of situated knowledge and as a particularly compelling form of embedded universalism. Redescribing human rights discourse thus allows us to think differently about the contested issue of the grounding of human rights. I challenge the traditional assumption that the viability of human rights discourse depends on the articulation of a single, universally persuasive account of its foundations and argue that the history of human rights has demonstrated that the discourse has endured precisely because it has been receptive to many different justifications. In this chapter my objective is not to construct a flawless epistemology but rather to develop a human rights ethic that can build upon the manifold ways in which values are embedded in culture, that can refine and redescribe our understandings of what justice entails, and that can continue to expand the range of our moral concern.

Chapter 5 focuses on the role of situated communities in the articulation of a human rights ethic. Building on the argument in chapters 3 and 4, I suggest that human rights discourse will flourish only when it accords proper recognition to comprehensive doctrines and when it acknowledges that there are different ways of accounting for why human beings can be said to have human rights. We are formed according to the rationalities of particular traditions and explain why we believe we can claim human rights by referring to specific religious or cultural categories. While acknowledging that we relate to human rights discourse from our specific "thick," culturally embedded vantage points, however, I also argue that we must avoid the tendency to essentialize communities or to reify traditions and cultures, whether they be religious or secular. Thus, in chapter 5 I bring a genealogical critique to bear on our discussion of the role of community and tradition in the construction of a shared ethic. A genealogical critique begins by accepting that the articulation of each community's distinctive world view and ethic is embedded in political processes. The historical processes that shape religious and other traditions involve choices between various and varying interpretations of the community's history, power struggles over the authorization and legitimation of the community's traditions, and disagreements about the criteria for belonging. Inevitably, therefore, there will be divergent views about the nature and status of particular beliefs and, perhaps more importantly, about where the power to define the limits of the tradition resides. So while it is vital that situated communities are acknowledged as having a role in the discourse of human rights, these communities and traditions should not be thought of as prediscursive entities that provide a refuge from the politics of knowledge. Rather, they must be acknowledged as being the products of historical and political processes through which their distinctiveness is constructed and according to which the parameters of orthodoxy are drawn. Of course, the politics of this history, especially the politics of the history of doctrine, is often obscured, or even denied by religious authorities who prefer to present an apolitical account of how the parameters of the tradition were and continue to be drawn. The fact that religious authorities frequently refuse to recognize the inescapably constructed nature of their traditions does not make it less true.

A community's ethic emerges in a discursive process and involves self-critical reflection in light of multiple interpretations. It is, therefore, a story of history and power. That it is a story of history and power creates the space wherein the debate about human rights can continue to occur. There will, of course, be conflicts, not only about whether particular human rights claims are appropriate but also about who speaks for a tradition and about the role of alternative interpretations and dissident voices. However, if we are to have a viable politics of human rights—one that will generate a consensus on which values must be secured for all people—then the manner in which we seek this consensus is of critical importance. It is possible that certain views will turn out to be incommensurable, and that claims about particular rights will continue to be contested. But human rights politics cannot shy away from these areas of dissonance and ambiguity. Nor can it expect that individuals will eventually exchange their inherited values for a human rights ethic that is developed independently of their respective comprehensive doctrines. Rather, a viable human rights ethic can only proceed on the basis that shared values will emerge through a dialogical engagement between multiple situated, historical communities, including religious communities, that are open to internally and externally generated social criticism.

Chapter 6 focuses on the challenges involved in building a durable culture of human rights. While the challenges are manifold, I have chosen to concentrate on the role that aesthetic resources can play in the creation of such a culture. Within the context of the aesthetic, I discuss the contribution that the literary and visual arts can make to the task of creating an imaginative space in which established parameters of moral concern can be challenged and expanded and from which a durable culture of human rights can be constructed. The chapter then considers in more detail how these art forms can help to expand the moral imagination and can enable a level of understanding that is qualitatively different from other more theoretical forms of discourse and argument. In particular, I discuss how the arts can provide a compelling account of where the threshold lies below which human dignity is irrevocably compromised, and how it can require us to confront more honestly the destructive nature of violence. In drawing out these particular dimensions of the ways in which the arts can expand the moral imagination, I argue that the arts can articulate registers of truth beyond the scientific and philosophical, thus making a unique contribution to the task of building a durable culture of human rights.

Human rights politics will only flourish if we can forge a genuinely inclusive, deliberative, cross-cultural conversation through which agreement on contested issues can be pursued. Given that our global and local conversations about human rights are shaped by the irreducible plurality of human religious experience, human rights politics must develop the capacity to engage with and facilitate intercultural and interreligious dialogue in this context. The practice of comparative theology and ethics will be an important component in this regard and will need to be pursued in parallel with intercultural hermeneutics as well as with processes that are analogous to "scriptural reasoning," wherein the rationalities embedded in the various ethical traditions can be engaged in the pursuit of greater understanding. The patterns we have adopted in the past do not suffice. Thus, even as we devise new methodologies and hermeneutical practices, we will need to guard against the construction of new stereotypes and mythologies. Nor should we expect too much from these rational discursive processes. Notwithstanding their potential, as I have argued, it is unlikely that reason alone will deliver consensus on such fundamental issues. Indeed, it may be that, ultimately, it will be not so much our ability to engage in intellectual debate but rather our capacity to imaginatively inhabit the world of the other that will secure the kind of shared political culture about which we have spoken. We cannot short-circuit this process of intercultural and interreligious communication; nor can we rely on frameworks that have been built on essentialist foundations; and nor can we forget that colonialism has been the vehicle through which adherents of other religions first encountered the language of human rights. Thus, we must proceed with caution, aware that as we build this interreligious and intercultural culture of human rights, we will need not only to learn but also to unlearn.

One of the critical concerns for citizens worldwide relates to how we should go about the task of building a shared political life. This work recommends a discursive, dialectical process that forges a variegated and nuanced consensus by engagement rather than by avoidance and argues that insofar as contemporary human rights discourse proceeds in this manner, it has the potential to provide a means by which we can articulate a vision of the global public good (and goods) in a pluralistic world. And as such, it is worth defending, securing, and promoting.

Notes

1. United Nations Declaration of Human Rights, Preamble. www.un.org/en/documents/udhr/index.shtml/.

2. See J. Waldron, ed. *"Nonsense upon Stilts": Bentham, Burke and Marx on the Rights of Man* (London: Metheun Books, 1987), 53.

3. Tracey Rowland, *Culture and the Thomist Tradition after Vatican II* (London: Routledge, 2003), 150, commenting positively on MacIntyre. The context here is a discussion of the use of rights language by the "masters of the Thomist tradition" like Jacques Maritain; however, the criticism is also made more widely.

4. Conor Gearty, *Can Human Rights Survive?* (Cambridge: Cambridge University Press, 2006), esp. 1–16.

5. Johannes Morsink, *Inherent Human Rights: Philosophical Roots of the Universal Declaration* (Philadelphia: University of Pennsylvania Press, 2009), esp. the introduction, 1–15, where he makes this case forcefully.

6. David Hollenbach, *The Global Face of Public Faith: Politics, Human Rights, and Christian Ethics* (Washington, DC: Georgetown University Press, 2003); John Mahoney, *The Challenge of Human Rights: Origin, Development and Significance*

(Oxford: Blackwell, 2006); Ethne Regan, *Theology and the Boundary Discourse of Human Rights* (Washington, DC: Georgetown University Press, 2010); George Newlands, *Christ and Human Rights: The Transformative Engagement* (Aldershot, UK: Ashgate, 1988); John Nurser, *For All Nations and Peoples: The Ecumenical Church and Human Rights* (Washington, DC: Georgetown University Press, 2005); and Esther Reed, *The Ethics of Human Rights: Contested Doctrinal and Moral Issues* (Waco, TX: Baylor University Press, 2007).

7. Brian Tierney, *The Idea of Natural Rights: Studies in Natural Rights, Natural Law and Church Law, 1150–1625* (Atlanta: Scholars Press, 1997).

8. The history of human rights is not a linear one, notwithstanding the tendency for it to be treated thus in many quarters. This work takes a similar view on the historical development to that of Samuel Moyn in *The Last Utopia: Human Rights in History* (Cambridge, MA: Harvard University Press, 2010). However, I argue that the contingent character of their development can be harnessed as a strength rather than seen as an impediment to their viability.

9. This is a paraphrase of Sumner Twiss and Bruce Grelle's formulation in "Human Rights and Comparative Religious Ethics: A New Venue," *Annual of the Society of Christian Ethics* 33 (1995): 21–48, although my approach differs from theirs in a number of respects.

10. This is Miranda Fricker's phrase, in "Feminism in Epistemology: Pluralism without Postmodernism," in *The Cambridge Companion to Feminism in Philosophy*, ed. Miranda Fricker and Jennifer Hornsby, 146–65 (Cambridge: Cambridge University Press, 2000), 156.

1

The Crisis of Legitimacy

Political and Philosophical Perspectives

The language of human rights pervades contemporary politics. Its categories shape our responses to the manifold forms of economic inequality and social exclusion, and provide the legal basis of our attempts to stem the tide of political violence, crimes against humanity, and genocide. Indeed, human rights categories carry a significant moral burden today since they both enumerate what we regard as the critical safeguards of human dignity in the form of protections from enslavement, torture, and destitution, and they articulate an account of the social and economic conditions that are necessary for human beings to flourish. The transformative impact of globalization has rendered human rights discourse even more crucial since it also now functions as *the* primary language through which the goods that can only be pursued through global political action are sought and secured. Human rights discourse has supplanted most other ethical languages, has been the platform upon which thousands of civil society organizations have built their varied agendas, and has increasingly become the vehicle through which victims of violence and injustice command our attention.

Yet a paradox remains. Notwithstanding the moral and political expectations that are placed upon the category of human rights, its legitimacy and meaning continues to be a source of political, philosophical, and theological controversy. While Boutros Boutros-Ghali's description of human rights as the "common language of humanity" has a certain resonance, its appeal is far from universal.[1] Thus, for every optimistic statement declaring a bright future for human rights, there is another one announcing the demise of human rights.[2] Indeed, Upendra Baxi characterizes the contemporary situation as being "riven with tensions and contradictions" about what it means to speak of humans or to claim that persons have rights, with endless contestations "over the nature, number, limits and scope of human rights," pursued amid what he regards as "the rather endless and unproductive contention about their universality."[3] Whether or not one agrees with Baxi's conclusions about the value of certain debates, however, his depiction of the nature, depth, and extent of the contestation is certainly apposite. It captures well the range of Conor Gearty's concerns when he speaks about a crisis of meaning and legitimacy that, if ignored, could damage human rights politics irrevocably.

Taking my cue from Gearty's analysis, in chapters 1 and 2 I focus on some of the most enduring criticisms of human rights discourse. Chapter 1 discusses these critiques as they arise in the political and philosophical realms while chapter 2 focuses on the theological critiques. I begin with a consideration of the political contestations of human rights. My concern is with debates about the universality of human rights, since this is the primary lens through which the political critique is pursued. I then move on to discuss the philosophical objections to the concept of human rights, focusing on the two most fundamental criticisms—namely, the anthropological and the epistemological. In chapter 2 I consider the long-standing theological critiques of human rights discourse. There the focus is on both the theological critiques of the concept of human rights itself and the objections to the manner in which it has been appropriated in theological discourse. Although I examine political, philosophical, and theological critiques separately, each discussion overlaps and reinforces the other in significant ways. There is no doubt that the cumulative weight of these critiques raises serious concerns about the viability of the discourse. Moreover, a historical perspective suggests that these critiques are likely to gain momentum since the philosophical mood of late modernity continues to be shaped by indeterminacy and its politics dominated by instability. Human rights theory has never been more insecure, yet human rights politics have never been more important. This ambiguous situation frames the discussions in these first two chapters, the purpose of which is to engage with and evaluate the criticisms (political and philosophical in this chapter, and theological in the next) in order to build a more convincing account of the nature and scope of human rights, both in itself and as a moral language of Christian social ethics.

Human Rights and the Politics of Universality

Its early promise notwithstanding, human rights discourse is now deeply contested and often regarded as a code word for political imperialism, Western individualism, and global homogenization. Much of this disquiet arises from the perception that the human rights apparatus of declarations, conventions, and treaties perpetuates the political dominance of Western countries, a dominance that was evident even at the inception of the current "regime." Behind this concern that human rights discourse reflects and extends the political hegemony of the West is the view that the concept of human rights is so embedded in the philosophical categories of the Enlightenment that it cannot be rendered meaningful apart from these grounding assumptions and commitments. Therefore, human rights are seen as the embodiment of the Enlightenment's grand narrative of order and progress whose core project, according to historian John Gray, has been "the displacement of local, customary or traditional moralities and all forms of transcendental faiths . . . by a critical or rational morality which was projected as the basis of a universal civilisation . . . and binding on all human beings."[4] Edward Said argues that this grand narrative has been fundamentally ethnocentric, with Western norms operating as the sole standards according to which diverse societies are judged. Said insists that this marginalization of non-Western perspectives has been accomplished most successfully through the representation of non-Western cultures solely through the categories of Western thought, and—in a process that further undermines the validity of non-Western cultures—Enlightenment discourse imposes on all others a sense of "otherness" and an assumption that they embody a negation of everything for which the West stands.[5] Stuart Hall supports this characterization, arguing that "in Enlightenment discourse the West was the model, the prototype and the measure of social progress. It was western progress, civilisation, rationality and development that were celebrated. . . . The 'Other' was the 'dark' side—forgotten, repressed and denied; the reverse image of enlightenment and modernity."[6] Although the imposition of this sense of otherness and inferiority was evident from the renaissance onward, as documented by Hall, it achieved the high point of its expression in enlightenment philosophy and in the colonialism of the nineteenth century.

The merits of the philosophical dimensions of this argument will be considered separately since they form an intrinsic part of the political debate about whether human rights are universal or whether they are, in Adamantia Pollis's iconic phrase, "a Western construct of limited applicability."[7] Few would dispute the claim that the liberal concept of human rights emerged within the context of the Western philosophical tradition and acquired its contemporary articulation at the high point of modernity. The critical question, however, is the degree to which these political and philosophical antecedents have shaped the current discourse and the extent to which other political, philosophical, and religious contexts have had a formative and continuing impact on its evolution.

The difficulties involved in answering this question are immense. In the first place, modern human rights discourse evolved over a period of two centuries and does not follow a linear pattern. As a result the rights talk of the late-eighteenth-century revolutionary movements in France and the United States is of a very different nature than the rights talk associated with the UN Declaration on Human Rights, which in turn is significantly different from the contemporary discourse.[8] Thus, one's assessment of the relative influence of the Western philosophical antecedents must be nuanced in line with the historical evolution of human rights discourse. The perspective that underpins the argument in this work is that although philosophical anchors of the human rights movement are Western in origin, from the late nineteenth century onward a pluralism of different political, cultural, philosophical, and religious perspectives began to impact on the substantive meaning of the category of human rights. Thus, although the human rights discourse of the eighteenth and nineteenth centuries was essentially Western, liberal, and primarily (although not exclusively) individualistic, and was focused on civil and political rights, by the beginning of the twentieth century the influence of non-Western political aspirations had begun to transform the discourse. Indeed, by the time the UN Declaration had been promulgated, this pluralism of perspectives had already been embedded in the discourse. A particular consequence of the embedding of this pluralism of perspectives was the subsequent prominence given to social and economic rights within the emerging human rights discourse—a move that was not without controversy. Neither can the impact that the politics of the Cold War has had on the concept be underestimated, since through the late 1970s there was a further transformation of human rights thinking that saw its remit expand even further. There are other complicating elements when one attempts to establish the extent to which the Western antecedents have shaped the current discourse of human rights. Many of these revolve around the complex and often contradictory positions that nation-states, nongovernmental organizations, activists, and academics adopted at different points in the evolution of the debates, and also arise from the multiple national, transnational, legal, and institutional contexts in which human rights politics has been pursued, particularly in the twentieth century.

In this section, I focus on the political critiques and, for the sake of clarity, concentrate on the debate as it has unfolded in relation to the signature project of human rights discourse, that is, the 1948 UN Declaration of Human Rights. In this context, I focus on four critical phases during which the question of the universality of human rights was debated: (1) the adoption of the Declaration in 1948; (2) the debate about the inclusion of a "colonial clause" in the draft covenant in 1950; (3) the controversy surrounding the creation of the role of High Commissioner for Human Rights in the 1970s; and (4) the Asian values debate in the 1990s. These four critical moments in human rights politics illustrate that the debate about universality does not follow a single trajectory in which Western imperialists are pitted against postcolonial "relativists." Rather, the historical record reveals a more complex narrative in which ethical idealism, political opportunism, and social protectionism each played a part.

The Adoption of the UN Declaration of Human Rights in 1948

Even as the UN Declaration was being drafted and debated, charges of ethnocentrism and political imperialism abounded. The fact that the General Assembly was composed of only fifty-eight states, and that the peoples of Asia and Africa were grossly underrepresented was undoubtedly a cause for concern.[9] Moreover, these imbalances in representation were accentuated by the power differentials between the major global players and the smaller nations. The submission of the American Anthropological Association (AAA) to the Human Rights Commission, in 1947, drew attention to these issues. It claimed that the draft Declaration was flawed because it was ethnocentric, and it also challenged the aspirations of the Commission on the basis of cultural relativism. It argued that if a Declaration of this sort was to have worldwide applicability, then it must embrace and recognize the validity of many different ways of life. "It will not be convincing to the Indonesian, the African, the Indian, the Chinese," it warned, if it replicated the patterns of earlier statements (it mentioned the declarations of the American and French revolutions).[10] The AAA's submission also asked how a proposed declaration could be applicable to all human beings and not fall into the trap of being no more than "a statement of the rights conceived only in terms of values prevalent in the countries of Western Europe and America."[11] Contextualizing its broader objections in the history of colonialism, the AAA argued that "the Rights of Man in the twentieth century cannot be circumscribed by the standards of any single culture or be dictated by the aspirations of any single people."[12] It observed that "what is held to be a right in one society may be regarded as anti-social by another people, or by the same people in a different period," and that "a man is free only when he lives as his society defines freedom."[13] Change is possible, according to the AAA, where people are being oppressed. However, such change ought not to be shaped by a set of externally imposed standards. Rather, a society's "underlying cultural values may be called on to bring the people of such states to a realization of the consequences of the acts of their governments, and thus enforce a brake upon discrimination and conquest."[14] It is not surprising that the AAA took this position, given the important role that its members played both in documenting the cultural pluralism that had been obscured by colonialism and in challenging the ethnocentrism of Western thought. One thinks, for example, of Franz Boas and his pupils in this regard. Whether the AAA's articulation of the nature and depth of cultural pluralism necessitated this thorough-going relativist stance regarding ethics is debatable, however. Its consistent and vocal message to the drafters of the Declaration was that ethical norms are relative to each culture and that criticism and change are legitimate only when they are generated internally and according to preexisting values. But the AAA's position has been modified over the years. In 1988 it argued for a new declaration on human rights, stating, quite remarkably, that "the AAA has long been, and should continue to be, concerned whenever human difference is made the basis for a denial of human rights."[15] Moreover, in

1999 it officially reversed its position on cultural relativism and endorsed the concept of universal human rights.[16]

The AAA's objections both to the content of the draft Declaration and, more significantly, to the project itself have been reiterated consistently in the intervening decades. Issa Shivji describes human rights as "a very important component in the armoury of imperialist ideology," while Abdullahi Ahmed An-Na'im defends the project but concedes that "given the historical context within which the present standards [of international human rights] have been formulated, it was unavoidable that they were initially based on Western cultural and philosophical assumptions."[17] However, a historical analysis of the debates, during both the drafting and the adoption of the Declaration, suggests that a more nuanced conclusion is possible. Certainly the Declaration was drafted and debated against the backdrop of significant Western power and influence, the effect of which power was moderated by the prominent roles that drafters and delegates from the global South played in the process. In the last decade in particular, the scholarship of Mary Ann Glendon, Paul Gordon Lauren, Johannes Morsink, and Susan Waltz has drawn attention to the significant roles that individuals and delegations from Arab, Asian, and Latin American countries played at every stage of the process.[18] This scholarship challenges the assumption that the Declaration is primarily and essentially the accomplishment of the big Western powers. Thus, while it is true that Europe, North America, and South America were not only disproportionately represented but also exercised significant political clout, nonetheless one is persuaded by the conclusion that the final text was generated through a genuinely international consensus. The celebrated roles of Chinese negotiator Peng Chung Chang, Indian delegate Hansa Mehta, and Lebanese diplomat Charles Malik in the articulation of the Declaration are now well known, thanks especially to the work of Lauren and Morsink. Less widely acknowledged are the more low-key but nonetheless important contributions of a variety of individuals and delegations to debates on specific articles of the Declaration. For example, Morsink mentions the important contribution made by the delegate from Syria, Abdul Rahman Kayala, to the argument about the inherence of human rights, while Susan Waltz's analysis of the debate in the Third Committee on Article 21 indicates that the final text was the product of views from the delegates of Belgium, Uruguay, the United States, Greece, Brazil, Venezuela, Iraq, China, Haiti,

Cuba, Sweden, the former Soviet Union, Lebanon, the Philippines, and Saudi Arabia.[19]

The historical record of these debates allows for a number of different interpretations on the question of whether the composition of the Third Committee (which was the context in which most of the drafting took place) was such that it compromised any aspiration to universality. It would be foolish to underestimate the impact on the process of the underrepresentation of the colonies in Africa and Asia, and of the failure to ensure that indigenous and tribal peoples on the different continents were appropriately represented by those who governed them. Nor should one ignore the impact that the political, economic, and cultural weight of the larger powers had on the negotiations. Within these limits, however, there are grounds for concluding that the Declaration was indeed the result of a process of international consensus-building and that claims that it was a Western imposition are not supported by the historical evidence. Not only was there significant international support for the concept of universal human rights but, as Lauren, Waltz, and Morsink demonstrate, the epistemological basis of such a claim was articulated not only by John Humphrey and René Cassin (the famed British and French drafters) but also by China's Peng Chung Chang and by Pakistani delegate Shaista Ikramullah, who declared that she and her delegation "fully supported the adoption of the declaration because it believed in the dignity and worth of man" and argued that it was imperative "that the peoples of the world should recognise a code of civilized behaviour that would apply not only in international relations but also in domestic affairs."[20] The inclusion of economic and social rights in the Declaration against the strongly expressed wishes of the United States, Britain, and France is a further indication of the influence of the non-Western powers. Neither should the significance of the eight countries who abstained from the final vote be overinterpreted since there were different political and philosophical imperatives at stake for each of the nations at that crucial period in international politics. South Africa was building the edifice of its apartheid system and would only accept a shortened list of human rights, a list that excluded the right to freedom of movement and therefore allowed it to pursue its policy of establishing homelands. In this case, narrow political interests trumped the ethical imperatives of the Declaration. For the six countries of the communist bloc (USSR, Czechoslovakia, Poland, Byelorussia, Ukraine, and Yugoslavia), the problem was the issue of the compatibility of the concept of individual rights with Marxist philosophy. Nonetheless, each of the delegations from the communist bloc made a substantial contribution to the drafting itself and, en masse, played a significant role in ensuring the inclusion of social and economic rights in the text, and eventually all signed and ratified the Declaration. Saudi Arabia's abstention hung on whether or not Shar'ia should be regarded as having a prior claim over against international human rights. Interestingly, only one of the ten Arab delegations concluded that there was a conflict between the two, with the nine other Arab countries adopting the Declaration.

The historical evidence at this critical moment, therefore, paints a complex picture, one that belies the claim that the UN Declaration was nothing more than the "advocacy of American ideological imperialism."[21] There is no doubt that its claims to universality were not only exaggerated but also based on a lack of self-reflexivity on the part of the major powers. Nonetheless, the record does suggest that the emerging nations of Africa, Asia, and many of the Arab countries were enthusiastic about both the concept and content of the UN Declaration of Human Rights. Moreover, this trajectory is confirmed in the second critical moment, to which we now turn our attention.

The Inclusion of a "Colonial Clause"

The agreement established through the adoption of the Declaration did not last long. Immediately following on its adoption, the issue of the Declaration's universality was reopened. However, the debate was reopened not because of lobbying by African and Arab states concerned about the putative Western bias of the Declaration but rather by the colonial powers who were concerned about the political implications of the Declaration in the territories that they continued to control. Roland Burke's *Decolonization and the Evolution of International Human Rights* is interesting in this regard. He assembles historical evidence that demonstrates that the first battle over universality in the newly established United Nations was between the imperial powers and the few third world delegates present at the time, and "was the exact opposite of what academic proponents of cultural relativism hold as orthodoxy."[22] Burke draws attention to two interrelated debates during which the issue of the universality of human rights was again discussed: namely, the debate that began in October 1950 about the inclusion of a "colonial clause" in a covenant on human rights that was intended to be the successor to the UN Declaration, and the continuation of that discussion in 1952 through the lens of the Convention on the Political Rights of Women.

The proposal that the draft covenant on human rights should include a colonial exemption clause was made in October 1950 by the same European powers who a few years earlier had led the efforts to establish the universal declaration. This clause was intended to allow the colonial governments to exclude their colonies from claiming the rights that were in the covenant and was motivated primarily by their need to resist the claims to the right to self-determination on the part of the peoples of the colonies. Arguing his country's case, Soudan of Belgium suggested that exempting the colonies from the demands of the Universal Declaration was essential because its purpose "was to prescribe . . . rules of conduct which, as they supposed a high degree of civilization, were often incompatible with the ideas of peoples who had not yet reached a high degree of development." In fact, he claimed, the rights in the covenant "ran the risk of destroying the very basis of their society" and, drawing a contrast between the "civilized nations of today" and "the indigenous inhabitants" of the colonies, Soudan proposed that the peoples of the colonies "should only be led towards civilization in a progressive manner which was adapted to their varying degrees of development and to the special conditions in each country."[23] René Cassin, one of the undisputed architects of the UN Declaration, also followed this line in the debate. Contradicting his earlier position, he argued for an approach that distinguished between the rights that were basic and that should be applied universally and those to which the claim to universality did not apply. The Summary Records describe Cassin as using the example of the rights of the family as a situation in which universality did not apply. He is reported as urging the committee to anticipate a situation that would likely arise in relation to a convention to protect the rights of the family. In the case of protecting the rights of families in France, for example, it would not be the same for a Christian family as for a Muslim family. He warned the committee against omitting any territorial clause that would represent a double disadvantage alternative. "It might subject countries inhabited by different peoples to uniform obligations, and the standards they adopted for legislation would be those applicable to peoples still in the lowest stage of development."[24]

This argument for cultural relativism was immediately and vigorously resisted. The insight provided by the diaries and analysis of British diplomat John Humphrey on this matter is fascinating and confirms Burke's conclusion that, in the years immediately following the adoption of the Declaration, it was the non-Western countries that held the line on the universality of human rights.[25] Peng Chung Chang resisted the argument of the colonial powers, claiming that it was "something that had been dignified by the name 'levels of civilization,' but represented little more than European prejudices."[26] Lakshmi Menon of India meanwhile argued that the positions advanced in support of the colonial clause "attempted to justify what could not be justified."[27] However, according to Burke, it was the Iraqi Bedia Afnan who most effectively exposed the incoherence of Cassin's position and that of the other colonial powers. Afnan insisted that "differences of culture and tradition were no obstacle whatever to the universal application of the provisions of the covenant" and concluded that "the Moslem world would certainly be able to respect human rights."[28] Representatives from Indonesia, Lebanon, Cuba, the Philippines, and Chile also argued forcefully for the universality of human rights and against giving official sanction to the idea that there was "a second category of people in the world . . . called natives . . . regarded as unfit to enjoy the minimum rights which the covenant was to guarantee."[29] The colonial exemption was, according to Egyptian Mahund Amzi, "only too reminiscent of the Hitlerian concept which divided mankind into groups of varying worth."[30] The exemption clause was defeated on November 2, 1950.

A comparable and no less acrimonious debate took place a mere two years later, also in the Third Committee, this time through the lens of a debate about the political rights of women. The proposed Convention on the Political Rights of Women consisted of three substantive articles that together reiterated and detailed the political implications of Articles 2 and 21 of the UN Declaration. It declared that women had the right to vote in elections, to be eligible for election to all public bodies, and to hold public office and exercise all public functions, all on an equal basis to men.[31] Britain and France once again argued for a colonial exemption clause, rehearsing the now familiar argument that "customs could not be radically changed overnight without damaging the body politic."[32] South Africa also argued against the extension of political rights to all women, supporting this position with its by then well-established argument for cultural relativism. Meanwhile, various Arab countries that two years earlier had been vociferous opponents of cultural relativism now argued for a gradualist approach to political rights for women, thus moderating their earlier support for the universality of human rights. The case for the universality of human rights, including women's human rights, was once again made by a significant number of delegates from the third world. Bedia Afnan of Iraq was once again a vocal proponent of human rights. She made a persuasive case that women's political rights were compatible with Islamic belief. Women's oppression, she argued, was not based on tradition or the laws of Islam but rather on an abuse of culture by Muslims.[33] Pakistan's Begum Ra'ana Liaquat Ali Khan supported Afnan's position, adding yet another voice to challenge what she regarded as the widespread misconception of the inequality of rights in Islam.[34]

As with the debate in 1950, the major powers failed to achieve an exemption to the obligation to extend women's political rights to all the peoples in their colonies. The argument for universality prevailed, with its most ardent advocates drawn not from Europe and the West but rather from Africa, Asia, and the Arab world. Moreover, not only was the concept of universality defended but the substance of the Declaration's enumeration of rights was also, with very few exceptions, supported by the non-Western powers. The point at which the consensus seemed most fragile was on the issue of women's rights. This is not surprising, given that this debate about women's rights predated the modern women's movement by over a decade. The relativism/universality divide has thus been a feature of the debate about international human rights since they were formally promulgated in the UN Declaration in 1948. However, one cannot assume that a line can be drawn between "the West and the rest" on the question of human rights since, as these two critical moments have illustrated, political pragmatism commingled with ethical principles to create a complex and oftentimes contradictory picture of the commitments of different countries. Within this multifaceted narrative, however, it is clear that, during the 1950s and '60s, the newly independent countries in Africa and Asia along with the Arab nations were among the most enthusiastic champions of human rights. Indeed, Burke characterizes this phase, especially as the decades advanced, as one of "militant third world universalism." In this phase newly elected postcolonial elites, drawing on strong democratic mandates, challenged and sought to eliminate customs and practices that were regarded as inconsistent with human rights. The flash points were predominantly associated with gender roles and with practices relating to marriage and the family. However, the dominant position of these delegates and governments was that self-determination and human rights were "all of a piece," and that each reflected the aspirations and commitments of these newly represented peoples.

The Creation of the Position of High Commissioner for Human Rights

The politics of decolonization continued to have an impact on the debates about the universality of human rights as the decades passed. However, as the character of the governance in many former colonies changed, so too did the nature of the debate about universality. The late 1960s and early '70s was a period of significant instability globally, with the rise of political unrest in the Arab world and of authoritarian regimes across Asia and Africa. Within this fractious political context, a proposal to establish the post of High Commissioner for Human Rights reemerged and quickly became the catalyst for yet another debate about the universality of human rights, although on this occasion the spotlight was on the role of the United Nations itself. In the background was the ongoing issue of the extent to which the United Nations should monitor member states' records with respect to human rights. In 1947 the newly established Commission on Human Rights had taken the decision not to investigate the thousands of complaints that it was receiving annually. In fact, the UN Economic and Social Council Resolution 75 even denied the Commission the right to see these allegations of human rights abuses worldwide. Instead of investigating these complaints, the secretariat recorded, acknowledged, and filed them. This resistance to the United Nations having a monitoring and investigative role with respect to human rights united all of the Cold War enemies, although it was a source of embarrassment for the Committee on Human Rights itself. The situation improved somewhat with the passing of Resolution 1235 in 1967, which authorized the Commission to discuss human rights violations in particular countries, and a further incremental improvement came with the adoption of Resolution 1503 in 1970, which authorized the Commission to investigate "communications" (complaints) that suggested "a consistent pattern of gross and reliably attested violations of human rights and fundamental freedoms." The effectiveness of this 1503 procedure has been much debated and need not concern us here. Of significance, rather, is that the proposal to establish a High Commissioner for Human Rights represented an attempt to establish a genuinely independent body that would be empowered to investigate human rights abuses in any country. Initial hostility toward this proposal was widespread, with Western powers as determined as others to avoid the kind of scrutiny envisaged through the Office of the High Commissioner. However, the more serious opposition came from an alliance of the Arab and Soviet countries, which deployed the rhetoric of cultural relativism to resist the initiative.

In many respects the substance of the debate about the establishment of a High Commissioner for Human Rights is similar to those discussed earlier. Jamil Baroody, the Saudi delegate who during his thirty-one years at the United Nations was the most consistent advocate of relativism, led the charge, insisting that human rights are a Western imposition, and even claiming that slavery "is a relative concept."[35] The intensity and ferocity of the debate was new, however, as was the posture of many of the former colonies who, during the period of debate over the proposal, began to oppose the idea of human rights. Earlier champions of the universality of human rights began to question the supervisory function that the office would have, with many reacting to what they regarded as its neocolonialist associations. Ratnakirti Gunewardene of Ceylon, for example, argued that the proposal was an attempt by the imperial West to "limit their sovereign rights."[36] Moreover, those countries that were at best ambivalent in the early decades hardened their resistance during the 1970s. Yemen's delegate, for example, argued that "the unproclaimed intention behind the creation of the post . . . [is an] attempt of certain western powers to impose their conceptions of human rights on other states."[37] By 1977 even Iran, which had earlier been a supporter of both the concept of universal human rights and the establishment of the Office of High Commissioner, was resisting the implementation of particular human rights and was making its case through the language of cultural relativism. In speech that foreshadowed the Asian values debate of the 1990s, Princess Ashraf of Iran insisted that "while the Western countries stressed the rights of the individual, the developing countries were thinking of the rights of entire peoples. The former spoke of the immediate implementation of civil and political rights, while the latter strove to establish economic ones." She argued that the machinery of the United Nations could not be based on "a narrow interpretation of concepts that were understood differently in a world which was divided by such great differences."[38] By 1977 the proposal to establish a High Commissioner for Human Rights had once again been abandoned, and the consensus on universal human rights, which at one time had been so strongly supported by the emerging nations in Africa and Asia, was beginning to unravel.

The Asian Values Debate

The Asian values debate of the 1990s further reinforced this skeptical trend, and although the debate was confined to one region, it also became a catalyst for some Arab and African nations to continue the antiuniversalist arguments that had begun to emerge in the 1970s. The Asian values debate reflects the pattern of earlier contestations and includes those who accept the universality of certain values but who have concerns about the current list of universal human rights as well as the appropriateness of the language of rights as the vehicle for conveying these values. According to this position, the norms enshrined in the language of human rights can equally be promoted through the more "communitarian" language of duty and loyalty to one's community. The spectrum of debate also includes those who argue the relativist position that "concepts on democracy, on human rights and on freedoms are relative and specific ones."[39] The uniting thread among these varied positions is a resistance to what is regarded as a Western bias in the current articulation of international human rights. At the 1993 World Conference on Human Rights in Vienna, for example, the Singaporean delegation, endorsing the universality of human rights, insisted that the West should "not be so blinded by arrogance and certainties as to lose the capacity for imagination and sympathy," and thereby should be open to a rearticulation of the content of the 1948 Declaration.[40]

In the preparatory conferences for the Vienna Conference, the distinctiveness of Asian values was consistently promoted. A 1991 Singaporean white paper, for example, claimed that for Asians the natural pattern is "nation before community and society before self."[41] A central element of the distinctiveness of Asian values, it is claimed, resides in an alternative conceptualization of political life in which the individual occupies a secondary position to that of the community or state. Prime Minister Dr. Mahathir of Malaysia's now infamous attack on Western individualism illustrates this point well. Prime Minister Mahathir Mohamad argued that "the West's interpretation of human rights is that every individual can do what he likes, free from any restraints by government. Individuals soon decided that they should break every rule and code . . . beginning with the little things. . . . They went on to disregard marriage . . . extramarital sex became the norm . . . cohabitation with . . . frequent changes of partner. . . . Children were begotten without known fathers, which will in time lead to incest. But then incest is not wrong either, if that is what is desired by the individual."[42] According to Prime Minister Mahathir, this immorality is the direct result of the West's misinterpretation of human rights in which individual interests and rights are promoted over those of the community and the nation. Moreover, he argued, rather than seeking to extend their individualistic interpretation of rights, whether that be through diplomacy or through imposing human rights conditions on trade, political leaders in the West should deplore the chaos that this has begotten. Furthermore, Singapore's Lee Kuan Yew is reported to have claimed that Asians have "little doubt that a society with communitarian values where the interests of a society take precedence over that of the individual suits them better than the individualism of America."[43]

This claim that the current human rights regime is permissive, and that it promotes discordant relationships between individuals and their societies, is repeated by Asian political leaders. In his speech at the Vienna Conference, the Indonesian foreign minister Ali Alatas articulated this concern, claiming that "Indonesian culture, as well as its ancient well-developed customary laws have traditionally put high priority on the rights and interests of the society or nation, without, however, in any way minimising or ignoring the rights and interests of individuals and groups."[44] In this context the importance of civil and political rights was often downgraded, while economic and social rights were accorded more significance. President Suharto of Indonesia, for example, insisted that "the principle of the indivisibility of all rights . . . implies the need for a balanced relationship between individual and community rights."[45] To date, politicians as different as Prime Minister Dr. Mahathir of Malaysia, President Suharto of Indonesia, and

Prime Minister Lee Kuan Yew of Singapore have argued that Westerners mistakenly equate good government with democratic government. In
contrast, they claim that as long as a government is just and accountable,
and it promotes economic prosperity and reflects the basic values of its
peoples, it can be regarded as a good government. Thus, while the notion
of universality is accepted, the articulation and prioritization of rights according to what has come to be regarded as Western preference is rejected.

The insistence on the distinctiveness of Asian values has frequently been
accompanied by skepticism about, and occasionally rejection of, the concept of universal human rights in itself. Associated particularly with Chinese leaders, this radical cultural relativism was especially championed in
the years immediately following the Tiananmen Square massacre. Yet even
within this context, the hard relativism is often interchanged for a more
nuanced position, describing the reality of cultural and ethical pluralism
and insisting that the current list of universal human rights needs to be
reconsidered and divested of its Western bias. Mr. Liu Huaqiu of China's
speech to the Vienna Conference exemplified this position and, while not
arguing a relativist case, nonetheless made the argument for an approach
to human rights that allows for a role for "the specific history, culture and
values of a particular country."[46]

The Asian values debate is best understood within the context of the
growing commitment to cultural relativism among the postcolonial nations, which had by the 1990s become a feature of global politics. It dominated both the preparations for and the proceedings of the 1993 Vienna
Conference, although it had its roots in the anti-imperialist agenda of
the 1970s wherein the dominance of Western philosophical and political categories was beginning to be challenged. Moreover, it has had many
corollaries, the most important being the analogous debate about the compatibility of human rights norms with Islamic values and especially with
Shar'ia law.[47] In that context, the Cairo Declaration of Rights on Human
Rights in Islam represents the most conclusive position of Muslim majority
governments thus far and is interesting in that it also attempts to combine
a qualified endorsement of the idea of universal human rights with an insistence that they must be implemented in ways that respect local customs,
including religious ones.[48] However, this question of how best to accommodate pluralism within the context of a commitment to human rights is
precisely where the debate begins.

There is no doubt that the crisis of legitimacy that has afflicted human rights discourse is fundamentally tied to the debate about its universality. For the most part this debate has been framed in terms of the contention that human rights categories are a Western imposition on the rest of the world. While this debate about their universality continues to be important, this analysis has shown that the debate cannot be framed solely in terms of "the West and the rest." My purpose in discussing these four critical "moments" in the recent history of human rights is to provide an insight into the nature of the political debate on the contested issue of universality. They reveal a complex and dynamic process in which political interests and ethical principle each play a part. Furthermore, they illustrate how the commitment to the principle of universality often became entangled in concrete political agendas and was either compromised or abandoned as a result. In particular, these moments challenge the conclusion that universal human rights were imposed by the West on the rest of the world. Rather, as is evidenced by the historical record, for the three decades immediately following the promulgation of the UN Declaration, the human rights framework was regarded by the emerging nations as a resource in their struggle for self-determination and as a protection from neocolonialism.[49] Even when subsequent governments of these new nations adopted a relativist stance, they were challenged from within by indigenous champions of human rights, although this internal contestation was rarely on view either in the General Assembly or in the Third Committee, where each country's official line on human rights was recorded. Thus, while the universality of human rights may continue to be contested, this brief historical analysis demonstrates that the commitment to a universal framework for human rights came from many different cultures, traditions, and regions; that it was not merely a Western project; and that the arguments against universal human rights were also made by Western nations when it was politically expedient to do so. That human rights subsequently came to be regarded as emblematic of a colonialist agenda is therefore both ironic and tragic.

Human Rights and Philosophical Skepticism

The crisis of meaning and legitimacy in human rights talk is also acute in the philosophical domain and has been the source of much commentary. Anthony Langlois's conclusion that the language of human rights is politically efficacious but philosophically bankrupt is echoed widely, although the prescriptions for remedying this situation vary.[50] Langlois's assessment can only be understood within the broader context of the disintegration of many of the claims of enlightenment rationalism and its replacement with skepticism, self-reflexivity, and genealogical critique. Analyses of the nature of this loss of confidence in "the enlightenment project" are many and will not be rehearsed here. Of critical importance for our discussion, however, is the impact that this loss of confidence has had on the categories upon which human rights discourse has been built—namely, the concept of an essential, shared human nature and the commitment to a concept of objective truth grounding all reasoning. In each case we discuss the criticisms leveled at these assumptions by both communitarian and postmodern theorists.

It is one of the paradoxes of human rights that, at the same time as it was growing in political appeal, the philosophical basis on which it was being constructed was being dismantled. Successive blows to the philosophy of human rights, in both the nineteenth and twentieth centuries, did not seem to undermine its political appeal to any great extent. This is changing, however, as philosophical skepticism gains popular cultural appeal, and as postcolonial politics increasingly throws in its lot with cultural relativism. As Gearty argues, "as post-modern uncertainty embeds itself more deeply in our culture, and as our memory of religious and Enlightenment time fades, so our commitment to this benign relic of both can be expected to recede."[51] It is in this context that we consider the challenges to two of the critical philosophical foundations on which human rights thinking depends, the concept of a shared, fixed human nature and the notion of objective, universal moral truth.

Human Rights and Human Nature: The Problem of the Unencumbered Self

Classical human rights philosophy is premised on the belief that all human beings share a fixed and essential nature from which one can determine the existence of certain universal human rights. Indeed, this concept of a shared human nature has been one of the cornerstones of even the earliest articulations of what we would now recognize as human rights claims. Stoic and Christian natural law theories depended heavily on this concept of human nature as they drew conclusions about how all human beings ought to be treated. Maritain's *The Rights of Man and Natural Law* is typical of this approach, insisting, as he does, that "there is a human nature and this human nature is the same for all men . . . and possessed of a nature, constituted in a given determinate fashion, man obviously possesses ends which correspond to his natural constitution and which are the same for all."[52] This commitment to the idea of an essential human nature persists even though the language of human nature has, for the most part, been replaced by the language of human person in human rights discourse.[53] The transition from the language of nature to the language of person is a consequence of the secularization of human rights philosophy, a transition that tends to be seen in a positive light since it is associated with the consolidation of human rights categories within the culture of modernity. Notwithstanding this transition, however, the philosophical basis of this anthropology (whether it be expressed through the language of nature or of person) continues to be called into question. Writing in 1984, philosopher Margaret MacDonald simply says that thinking in such terms is a "complete mistake . . . that human beings are not like exactly similar bottles of whiskey each marked 'for export only' . . . that men do not share a fixed nature, nor, therefore, are there any ends which they must necessarily pursue in fulfillment of such nature. There is no definition of 'man . . . only a more or less vague set of properties which characterize in varying degrees and proportions those creatures which are called 'human'."[54] In this section I discuss the most significant of these contestations as they impact on human rights theory. I focus on two major strands of criticism, the communitarian and the postmodern, both of which raise serious doubts about the durability of the anthropological assumptions enshrined in the philosophy of human rights.

A frequently heard criticism of human rights language relates to the manner in which it conceptualizes the human person as detached, autonomous, and free. The UN Declaration and the ancillary treaties each focus on the rights due to each person, without any mention of the groups or communities to which individuals belong. In this, the Declaration reflects liberalism's normative conception of the person as an individual, whose attachments are supplementary to her essential nature and whose identity can be articulated apart from her relationships, loyalties, and encumbrances. Michael Sandel's classic phrase "the unencumbered self" captures the essence of this anthropology.[55] In his view, liberalism assumes that one can speak of an original, unencumbered, antecedent self or nature, upon which is laid a veneer of attachment. This essential nature is taken to be shared by all human beings, to exist independently of and prior to the values and interests that each individual possesses, and to provide the basis upon which the various affiliations, commitments, and values are inscribed.[56] Crucially, the unity and identity of the self is regarded as being accomplished prior to the commitments chosen. The result, according to Sandel, is an anthropology in which "there is always a distinction between the values I *have* and the person I *am*. To identify any characteristics as *my* aims, ambitions, desires and so on is always to imply some subject 'me' standing behind them, at a certain distance, and the shape of this 'me' must be given prior to any of the aims or attributes I bear. One consequence of this distance is to put the self itself *beyond* the reach of its experience, to secure its identity once and for all."[57] Critics of liberalism's normative anthropology, including Sandel, Charles Taylor, and Alasdair MacIntyre, have disputed its adequacy, insisting that one cannot speak of an essential self that is distinct from the processes of social embodiment through which human identity is constructed.[58] In drawing attention to these processes of social embodiment, their primary concern is to resist what they regard as the inappropriately individualistic account of human identity contained within human rights discourse. Michael Walzer's *Politics and Passion* makes this point forcefully when he argues that the structure of human life is essentially communitarian; that all human beings inhabit "biographically and historically prior," unchosen, associational contexts; and that it is from within these contexts, and not as unencumbered individuals, that we develop our identities, articulate our values, and forge our social interactions.[59] It is clear that the UN Declaration speaks of human beings primarily in terms of distinct, autonomous individuals and does not grant that social and political context or cultural and religious beliefs should have an impact on the realization of an individual's human rights. Nor does it give any recognition to the notion that cultures and communities can profoundly shape whether and how an individual recognizes, claims, or believes that she has an entitlement to particular rights. Community and culture are mentioned rarely, and even when they are, there is very little recognition that the communities that individuals inhabit play a normative and formative role in shaping and constructing that person's identity. Indeed, it is precisely because of this normative disjunction between the self and the individual's attachments that the UN Declaration can confidently declare that "everyone is entitled to all the rights and freedoms set forth . . . without distinction of any kind, such as race, colour, sex, language, religion, political or other opinion, national or social origin, property, birth or other status" (Article 2). The "I" of popular human rights discourse, then, is an "I" that is conceived of as existing independently of the values, experiences, encumbrances, and beliefs that "I" have. It is an "I" that, according to communitarians, is based on a mistaken understanding of human identity.

According to its communitarian critics, this classical liberal concept of "a human nature upon which individuating elements are overlaid" is based on a fundamental misunderstanding of how human identity is formed. Communitarians resist the idea of an essential self, or nature, upon which identity is inscribed and argue instead that our identities are shaped in and through the multifaceted commitments and contexts that ground us. Delineating the contours of these multifaceted relationships cannot detain us here. What is clear, however, is that this communitarian critique has serious implications for the manner in which the person is understood within human rights discourse. In particular, it suggests that human rights theory will need to develop a more complex and nuanced account of the relationship between the individual and her encumbrances. It will also require that greater attention be given to the increasingly complex nature of her situatedness and the forms of belonging that it generates. In so doing, human rights theory will need to revisit the anthropological assumptions on which it is based.

Human Rights and Universal Humanity: The Politics of the Self

The communitarian critique of human rights discourse focuses on liberalism's impoverished account of the manner in which human subjectivity is fashioned, particularly on its failure to acknowledge the formative role of context in the structuring of identity. In so doing, it modifies rather than destabilizes the liberal account of the person. Michel Foucault and those who have pursued what he called "the critical attitude" develop this critique in a more radical way and argue that the manner in which modernity conceptualizes human life is fundamentally incorrect and implausible.[60]

Foucault, in particular, insists that human life cannot be understood apart from the cultural practices through which it is constructed. Both the communitarian and postmodern critiques share the determination to attend to the contexts within which the subject is formed. However, they do so in profoundly different ways. Thus, while Sandel and Walzer both develop what one might call a communitarian version of humanism, Foucault rejects such approaches. Rather, in announcing the "death of man," Foucault—particularly in his early work—argues that the modern understanding of the subject as autonomous and rational is no longer convincing. He developed his archaeological method specifically to demonstrate that the modern subject is established and maintained through particular discursive practices. According to Foucault, there are three different modes by which, in our culture, "human beings are made subjects."[61] The first are the disciplines of enquiry such as philosophy, linguistics, and biology, "which try to give themselves the status of science," and through which societies establish their most cherished and fundamental assumptions.[62] The second he identified as the "dividing practices," which he investigated in both *Discipline and Punish* and *Madness and Civilization*. These have an objectifying and normalizing function and are the processes by which the distinctions between "the mad and the sane, the sick and the healthy, the criminals and the good boys are identified and maintained."[63] The third mode focused on "how a human being turns him- or herself into a subject."[64] Within this mode Foucault concentrated on sexuality, although he regarded it as simply one of the many "technologies of the self" through which the subject is formed. For Foucault, the subject is constructed through these three overlapping modes—through the scientific and philosophical discourses of culture; through the disciplinary practices through which a society maintains the norms by which it differentiates and evaluates behavior; and, crucially, through "the technologies of the self" whereby the individual conforms her own identity to the institutions of the state. In this regard there is an evolution in Foucault's thought. The early work focused the technologies of domination through which the individual is constructed in modern societies. In his later work, however, especially through his focus on the technologies of the self, he began to interrogate the roles that subjects play in constructing their own identities through their daily lives. Notwithstanding this evolution, Foucault's basic point remains, namely, that the human subject is "made not born" and that the idea of a prediscursive, essential, shared human nature is an illusion.

This anti-essentialist notion of identity sits uncomfortably with the anthropological assumptions of liberal human rights discourse. Foucault's "politics of the self" implies that the subject of human rights discourse can no longer be conceptualized as the autonomous individual who encounters the given social world. Rather, the subject of human rights is one who constitutes herself in and through the disciplines or regimes of power. Indeed, viewed from a Foucauldian perspective, human rights discourse is itself implicated in these disciplinary practices and is yet another illusory humanistic narrative through which the subject is conformed to societal norms.[65] For Foucault, human rights discourse also constructs and regulates the idea of normative humanity through its philosophical ideals, legislative apparatus, and habituating practices. For example, he draws attention to what he regards as the implausible position occupied by the subject in human rights and other humanistic narratives. For Foucault, "man" cannot function as both guarantor and guaranteed, as both vindicator and vindicated. According to James Bernauer, "As transcendental he is constructor of the world . . . transparent thinker of his own unthought." But as "empirical he is like any other object: subject to prediction, to alien forces, to a history which antedates him."[66] While one might want to take issue with the totalizing character of the Foucauldian position, his genealogical critique is particularly illuminating when one examines the history of the concept of "the human." Even the most cursory glance at the history of the human reveals that the critical marks of humanness have changed over time. Such a history also confirms that the debates about who could or could not be regarded as human were deeply contested and were framed through what in Foucault's terms would be regarded as disciplines of power. One thinks, for example, of the philosophical and theological debates in the nineteenth century about whether the Africans brought to the United States as slaves should be regarded as human, and of comparable debates some centuries earlier about the anthropological status of the tribal and indigenous peoples of South America. What these debates suggest is that the qualities that today are regarded to be the "natural" or "constant" marks of human nature are themselves the products of historical and political practices.[67] These qualities cannot simply be read from the nature of things, cannot be assumed to be constant and universal. Foucault cautions further about the lure of humanistic discourses like those of human rights. He recalls modernity's ambiguous legacy in the eighteenth century when the rhetoric of equality flourished alongside greatly enhanced systems of surveillance and social control.[68] In doing so, he reminds us to pay attention to the potential blind spots and exclusions that contemporary human rights politics may perpetuate and to recognize that this too can be yet another regulative ideal, a form of disciplinary control.

This critical attitude is taken up by post-Foucauldian human rights scholars who attempt to develop a discourse that is not premised on the idea of a prediscursive, shared, and fixed human nature. As such, the work of these scholars, particularly those writing from a postcolonial perspective, represents an important break with the dominant liberal philosophy of human rights. Upendra Baxi, for example, follows Foucault in viewing the human dialectically, arguing that "the human is what in a large measure the apparatuses of power/knowledge designate as such by practices of violent social exclusion."[69] Baxi is particularly illuminating on the manner in which the "human" in human rights discourse is constituted by the power effects of its own histories. Thus, alongside the various emancipatory practices engendered by human rights politics, modern human rights discourse has also "provided the grammars of political experience for the domination of the non-European peoples and the ruthless unmaking of their lifeworlds."[70] Judith Butler also insists that the terms by which we are recognized as human are socially articulated and changeable.[71] Indeed, a historical analysis of the way in which the concept of the human has evolved in philosophical discourse will certainly confirm that "the human" is made and remade through what Foucault would call the insurrection of subjugated knowledges. Feminism illustrates this well and is discussed in more detail in the next chapter. Ernesto Laclau and Chantal Mouffe develop this point further, insisting that human rights politics does not require a concept of human nature in order to flourish.[72] They develop strategies for resisting oppression that are embedded within contingent discursive formations and that do not depend on such external and ostensibly universal referents. In chapter 3 I discuss in more detail this dialectical understanding of the human and its possibilities for the renewal of human rights discourse. For the moment, however, it is simply important to note that this rearticulation of the human within the power/knowledge axis challenges in a fundamental way the concept of the rational autonomous "agent" upon which modern human rights theory is premised.

Human Rights and Universal Rationality: Tradition-Dependent Reasoning

As Johannes Morsink rightly insists, the concept of inherent human rights involves two critical and interrelated claims: a metaphysical claim that says that all human beings have these rights because they share a human nature and an epistemic claim that says that human beings can come to know this is so by virtue of what he calls "their own epistemic (or knowledge) equipment."[73] This concept of what Morsink calls "epistemic universality" is a central component of the liberal philosophy of human rights but draws on an understanding of the nature of moral knowledge that is increasingly disputed. The proceedings of the debates that accompanied the Vienna Declaration's statement that the universal nature of human rights is "beyond question" provides an insight into the way in which this epistemic universality continues to be called into question.[74] The inclusion of this statement was a source of major controversy, with this concept of epistemic universality under attack from many quarters. The Asian delegates in particular argued that there is an integral connection between moral values and the historical and social contexts in which they are embedded, resisting the dominant liberal framework that, they claimed, strives to separate them. The objections to epistemic universality discussed at Vienna mirror MacIntyre's indictment of human rights thinking. MacIntyre's claim that contemporary society lacks a coherent moral framework, and that what we possess instead "are the fragments of a conceptual scheme . . . simulacra of morality," is well known.[75] However, his explanation for this arbitrary and fragmentary character of contemporary morality is of interest to human rights theorists because he locates the blame for this incoherence in the liberal polity's attempt to maintain an artificial separation between moral values and the contexts from which they emerge. Liberal philosophy, he argues, consistently and purposefully promotes the idea of moral values independent of human interests and bonds, and it aims to articulate a morality that transcends tradition. In the contemporary political context, human rights norms have become the culturally acceptable way of asserting this idea of a morality that transcends tradition. MacIntyre insists that this aspiration to a tradition-independent morality is a fiction that can be perpetuated only because liberalism refuses to acknowledge its own tradition-dependent nature. For MacIntyre, therefore, human rights discourse is just one more instance of the unhealthy legacy of "the enlightenment project" in which the social embeddedness of value is denied. Moreover, in an ironic twist that illustrates further the incoherence of this legacy, MacIntyre claims that the current difficulties with the category of human rights arise precisely because it has been cut adrift from its original philosophical hinterland of natural rights—that is, from the only foundations that could give it legitimacy.[76]

Not only does human rights discourse exemplify the incoherence of contemporary moral debate but, according to its critics, it also advances one of the fundamental errors of enlightenment thinking—a claim to universality. Human rights theory identifies what it takes to be a set of normative ethical principles that can be apprehended by each person who, engaging in a process of moral reasoning, can draw conclusions about universal morality based on the nature of the person. Kantian and natural law traditions have each pursued this line of epistemological justification to varying degrees, although the morphology of reason is different in each case. Within these philosophical traditions, there are, of course, nuances and developments. Cornelia Richter reminds us, for example, that only the first of Kant's two *Critiques* presents what is now taken to be the classic articulation of Enlightenment rationality, where reason seems to be completely independent of the surrounding context "content in and by itself and thereby able to guide human action according to the rules of the categorical imperative."[77] These nuances notwithstanding, there persisted a conviction that human beings could construct an account of morality, binding for all peoples and in all places, and that the content of this could be known via the practices of universal reason.[78] Alan Gewith's argument for the universality of human rights based on deductive reasoning from the Golden Rule is one such example of this argument of reason.[79]

This idea of an abstract and universal rationality that exists independent of the social matrices in which it is exercised is rejected today not only by MacIntyre and other communitarian critics of liberalism but also by feminist and postcolonial scholars. What unites these otherwise disparate philosophies is the belief that what are taken as the objective standards of reason are themselves the result of socially embedded assumptions about what is reasonable, logical, coherent, and self-evident. They argue that what counts as evidence, how evidence is evaluated, the relative merits of one piece of evidence over against another, and other evaluative concerns shape the trajectory of reason to such a degree that reason is more appropriately regarded as itself enmeshed in the historical and social contingencies of each age. The feminist critique, for example, draws attention to the fact that these putatively objective and impartial standards, premised as they are on the belief in a hierarchical opposition between "mind" and "nature," are essentially "historically situated and contingent terms, often extrapolations of masculine characteristics and values that serve to legitimize and reproduce a dominantly masculine culture."[80] Thus all moral reasoning is tradition dependent. There are no objective criteria that allow one to identify the norms of rationality separately from the lived traditions of enquiry. Indeed, this desire to escape particularity "into a realm of entirely universal maxims which belong to man as such" is rejected as "an illusion and an illusion with painful consequences."[81] Moral values and the traditions of enquiry (rationality) through which they are articulated are more appropriately understood as, simultaneously, the products and the producers of particular moral traditions.

Communitarian, feminist, and postcolonial theorists each believe that the norms of rationality cannot be detached from their historical and cultural contexts. Indeed, *After Virtue* asserts this to the extent that it foregrounds incommensurability as a central feature of moral values. Undoubtedly, the language of incommensurability is challenging for human rights theorists who either assume or argue for a significant degree of commensurability and translatability, whether this is expressed in terms of rights, needs, capabilities, dignity, or overlapping consensus.[82] Yet, as I argued later, this stress on the tradition-dependent character of reason does not inevitably result in an epistemological relativism. As I discuss later, theorists as diverse as Upendra Baxi, Jeffrey Stout, and Michael Walzer acknowledge that rationality is tradition dependent while they also hold to the belief that human beings can communicate across their "thick" embedded traditions and can arrive at an account of shared value and values. Far from being simply a rearticulation of the abstract and universality reasoning of classic human rights discourse, these approaches share a conviction and a hope that in among the plurality of thick, located, and culturally embedded moral traditions, we may be able to identify shared principles that could be regarded as indispensable for our global social well-being.

Human Rights and Universal Rationality: Challenging Idealization

Critics who reject liberal conceptions of universal rationality have dealt a blow to the epistemological foundations of human rights discourse. Yet, although dismissive of universalist positions that are derived from abstract, transcendent reason, many critics retain a realist conception of truth and endorse a pluralist stance regarding moral values. MacIntyre, for example, rejects approaches that have attempted "to eliminate the notion of truth from that of enquiry."[83] The communitarian difficulty is with the quest to identify norms independent of social practice and not so much with the desire to identify norms that may emerge as shared or common among cultures.[84] Thus, it is abstraction rather than universalism that is the basic stumbling block. Neither do critics reject the idea of assessing the adequacy of competing traditions of enquiry. MacIntyre is quite explicit on this point when he insists that we can assess the relative worth of a tradition by examining its performance when it encounters an epistemological crisis.[85] The test of a tradition, he argues, lies in its internal capacity to respond to the difficulties it encounters, that is, the extent to which it contains the seeds of its transcendence.

Both pragmatist and postmodern philosophers extend the epistemological critique still further. Following Ludwig Wittgenstein, each school rejects correspondence theories of truth, insisting that there is no place to stand from where the alleged correspondence between language and "reality" can be discerned. With his groundbreaking *Philosophy and the Mirror of Nature*, the pragmatist philosopher Richard Rorty rejected the representational theory of knowledge that is embedded in realism.[86] He characterized this realism as being based on the belief that "the mind's task is to take the empirical input—'the given'—and for the generated thoughts to then represent, or 'mirror the reality,' of the exterior world." In realism, this exercise of the mind's mirroring the world by representation becomes "a rational reconstruction of our knowledge" and that "by means of this representation, if done rightly, we will have then established a correspondence with the world, deriving truth."[87] Rorty insists that this approach has characterized philosophical inquiry from Plato to Kant, and, in his view, the two thousand years of philosophizing in between has not paid any dividends because it is premised on mistaken assumptions about what we can know and how we can know. Rorty takes up and develops the pragmatic approach of Dewey and proposes that "if ideas, meanings, conceptions, notions, theories, systems are instrumental to an active reorganization of the given environment, to a removal of some specific trouble and perplexity, then the test of their validity and value lies in accomplishing this work."[88] This emphasis on contingency means "ceasing to ask both metaphysical questions about the ground or source of our ideals and epistemological questions about how one can be certain that one has chosen the correct ideal."[89] Philosophers should therefore give up this idea that there is "the really real to be uncovered" through reason and focus instead on the value that a truth claim can bring.[90] Indeed, as Gianni Vattimo observes, "Rorty's stance imposed a different horizon on the problem of observational truth: no longer that of inspecting how things are but that of operating in (and on) reality." For Rorty, "the highest value is not truth as objective description; the highest value is accord with others."[91]

Rorty's develops the implications of this position for the politics of human rights in his celebrated Amnesty Lecture.[92] He argues against what he calls human rights foundationalism, rejecting theories that are based on either human nature or universal reason, or a combination of both. His rejection of human rights foundationalism is based on his insistence that, since its metaphysical claims are no longer credible, therefore they are no longer efficacious. Thus he replaces the question "what is our nature" with the question "what can we make of ourselves," and he argues that our focus ought to be on how "we can grab hold of history" and discern "how best to bring about the utopia sketched by the Enlightenment."[93] Rorty insists that "we are now in a good position to put aside the last vestiges of the ideas that human beings are distinguished by their capacity to know rather than the capacities for friendship and inter-marriage, distinguished by rigorous rationality rather than by flexible sentimentality."[94] As a result, as I discuss in more detail in chapter 6, Rorty believes the politics of human rights can best be secured not by "our becoming more aware of the requirements of the moral law" but rather through what Annette Baier, following David Hume, describes as "a progress of sentiments" that consists in an increasing ability to see the similarities between ourselves and people very unlike us as outweighing the differences.[95] Moreover, within this framework of developing our sentiments and expanding the circles of our moral concern, the arts—rather than rational argumentation—can play an important educative role.

Although pragmatist and postmodern theorists agree that human rights foundationalism is unconvincing, they differ in their evaluation of what Rorty admiringly termed "the utopia sketched by the Enlightenment." Foucault holds no such admiration for the Enlightenment project and argues, instead, that the production of knowledge is always bound up with regimes of power, and that every society produces its own truths which have a normalizing and regulatory function.[96] He saw modernity's great civilizing projects as exemplifying these regimes of power through which societies are regulated. One example will suffice. In *Madness and Civilization: A History of Insanity in the Age of Reason*, Foucault develops his argument that, in modernity, classical reason and social practices combine to create a discourse and apparatus of repression. In this case, he argues that the categorization and subsequent incarceration of the insane is a direct effect of the formulation of Cartesian reason. His analysis of Descartes's meditation on doubt leads him to conclude that "reason" is only recognizable through the absence of its opposite, unreason, and that the rationalism of the enlightenment is thus predicated on the exclusion of other forms of thought. In *Discipline and Punish* and *The History of Sexuality*, Foucault extends his analysis of the contexts in which the marginalizing and repressive functions of power operate. For Foucault, enlightenment rationality is both constituted by and implicated in the marginalization of the insane and other "outsiders" and can never be read apart from its authoritarian effects. Zygmunt Bauman's *Modernity and the Holocaust* makes a similar argument about the way in which the philosophical, technological, and procedural dimensions of modernity both facilitated and enabled the perpetration of the atrocity. In fact, it has led to a situation in which, according to Simon Chesterman, "the ends of modernity in securing international recognition of norms born of the European Enlightenment have been subverted by the end of modernity and the concomitant scepticism of the power of reason to herald in a new World Order."[97]

This Foucauldian conviction that all knowledge is enmeshed in power relations is again taken up by feminist and postcolonial scholars who reject traditional conceptualizations of reason on the grounds that reason is marred by masculinist, racist, and Western biases. As such, this Foucauldian perspective provides a legitimate and important critique of the marginalizing and silencing functions of power and has the effect of undercutting false universals and exclusionary idealizations. In this context it is possible that the concept of human rights will be seen to be so contaminated by dominatory power that it will be regarded as nothing more than a "pretentious local narrative."[98] However, this is not the full story, either for Foucault or for those who desire to keep faith with human rights politics while recognizing these limitations. In his later work, Foucault develops the idea of "subjugated knowledges"—that is, the knowledge produced from the experiences of those who have been marginalized and whose perspectives have never been properly articulated or accorded "official" status. Although subjugated knowledges do not have any special epistemic status, they do have a progressive role in that they function as "struggles against secrecy, deformation, and mystifying representation imposed on the people."[99]

Foucault's critique is ultimately unsatisfactory because he does not explain the basis on which he can hold out hope for a more progressive ethics and politics. Nonetheless, his insistence that we pay attention to the normalizing functions of knowledge is important as we attempt to develop an understanding of human rights that is more aware of its own discursive character. It is important to remember that human rights politics has functioned both as a form of subjugated knowledge and as a dominatory discourse. Inevitably, we will need to address the question of whether and how it can be rearticulated to retain its ethical force while also recognizing its contingent character.

Conclusion

Human rights discourse must be divested of its anthropological essentialism and its transcendent rationalism. In addition, it will need to acknowledge the moral significance of diversity while developing practices that enable cross-cultural ethical discourse. Moreover, it will need to accomplish this while resisting the tendency to essentialize cultures, communities, and traditions. Many of the political and philosophical critiques of human rights discourse considered here are coherent and compelling. They demand our attention if we are to renew discourse of human rights. Conor Gearty is correct when he insists that we cannot unlearn the skepticism about truth that has made the liberal version of human rights untenable.[100] It is, therefore, only by engaging with these philosophical critiques that a discourse that is more in sync with the mood of late modernity can be developed.

Notes

1. Boutros Boutros-Ghali, "The Common Language of Humanity," *United Nations World Conference on Human Rights: The Vienna Declaration and the Programme of Action* (New York: United Nations, 1993).

2. Michael Ignatieff, "The End of Human Rights," *New York Times*, February 5, 2002.

3. Upendra Baxi, *The Future of Human Rights*, 3rd ed. (Oxford: Oxford University Press, 2008), x.

4. John Gray, *Enlightenment's Wake* (London: Routledge, 1995), 123.

5. Edward Said, *Culture and Imperialism* (London: Chatto & Windus, 1993), 58.

6. Stuart Hall, "The West and the Rest: Discourse and Power," in *Formations of Modernity*, ed. Stuart Hall and Brian Gieben, 275–320 (Cambridge: Polity Press, 1992), 312.

7. Adamantia Pollis, "Human Rights: A Western Construct with Limited Applicability," in *Human Rights: Cultural and Ideological Perspectives*, ed. Adamantia Pollis and Peter Schwab, 1–18 (New York: Praeger, 1979), 1.

8. See Samuel Moyn's discussion of this in *The Last Utopia: Human Rights in History* (Cambridge, MA: Harvard University Press, 2010).

9. This is Roland Burke's calculation in *Decolonization and the Evolution of International Human Rights* (Philadelphia: University of Pennsylvania Press, 2010), 1. Philippe de la Chapelle estimates that fifty-six nations participated in the drafting of the Declaration and describes the nature of the representation thus: "North and South America with 21 countries represented 36 percent of the total, Europe with 16 countries 27 percent, Asia with 14 countries 24 percent, Africa with 4 countries a mere 6 percent and the South Sea Islands with 3 countries 5 percent." See *La Déclaration universelle des droits de l'homme et le catholicisme* (Paris: Pinchon et Durand-Auzias, Librarie Générale de Droit et de Jurisprudence, 1967), 44.

10. American Anthropological Association, "Statement on Human Rights," *American Anthropologist* 49, no. 2 (1947): 543.

11. Ibid., 539.

12. Ibid., 543.

13. Ibid., 542, 543.

14. Ibid.

15. Cited in Sally Engle Merry, "Changing Rights, Changing Culture," in

Culture and Rights: Anthropological Perspectives, ed. Jane K. Cowan, Marie-Benedicte Dembour, and Richard Wilson, 31–55 (Cambridge: Cambridge University Press, 2001), 38–39.

16. "Declaration on Anthropology and Human Rights," Committee for Human Rights, American Anthropological Association, adopted by the American Anthropological Association membership, June 1999, www.aaanet.org/about/Policies/statements/Declaration-on-Anthropology-and-Human-Rights.cfm.

17. Issa Shivji, *The Concept of Human Rights in Africa* (London: Codesria Book Series, 1989), 3; and Abdullahi Ahmed An-Na'im, ed., *Human Rights in Cross-Cultural Perspectives: A Quest for Consensus* (Philadelphia: University of Pennsylvania Press, 1992), 427.

18. Mary Ann Glendon, *A World Made New: Eleanor Roosevelt and the United Nations Declaration of Human Rights* (New York: Random House, 2001); Paul Gordon Lauren, *The Evolution of International Human Rights: Visions Seen* (Philadelphia: University of Pennsylvania Press, 1998); Johannes Morsink, *The United Nations Declaration of Human Rights: Origins, Drafting, and Intent* (Philadelphia: University of Pennsylvania Press, 1999); Susan Waltz, "Reclaiming and Rebuilding the History of the Universal Declaration of Human Rights," *Third World Quarterly* 23, no. 3 (2002): 437–48; and Waltz, "Universal Human Rights: The Contribution of Muslim States," *Human Rights Quarterly* 26, no. 4 (2004): 799–844.

19. Johannes Morsink, *Inherent Human Rights: Philosophical Roots of the Universal Declaration* (Philadelphia: University of Pennsylvania Press, 2009), 28; and Third Committee Records, at 448–73, in Susan Waltz, "Universalizing Human Rights: The Role of Small States in the Construction of the Universal Declaration of Human Rights," *Human Rights Quarterly* 23, no. 1 (2001): 55. Article 21 declares that "(1) everyone has a right to take part in the government of his country, directly or through freely chosen representatives, (2) everyone has a right of equal access to public services in his country, and (3) the will of the people shall be the basis of the authority of government; this shall be expressed in periodic and genuine elections which shall be by universal and equal suffrage and shall be held by secret vote or by equivalent free voting procedures."

20. General Assembly Ordinary Record, Third (Humanitarian, Social and Cultural) Committee 1948, 36, quoted in Morsink, *Inherent Human Rights*, 76.

21. Julian Steward, "Comments on the Statement on Human Rights," *American Anthropologist* 50, no. 2 (1948): 351–52.

22. Burke, *Decolonization*, 114. See also the discussion in Evan Luard's *A History of the United Nations*, vol. 2, *The Age of Decolonization 1955–65* (London: Palgrave MacMillan, 1989), in which he discusses the impact that the third world states had on the agenda. See especially chapter 20, 514–48.

23. This is Burke's summary of the Summary Records of the sessions of the Human Rights Commission's drafting subcommittee, i.e., Third Committee, 292nd meeting, October 25, 1950, A/C.3/SR.292, para. 5, in *Decolonization*, 117. It is supported by the analysis in A. W. B. Simpson's *Human Rights and the End of Empire: Britain and the Genesis of the European Convention* (Oxford: Oxford University Press, 2001); and by Roger Normand and Sarah Zaidi's *Human Rights at the UN* (Bloomington: University of Indiana Press, 2008).

24. Burke, *Decolonization*, 117, quoting Summary Records of the Third Committee, 294th meeting, October 27, 1950, A/C.3/SR.294, para. 37–38.

25. See especially Humphrey's *Human Rights and the United Nations: A Great Adventure* (London: Transnational, 1984).

26. Burke, *Decolonization*, 118, quoting Summary Records of the Third Committee, 295th meeting, October 27, 1950, A/C.3/SR.295, para. 25.

27. Ibid., 118, quoting Summary Records of the Third Committee, 296th meeting, October 27, 1950, A/C.3/SR.296.

28. Ibid., 119, quoting Summary Records of the Third Committee, 296th meeting, October 27, 1950, A/C.3/SR.296, para. 6.

29. Carlos Valenzuela of Chile, quoted in ibid., 120, quoting Summary Records of the Third Committee, 296th meeting, October 27, 1950, A/C.3/SR.296, para. 69.

30. Ibid., 120, quoting Summary Records of the Third Committee, 296th meeting, October 27, 1950, A/C.3/SR.296, para. 81.

31. General Assembly Resolution, Convention on the Political Rights of Women, 640 (VII), December 20, 1952, www.un.org/en/ga/search/view_doc.asp?symbol=A/RES/640%28VII%29.

32. Burke, *Decolonization*, 121, quoting Summary Records of the Third Committee, 478th meeting, December 15, 1952, A/C.3/SR.478, para. 24.

33. Ibid., 124, quoting Summary Records of the Third Committee, 477th meeting, December 15, 1952, A/C.3/SR.477, paras. 47, 49.

34. Ibid., 124, quoting Summary Records of the Third Committee, 478th meeting, December 15, 1952, A/C.3/SR.478, para. 4.

35. Ibid., 132, quoting Summary Records of the Third Committee, 43rd meeting, 32nd session, November 10, 1977, A/C.3/32/SR.43, para. 38.

36. Ibid., 134, quoting Summary Records of the Third Committee, 1809th meeting, December 3, 1970, A/C.3/SR.1809, para. 3, 8.

37. Ibid., 136, quoting Summary Records of the Third Committee, 2049th meeting, December 4, 1973, A/C.3/SR.2049, para. 44.

38. Ibid., 138, quoting Summary Records of the Third Committee, 43rd meeting, 32nd session, November 10, 1977, A/C.3/32/SR.43, para. 26.

39. Premier Jiang Zemin of China, quoted in William Korey, *NGOs and the Universal Declaration of Human Rights: A Curious Grapevine* (New York: St. Martin's, 1998), 488.

40. Bhikhu Parekh, "Non-Ethnocentric Universalism," in *Human Rights in Global Politics*, ed. Tim Dunne and Nicholas Wheeler, 128–59 (Cambridge: Cambridge University Press, 1999), 154.

41. Andrew Hurrell, "Power, Principles and Prudence: Protecting Human Rights in a Deeply Divided World," in *Human Rights in Global Politics*, ed. Tim Dunne and Nicholas Wheeler, 277–302 (Cambridge: Cambridge University Press, 1999), 295. There are also similar discussions from a Cuban perspective. See, for example, Peter Schwab, *Cuba: Confronting the US Embargo* (London: Macmillan, 1998), 57.

42. Mahathir bin Mohammad, Keynote Address, 9, quoted in Anthony Langlois, *The Politics and Justice of Human Rights* (Cambridge: Cambridge University Press, 2001), 15.

43. Michael Ignatieff, *Human Rights as Politics and Idolatry* (Princeton, NJ: Princeton University Press, 2001), 63, quoting the *International Herald Tribune*, November 9–10, 1991.

44. Langlois, *Politics and Justice of Human Rights*, 19.

45. Ibid., 18.

46. See Stephen C. Angle, *Human Rights and Chinese Thought: A Cross-Cultural Inquiry* (New York: Cambridge University Press, 2002), 1.

47. Following the well-worn path of Baroody, the Saudi Arabian delegate at Vienna argued that for Muslims, human rights can only be derived from Shar'ia law. See Philip Alston, "The UN's Human Rights Record: From San Francisco to Vienna and Beyond," *Human Rights Quarterly* 16, no. 2 (1994): 278.

48. Cairo Declaration of Rights on Human Rights in Islam was adopted by the Organisation of the Islamic Conference in 1990. See Elisabeth Ann Mayer, "Universal versus Islamic Human Rights: A Clash of Cultures or a Clash with a Construct?" *Michigan Journal of International Law* 15, no. 2: 307–404, for an interesting consideration of the Cairo Declaration.

49. This effort culminated at the first UN International Conference on Human Rights in Tehran in 1968, whose final proclamation highlighted the two international covenants—the Declaration on Granting Independence to Colonial Countries and Peoples and the International Convention on the Elimination of All Forms of Racial Discrimination—as having "created new standards and obligations to which States should conform." Proclamation of Teheran, Final Act of the International Conference on Human Rights, Teheran, 22 April to 13 May 1968, UN Doc. A/Conf.32/41, at 3, Article 3, available on the ICTY website www.un.org

/icty. Moyn's *The Last Utopia* highlights that there was a crucial transition from the 1948 UN Declaration's understanding of human rights that pertains today and that national and international politics of the 1970s were key to this transition.

50. Langlois, *Politics and Justice of Human Rights*, 80.

51. Conor Gearty, *Can Human Rights Survive?* (Cambridge: Cambridge University Press, 2006), 20.

52. Jacques Maritain, *The Rights of Man and Natural Law* (New York: Charles Scribner's Sons, 1944), 35.

53. This separation of human rights language from its original theocentric framework will be discussed later in this chapter.

54. Margaret MacDonald, "Natural Rights," in *Theories of Rights*, ed. Jeremy Waldron, 21–40 (Oxford: Oxford University Press, 1984), 29, 30.

55. Michael Sandel, "The Procedural Republic and the Unencumbered Self," in *Communitarianism and Individualism*, ed. Shlomo Avineri and Avner de-Shalit, 12–28 (Oxford: Oxford University Press, 1992).

56. In his *Anarchy, State, and Utopia* (New York: Basic Books, 1974), 32, Robert Nozick proposes an even more exaggerated form of individual identity in which there are "only different individual people, with their own individual lives."

57. Sandel, "Procedural Republic," 18.

58. Sandel argues that in proposing this anthropology liberalism embodies and extends one of its fatal flaws—that is, its inability to recognize that what it recommends as purely procedural is in fact substantive. See especially Charles Taylor, *Sources of the Self: The Making of the Modern Identity* (Cambridge: Cambridge University Press, 1989), particularly chapter 2, "The Self in Moral Space," 25–52; and Alasdair MacIntyre, *After Virtue: A Study in Moral Theory* (London: Duckworth, 1981), 31.

59. Michael Walzer, *Politics and Passion: Towards a More Egalitarian Liberalism* (New Haven, CT: Yale University Press, 2004).

60. Silvere Lotringer, ed. *The Politics of Truth: Michel Foucault* (Los Angeles: Semiotext(e), 2007), 42. I am grateful to Celia Kenny for this reference.

61. Michel Foucault, "Afterword: The Subject and Power," in *Michel Foucault: Beyond Structuralism and Hermeneutics*, ed. Hubert Dreyfus and Paul Rabinow, 208–28 (New York: Harvester Wheatsheaf, 1982), 208.

62. Ibid.

63. Ibid.

64. Ibid.

65. Hubert Dreyfus and Paul Rabinow, "The Methodological Failure of Archaeology," in *Michel Foucault: Beyond Structuralism and Hermeneutics*, ed. Hubert Dreyfus and Paul Rabinow (New York: Harvester Wheatsheaf, 1982), 96.

66. See Charles Davis, *Religion and the Making of Society: Essays in Social Theology* (Cambridge: Cambridge University Press, 1994), 161. See also James Bernauer, "The Prisons of Man: Foucault's Negative Theology," *International Philosophical Quarterly* 27 (1987): 365–80.

67. Foucault argues this case in a much-quoted passage from *The Order of Things*, in which he quotes from a particular Chinese encyclopedia that divided animals into "(a) belonging to the Emperor, (b) embalmed, (c) tame, (d) sucking pigs, (e) sirens, (f) fabulous, (g) stray dogs, (h) included in the present classification, (i) frenzied, (j) innumerable, (k) drawn with a fine camelhair brush, (l) *et cetera*, (m) having just broken the water pitcher, (n) that a long way off look like flies." To the modern eye, this classification system is bizarre and arbitrary. Foucault's argument, however, is that the "natural" classifications of every order are similarly arbitrary and that the regimes of power/knowledge through which our categories of thought are classified are radically contingent and cannot be regarded as natural. Foucault, *The Order of Things: An Archaeology of the Human Sciences* (New York: Vintage, 1994), xv.

68. In *Discipline and Punish*, Foucault points out that at the same time that the humanist discourse of equality was gaining currency, at every level of society there was increased surveillance—in manufacturing workshops, prisons, hospitals, among the poor and indigent. Thus, the practices that were ostensibly concerned with economic efficiency or the provision of welfare had the practical effect of undermining the widely prevailing aspiration to "liberty, equality and fraternity." Foucault, *Discipline and Punish: The Birth of the Prison*, 2nd ed. (New York: Vintage, 1995), 222.

69. Upendra Baxi, *Human Rights in a Posthuman World: Critical Essays* (Oxford: Oxford University Press, 2007), 24.

70. Baxi, *Future of Human Rights*, 118.

71. Judith Butler, *Undoing Gender* (London: Routledge, 2004), 2.

72. See, in particular, Ernesto Laclau and Chantal Mouffe, *Hegemony and Socialist Strategy: Towards a Radical Democratic Politics* (London: Verso, 2001), 153–54.

73. Morsink, *Inherent Human Rights*, 55.

74. Paragraph 1 of Vienna Declaration (UN Doc. A/CONF.157/22, July 6, 1993), http://www1.umn.edu/humanrts/instree/l1viedec.html.

75. MacIntyre, *After Virtue*, 8.

76. MacIntyre believes that it may be plausible to speak about "inalienable human rights" in the context of belief in a natural law, complete with a divine author as its guarantor. However, as early as the eighteenth century, philosophers began to distance themselves from this practice of anchoring human rights in a theistic world view. Nor did later proponents of rights-based philosophies address

this problem of origins. More often than not, they simply ignored the fact that this concept of "right" was once parasitic on religion. Although once parasitic on religion, in the twentieth century it began to flourish without that God, or any other replacement. See, for example, Peter Gay, *The Enlightenment: An Interpretation*, vol. 2, *The Science of Freedom* (London: Weidenfeld & Nicolson, 1969), 456–57. See also Charles Taylor's *Sources of the Self*, especially the chapter "Rationalised Christianity," 235–47, in which he argues that Locke's theory of natural rights plays a significant role in this transition toward the internalization of the moral sources of human rights. This will be discussed in more detail in the section on theological objections to human rights theory.

77. Cornelia Richter, "The Productive Power of Reason," in *Faith in the Enlightenment? The Critique of the Enlightenment Revisited*, ed. Lieven Boeve, Joeri Schrijvers, Wessel Stoker, and Hendrik M. Vroom, 23–38 (New York: Rodopi, 2006), 28.

78. This idea of objective reason is the most frequent and long-standing epistemological justification for universal human rights. In an interesting historical analysis of the debates during the drafting of the UN Declaration, Morsink proposes an alternative epistemological ground—namely, moral intuitionism. He suggests that the arguments from reason and from intuition were present side by side in the debates, and he goes on to justify the content of the Declaration on the basis of an argument from the framework of shared moral intuitions. This is discussed in more detail in chapter 4.

79. Alan Gewith, "The Golden Rule Rationalized," in *Human Rights: Essays on Justification and Applications* (Chicago: University of Chicago Press, 1992); and Gewith, *The Community of Rights* (Chicago: University of Chicago Press, 1996).

80. Lois McNay, *Foucault and Feminism* (Oxford: Polity Press, 1992), 91.

81. MacIntyre, *After Virtue*, 205–6.

82. Martha Nussbaum has been associated with this approach for many years. See her most recent book, *Creating Capabilities: The Human Development Approach* (Cambridge, MA: Harvard University Press, 2011). See also Jack Donnelly, *Universal Human Rights in Theory and Practice* (Ithaca, NY: Cornell University Press, 1989).

83. See Alasdair MacIntyre, "A Partial Response to My Critics," in *After MacIntyre: Critical Perspectives on the Work of Alasdair MacIntyre*, ed. John Horton and Susan Mendus, 283–304 (Cambridge, UK: Polity Press, 1996), 298.

84. For the most part, communitarians have not included this "intercultural" or "global" perspective. However, there is nothing within the communitarian framework that would reject such an approach in principle.

85. See the extensive discussion in chapter 18 of Alasdair MacIntyre's *Whose Justice? Which Rationality?* (Notre Dame, IN: University of Notre Dame Press, 1989).

86. Richard Rorty, *Philosophy and the Mirror of Nature* (Princeton, NJ: Princeton University Press, 1979).

87. Rorty quoted in G. Elijah Dann, "Philosophy, Religion and Religious Belief after Rorty," in *An Ethics for Today: Finding Common Ground between Philosophy and Religion*, by Richard Rorty (New York: Columbia University Press, 2008), 29; discussing Rorty's *Objectivity, Relativism, and Truth* (Cambridge: Cambridge University Press, 1991).

88. John Dewey, quoted in Dann, "Philosophy, Religion and Religious Belief," 34.

89. Rorty, *An Ethics for Today*, 9.

90. Richard Rorty, *Truth and Progress: Philosophical Papers* (New York: Cambridge University Press, 1998), 116–17.

91. Gianni Vattimo, "Introduction," in *An Ethics for Today: Finding Common Ground between Philosophy and Religion*, by Richard Rorty, 1–6 (New York: Columbia University Press, 2008), 3.

92. Richard Rorty, "Human Rights, Rationality, and Sentimentality," in *On Human Rights: The Oxford Amnesty Lectures*, ed. Stephen Shute & Susan Hurley, 112–34 (Oxford: Basic Books, 1993), reprinted in Christopher J. Voparil and Richard J. Bernstein, eds., *The Rorty Reader* (Oxford: Wylie-Blackwell, 2010), 351–65.

93. Voparil and Bernstein, *Rorty Reader*, 353, 355.

94. Ibid., 365.

95. Ibid., 362.

96. McNay, *Foucault and Feminism*, 25, commenting on Foucault's *The Archaeology of Knowledge* (London: Tavistock, 1972), 185.

97. Simon Chesterman, "Human Rights as Subjectivity," *Millennium: Journal of International Studies* 27, no. 1 (1998): 97–118, at 97.

98. This is an adaptation of Charlotte Witt's phrase in "Feminist Metaphysics," in *A Mind of One's Own: Feminist Essays on Reason and Objectivity*, eds. Louise M. Anthony and Charlotte Witt, 273–87 (Boulder, CO: Westview Press, 1993), 276.

99. Michel Foucault, *Power: Essential Works of Foucault 1954–1984*, vol. 3, ed. Michel James D. Faubion (New York: New Press, 2000), 330.

100. Gearty, *Can Human Rights Survive?* 40.

2

The Crisis of Meaning

Theological Perspectives

The political and philosophical critiques of human rights are profound and persuasive and must be addressed if human rights are to flourish. However, a series of theological critiques of human rights have further destabilized the confidence with which Christians have engaged with the politics of human rights. Richard Rorty is very clear that the symbiotic relationship between philosophy and theology means that his pragmatist critique (see chapter 1) applies equally to the truth claims of Christianity since "its theological language, woven from the same Platonic assumptions as traditional philosophy, shares a conceptual framework about the True and the Good."[1] His rejection of foundationalism has purchase in the theological as well as in the philosophical realm, and, insofar as theological justifications of human rights depend on the twin concepts of human nature and of universal rationality, they too are under fire from Rorty and others who share his critical perspective. These objections to the liberal philosophical framework are also found among theologians, including William Cavanaugh, Stanley Hauerwas, and John Milbank, who are equally critical of its universalist and rationalist claims. However, this represents just one strand of the contemporary theological resistance to liberal human rights discourse. The other prominent strand of criticism focuses, ironically, on what is taken to be its failure to provide an adequate metaphysical foundation once liberal human rights theory has abandoned its original theistic framework in favor of a secular grounding. These strands interpret the history of human rights differently and have diverse understandings of the nature of, and justification for, human rights claims. In many respects they run along parallel lines, each suspicious of liberal human rights discourse but for very different reasons.

In this chapter I discuss the most prominent of these theological critiques of contemporary human rights theory. I begin by considering the objections to the various attempts to establish a nonreligious basis for human rights politics. This argument draws on philosophical reasoning and historical evidence to propose an account of human rights that is situated firmly within a theistic framework. However, in the process of doing this, it undermines all secular theories. Most historians agree that the antecedent of the concept of the human right—that is, the natural right—functioned within a theistic framework, but the theological significance of this historical fact is deeply contested. Some, including Michael Perry and Nicholas Wolterstorff, whose work will be considered later, argue that contemporary discourse is incoherent because it has abandoned this theistic frame of reference, and they advocate a retrieval of this Christian tradition and the reestablishment of a religious grounding for human rights discourse.[2] Others see no prospect of a rapprochement because, they claim, liberal human rights discourse is premised on the maintenance of this radical rupture with its Christian antecedents. I go on to discuss the historical arguments and their theological development by focusing on debates about the politics of accommodation. I conclude by suggesting that, notwithstanding Christianity's complex and contested relationship with the language of human rights, there are good historical and theological reasons to keep faith with human rights. In making this case, however, I am not endorsing the classical liberal theory but rather expressing a conviction that human rights discourse has both the potential and the means to transcend its historical and conceptual limitations and, by so doing, can become a genuinely cross-cultural moral discourse that can draw on theological or secular foundations and through which the politics of exclusion and of violence can be challenged.

Human Rights without God?

With her description of human rights as "values for a godless age," Francesca Klug captures an important change in the way that human rights have come to be understood in the post–Cold War period.[3] While she later explained that it was not her intention to suggest that the concept of human rights is an exclusively secular one, her title nonetheless exemplifies the growing tendency to ignore its theological antecedents. This secularizing process has, for the most part, been welcomed by philosophers and political activists who regard human rights as providing the basis of consensus on fundamental values in the absence of agreement on shared comprehensive doctrines. However, this tendency to divorce the concept of human rights from its theological moorings has also been the subject of substantial criticism on both philosophical and historical grounds. In this section I discuss the philosophical critique as it is developed within the Christian tradition. Although one finds comparable, if less frequent, critiques of the abandonment of the theistic framework from Jewish and Islamic perspectives, these will not be discussed here.[4] Michael Perry argues that, while there may be grounds for the morality of human rights in different religious traditions, all secular attempts to ground or justify human rights are unconvincing. His case focuses on the premises underlying human rights claims—namely, that each human being has an inherent dignity, and that this dignity is inviolable. The core of Perry's argument is that the basis of this twofold claim—that human beings have an inherent dignity and that this dignity is inviolable—requires an explanation, and the only convincing explanations are religiously based ones. He notes that the International Bill of Rights is silent on the grounding of these claims, but he insists that in order to have moral force, human rights morality must be able to give an answer to the question "what is the source, the ground, of this dignity—and of the normative force this dignity has for us?"[5] Perry sketches a religious defense of the claim that human beings have an inherent dignity that is inviolable, structured around the Christian belief in a loving creator God. Using the motif of a person called Sarah, Perry explains the nature of the normative claim thus: "Sarah believes that because God is who God is, because the universe is what it is, and because we are who we are, and not because of anything commanded by God as supreme legislator, the most fitting way of life for us human beings—the most deeply satisfying way of life of which we are capable—is one in which we children of God, we sisters and brothers, 'love one another just as I have loved you.'"[6] He does concede that other religious grounds can be developed, and thereby confers legitimacy on the work of Jewish, Islamic, and Christian scholars who are developing theological arguments in support of contemporary human rights claims.[7] He is silent, however, on whether he believes that the nontheistic religious traditions, like Buddhism or Confucianism, can provide a coherent basis for human rights claims, and as far as secular groundings are concerned, he is unconvinced by any such attempts thus far.

Max Stackhouse and Nicholas Wolterstorff also address this issue of the grounding of human rights, each confirming, with Perry, that the resources of other religions, especially the theistic traditions, can be deployed in support of human rights but that all secular attempts at grounding are unlikely to be successful.[8] Wolterstorff concludes that the secular attempts of Immanuel Kant, Gerald Dworkin, and Alan Gewith are not convincing, while Perry draws the same conclusion in respect of the theories of John Finnis, Dworkin, and Martha Nussbaum as well as accounts that draw on evolutionary biology.[9] Wolterstorff's rather stark assessment is that, if the Judaic and Christian heritage of Western society erodes, then we can expect that our moral subculture of rights will also eventually erode, and we will eventually slide back into tribalism.[10] Perry similarly concludes that the morality of human rights cannot survive "the death of God" and that secular attempts at grounding human rights in ideas such that human beings are inestimably precious—or that they are ends in themselves, or that they are owed unconditional respect—are simply not viable without being underwritten by belief in a loving God.

But Perry fails to note that both religious and secular groundings of human rights are each, ultimately, articles of faith. Neither the theological claim to dignity based in belief in a creator God nor the ethical conviction that human beings are due unconditional respect can be established or proved through rational argumentation. What distinguishes the theological from the secular grounding is not that one can give a more convincing answer to the question "why is this the case—in virtue of what is it the case." Both the theological and the secular moralities give tradition-specific intelligible answers to this question, and each depends ultimately on a conviction that cannot be proved. Perry, and others who follow this line of argumentation, construe the foundations of human rights too narrowly. They transform a historical fact into a philosophical necessity and, consequently, imply that there can only be one tradition-specific grounding for human rights—namely, a Christian theological grounding. This conclusion that human rights morality requires a religious grounding also raises fundamental questions about the legitimacy of the last six decades of human rights politics. In particular, it seems to dismiss the significance of the radical transformation that has seen human rights evolve from a theory anchored in a now-neglected theistic framework into a vibrant multireligious, cross-cultural one. Michael Ignatieff correctly characterizes the transformation in terms of human rights having gone global by going local, where going local has involved human rights connecting with the extraordinary diversity of moral languages and narrative traditions—both religious and secular—worldwide and finding comparable justifications for human rights claims therein.[11] Already in 1947 at the UNESCO Symposium on Human Rights, there was a disagreement between those such as the Italian philosopher Benedetto Croce, who argued for a normative and universally agreed account of the grounding of human rights, and those who believed that the discourse would prosper only if the many different ways of grounding human rights (i.e., the comprehensive doctrines) were acknowledged.[12] Maritain's now-infamous comment that those present were able to agree on the existence of human rights but only on condition that no one asked them why, since the "why" is where the argument begins, illustrates the point.[13] Over the last six decades, human rights discourse has in fact welcomed the articulation of different tradition-specific accounts of the grounding of human rights—both secular and religious. Moreover, it was only when human rights discourse began to include these diverse "whys" and incorporate the various indigenous categories and narratives that it began to flourish.

The success of human rights politics over recent decades confirms Ignatieff's instinct that "we do not need to agree that we are all created in the image of God, or that we have natural rights that flow from our human essence, to agree that we do not want to be tortured by government officials, or that we do not want our lives, families and property forfeited."[14] Indeed, one might conclude that human rights discourse has flourished precisely because it has, albeit belatedly, valorized the role of different comprehensive doctrines and, consequently, has come to acknowledge that there are different ways of accounting for why human beings can be said to have universal human rights. We are formed according to the rationalities of particular traditions and, as a result, are likely to explain why we believe we ought to be immune from these kinds of threats by referring to specific religious or cultural categories. We relate to human rights discourse from our specific "thick," culturally embedded vantage points. Thus, David Hollen-bach argues for a new way of grounding human rights that "is in continuity with [Catholicism's] ancient stress on virtuous commitment to the good of community," while Stephen Angle explains how neo-Confucianism posits a nontheistic grounding of human rights, and Martha Nussbaum's secular grounding is focused on the basic social emotion of compassion.[15] Rorty also argues for a grounding of human rights that flows from empathy and compassion.[16] However, theologians must accept that their explanations of the grounding of human rights are also tradition-specific. Indeed, Wolter-storff's grounding of human rights on the conviction that they inhere in the worth bestowed on human beings by the love of God is no different from those of Angle, Nussbaum, or Rorty in being tradition-specific groundings of human rights claims that are intelligible and convincing only within its own frames of reference. In fact, the recent success of human rights discourse has depended, in no small measure, on particular religious and cultural traditions coming to believe that they have a stake in promot-ing these categories and that the narratives, values, and practices of such traditions—far from being marginalized—can be harnessed. Of course, there are significant differences between religious believers who assert that their relationship with God has a bearing on their commitment to human rights as well as those for whom such an assertion makes no sense. The last century has shown, however, that the morality of human rights becomes more, rather than less, durable when citizens can draw upon their manifold comprehensive doctrines—religious and secular—to ground their morali-ties of human rights.[17]

Human Rights, Christian Witness, and the Politics of Accommodation

An altogether different and more pervasive theological critique of human rights comes from those who argue that Christianity and liberalism are fundamentally incompatible, historical affinities notwithstanding. It is a view expressed by theologians described as "the new traditionalists," as well as by many Christian communities worldwide who are dismayed at the strident secularism of some liberal societies. This suspicion of liberalism and in particular of the politics of human rights has been evident in differ-ent forms through the entire modern period. When, in 1789, the National

Constituent Assembly of France declared that "men are born and remain free and equal in rights" and that "the aim of every political association is the preservation of the natural and inviolable rights of man," the Vatican reacted immediately to condemn it.[18] In 1791, in *Quod aliquantum*, Pius VI claimed that it was anathema for Catholics to accept this Declaration of the Rights of Man and of the Citizen and insisted that "this equality, this liberty, so highly exalted by the National Assembly, have then as their only result the overthrow of the Catholic religion."[19] Additionally, *Mirari vos* strongly condemned liberalism, individualism, and democracy as well as freedom of conscience, of speech, and of the press.[20] Reformed traditions have also expressed concern about the threats that liberalism poses to Christian values, with many denominations becoming progressively and vocally hostile to the liberal polity and to what they call "the human rights agenda." Today this multidenominational critique draws on both historical and theological arguments to insist that Christians should avoid politics of accommodation and should eschew liberal categories, including human rights, as they strive to promote the kingdom values of peace and justice in society. In this section, I evaluate the historical and theopolitical dimensions of this argument, recognizing, however, that they are mutually dependent.

It is paradoxical that traditions that have been so deeply intertwined, both conceptually and politically, now regard the other with such suspicion. Nonetheless, many Christians and secularists refuse to accept that the formative role that Christianity played in the articulation of liberal values continues to have relevance for today. Much of the debate centers on the extent to which the intellectual climate of Christendom endured after its political manifestations had disappeared, and on the degree of dependency that the emerging liberal categories, including human rights, had on a Christian moral framework. For many decades, the dominant view among theologians and philosophers was that the emergence of liberalism should be regarded as something startlingly new.[21] However, this view has been modified significantly within the last two decades. The historical studies of Roger Ruston, Brian Tierney, and John Witte Jr., in particular, have challenged this assessment with respect to human rights and have provided the basis for a new history of rights in which the enduring significance of its Christian antecedents is acknowledged.[22]

Much of the debate about the appropriation of human rights language in Christian social ethics revolves around the question of the extent to which original theological meanings have persisted in contemporary human rights discourse. Alasdair MacIntyre claims, for example, that "there is no expression in any ancient or medieval language correctly translated by our expression 'a right' until near the close of the middle ages: the concept lacks any means of expression in Hebrew, Greek, Latin or Arabic, classical or medieval, before about 1400."[23] Brian Tierney's analysis of the jurisprudence of the twelfth century seems to contradict this conclusion and refutes the view that human rights are a modern invention imposed on Christian political thought. According to Tierney, the early medieval discussions about natural rights represent a thoroughly theological foreshadowing of the concept of human rights. Tierney's discussion centers on the point at which *ius naturale,* which traditionally meant cosmic harmony or objective justice, began also to acquire the sense of a subjective natural right.[24] He remarks that the context of the evolving interpretation was a medieval society that was "saturated with a concern for rights," and this undoubtedly influenced academic jurisprudence.[25] Tierney assembles a host of textual sources that reveal how important individual subjective rights were to the canonists. Even Gratian wrote "of the rights of liberty that could never be lost, no matter how long a man was in bondage."[26] Moreover, in the discussions of whether the poor have a natural right to the superfluous goods of the rich, we find the articulation of a subjective natural right in the form of a welfare right, thereby contradicting Maurice Cranston's influential argument that rights of recipience were unknown even in the seventeenth and eighteenth centuries.[27] Though there are a host of different discussions, each with its specific emphasis, Tierney discerns a clear progression from the idea that a rich man has an obligation to share his superfluities with the poor, to the eventual articulation of a right to the material necessities of life. Alanus, Laurentius, and later Vincentius Hispanus, for example, each used the language of rights to refer to the poor man's claim. Later Godfrey of Fontaines wrote of this right as inalienable. "By law of nature (*ius naturae*) each one has a certain right (*ius*) in the common exterior goods of this world, which right cannot be licitly renounced," he claimed.[28] Many of the canonists also insisted that the procedure of evangelical denunciation should be available to the poor person in need. In this way the local bishop could then compel an intransigent rich man to give alms from his superfluities, "on pain of excommunication if necessary."[29] Nor was this purely a passive right because, in the case of necessity, the canonists recognized that the poor had a right to take what they needed. Evangelical denunciation thus became a means by which this right was justiciable, a remarkable accomplishment given that we are still struggling today to find ways to achieve justiciability in relation to welfare rights.

John Witte's analysis of the contributions that early modern Calvinists made in the history of human rights is also revealing and relevant in this regard. Although Witte's analysis focuses on a later period, the material he uncovers also confirms that this early language of rights was rooted in the language and practice of Christian social witness. Witte's history covers three centuries and two continents and illustrates how a host of Calvinist figures, including Theodore Beza, Johannes Althusius, John Milton, John Winthrop, and John Adams, played a significant but neglected role in the establishment of "rights talk" on both sides of the Atlantic. Witte's analysis suggests that these reformers drew on classical and Catholic resources, and that they worked in conjunction with scholastic and humanist reformers in order to pursue the concrete realization of civil and political rights as well as, to a more limited extent, economic, social, and cultural rights. Witte summarizes their concerns thus: "Early modern Calvinists were particularly ardent champions of the rights of life, liberty, property and the pursuit of happiness, rights of democratic election and representation, rights to political dissent and civil resistance, freedoms of religion, speech, press, petition and assembly, freedoms of contract and association, rights to marriage, family, divorce and inheritance, rights to form and dissolve corporations, partnerships and other voluntary associations."[30] They were also equally concerned about group rights. Of more significance in this context, however, is what Witte's analysis reveals about the manner in which these rights were framed, and the extent to which this theological framing persisted even as the voluntarist strand of the early Enlightenment began to be articulated. In the sixteenth and seventeenth centuries, Witte concludes, "they tended to assert Decalogue-based rights as inalienable rights whose abridgement could lead to resistance and revolt," whereas in the seventeenth and eighteenth centuries "they used both theological anthropology and covenant theology" to establish which rights were to be regarded as inalienable and which institutions were necessary for their vindication.[31]

Of course, the historical antecedents can be recognized without conceding either that the affinities between Christianity and liberalism should be seen in positive terms, or that the historical affinity implies that a particular form of politics should be adopted today. Yoder, for example, acknowledged what he called a "Constantinian synthesis" but described it as "this fallen condition of the church" and concluded that its role in the development of liberal political institutions signaled "the loss of the identity of the Christian community."[32] Joan Lockwood O'Donovan also acknowledges the historical affinity but questions its contemporary relevance on the basis that quite early on a "progressive antagonism [developed] between the older Christian tradition of political right and the newer voluntarist, individualist and subjectivist orientations."[33] According to Oliver O'Donovan, this is evident when we realize that in the new political order, subjective rights were mistakenly "taken to be original, not derived."[34] Lockwood O'Donovan takes up this point and argues that the absence of an overarching theocentric frame of reference radically differentiates the two world views, thus rendering them fundamentally incompatible. Furthermore, according to Lockwood O'Donovan, the category of natural rights is deeply implicated in this story of mutual antagonism since it was in the "theoretical elaborations of the concept of rights during the fifteenth to the eighteenth centuries, and especially in its classical and Enlightenment heydays, [when it was invested] with lasting intellectual content" that the context of divine providence and rule was abandoned.[35]

So what is the significance of this ambiguous legacy for Christianity's engagement with contemporary human rights discourse? That there was evolution in the concept of natural rights between the medieval and early modern period is not disputed. What continues to be debated, however, is its significance for the theological appropriation of rights talk. The loss of the theological horizon, together with an entrenchment of the dualism that has attempted to relegate religion to the private sphere, has led some to conclude that Christianity and liberalism now represent two incompatible ways of conceptualizing human social relationships. Lockwood O'Donovan makes this argument when she insists that the "western rights tradition" is incompatible with the biblical theological doctrines that are regularly invoked by Christians to ground the concept of rights.[36] This conclusion, which is widely shared, is based on her conviction that both the medieval and early modern traditions of natural rights were fatally compromised by "a progressive antagonism" toward theism. It also seems to assume that the later voluntaristic account of natural rights has dominated to such an extent that it is now the only viable one, and that any attempt to articulate a Christian tradition of rights is foolhardy.

This conclusion that the two traditions are fundamentally incompatible is, in my view, unwarranted. In the first place, it places too much emphasis on the discontinuities between the two and it tends to interpret the theological tradition of rights exclusively through the lens of the voluntarist one. It also gives undue attention to figures like Thomas Jefferson and Maximilien de Robespierre, who were deeply hostile to any theological account of rights, but who, as Wolterstorff reminds us, were not representative of eighteenth-century political thought but rather "were the odd men out."[37] Moreover, it fails to give due recognition to the fact that a theological language of rights has endured for a millennium and that in many different historical periods it represented a thoroughly theological response to the critical ethical challenges of the day. The texts discussed by Tierney, Witte, Roger Ruston, and others confirm that, in different historical periods, a theological language of rights was generated from within the life of the Christian community and was articulated in response to questions about the nature of Christian witness in the social context. The medieval canonists, the early Calvinists, and the Spanish Dominican reformers of the sixteenth century each moved effortlessly between the language of rights and the language of biblical texts and saw no conflict in so doing. Rights language was thus an indigenous theological language. It flourished within a religious world view and expressed a fundamental theological belief about human beings as social creatures in a divinely providential universe. It was, in effect, deeply and incontrovertibly Christian. Nor was it the case that, once the voluntarist interpretation took hold, it was the only frame through which rights language was refracted. For example, Tierney mentions Samuel von Pufendorf, John Locke, Jean-Jacques Burlamaqui, and Christian Wolff as thinkers in whom traces of this theological frame were still evident and who moderated the skeptical tenor of the emerging liberal rights theories.[38] Indeed, particularly in Locke, one can discern the continuing significance of the Christian tradition of rights even though he is often mistakenly perceived as "a prototype liberal individualist."[39] These early affinities, together with a myriad of albeit fragile continuities, account for the ease and fluency with which Christians in the twentieth century reappropriated the discourse of rights. One could argue not only that the reappropriation has a historical warrant but that it can be interpreted as the elaboration, not the abandonment, of a theological tradition. Thus, although the language of historic memory, of faithful witness, and of moral virtue is often invoked by Christian communitarians to indicate a conflict with liberal, including human rights, categories, it is clear that, at least historically, this situated memory, witness, and virtue can also be read as facilitating a more positive mode of engagement.

Over and above this discussion of the significance of these historical affinities has been a long-standing and often divisive debate about the specifically theological dimensions of the relationship between Christianity and liberalism. Within this context, an influential strand of thought is noted for its theological objections to the politics of accommodation within the modern liberal nation-state. Lockwood O'Donovan's claim that there is a fundamental incompatibility of world views is repeated by a number of authors, including both Oliver O'Donovan and John Milbank. Both are critical of the manner in which the liberal political order has divested itself of its original theological framework, although they differ in their respective evaluations of both the nature of this disruption and its impact. For Milbank, liberalism is the result of prior heretical developments on theology and ecclesial practice, whereas for O'Donovan it is "the child of Christianity," or, to be more precise, it is its prodigal child.[40] Each imply that liberalism and Christianity are incompatible.

In a somewhat similar vein, the theologies of Hauerwas, Yoder, and Cavanaugh draw attention both to the limitations of liberalism and to the hazards of a politics of accommodation.[41] Both Cavanaugh and Hauerwas construct compelling analyses of the embedded violence that lies at the heart of the liberal state, about which many of the theological advocates of liberalism are silent, and with which Christians must contend if they seek to witness to gospel values through active engagement with the liberal polity. Cavanaugh rightly acknowledges that an expressively theological politics is not immune to violence; however, he also gives pause for thought when he insists that "the separation of power from any transcendent moorings has not made the world less violent, but has only made the violence more arbitrary and more intense."[42] Whether this assessment is correct or not is, to a certain extent, beside the point, although Jonathan Glover's *Humanity: A Moral History of the Twentieth Century* seems to confirm Cavanaugh's conclusion.[43] The essential point is rather that we should see the Enlightenment myth of peace and progress for what it is, and ensure that the theopolitical imagination is neither domesticated nor compromised when Christians engage with the politics of liberalism. In a similar vein, Hauerwas's recognition of the uniquely corrupting nature of the putative legitimate violence of the state provides an essential corrective and caution to theologies that, in his own words, "seek to rescue the liberal project either in its epistemological or political form."[44]

Hauerwas is surely correct when he argues that the political question for Christians is "what kind of community the Church must be to be faithful to the narratives central to Christian convictions."[45] Drawing on Yoder's radical anti-Constantinianism, Hauerwas develops his theological politics as a response to the question of how Christians can be faithful to the narratives that are central to their convictions. For many years his motif has been of Christians as resident aliens, eschewing what he regards as the reductive and degraded politics of the nation-state. In my opinion, however, this is not the only way to answer to the political question of how Christians can witness to the narratives that are central to their convictions. Indeed, as is argued throughout this book, both historically and in the contemporary context, work for human rights is and can be one critical way of witnessing to the gospel of peace and justice. Hauerwas's dismissal of the language of justice and consequently of the politics of human rights is based on what I believe is his incorrect conclusion that Christian involvement in the politics of justice stems from "the church's attempt to remain a societal actor in societies that [they] feel are slipping away from [their] control," and that in pursuing this course of action Christians "lose the critical ability to stand against the limits of our social orders" and as a result "forget that the first thing as Christians [they] have to hold before any society is not justice but God."[46] To be sure, these are temptations. Moreover, there probably are contexts in which work for social justice has replaced evangelization as the church's primary mode of engagement with society. But I see these as temptations to be avoided rather than reasons why Christians should avoid the politics of justice and human rights.

In fact, the unique nature of Christian witness can be expressed through many different forms of political engagement. Historically, Christian political engagement has been embodied in a variety of models. Its thick, culturally embedded narratives have witnessed to the value of withdrawal and to the value of developing institutional and individual relationships with others. Anabaptist and Mennonite traditions as well as monastic and ascetic movements have expressed their faithfulness to the gospel through practices and institutions that stress separation.[47] Yet this faithfulness has also been witnessed through "accommodationist" modes of political engagement. Because of its pejorative overtones, the adjective "accommodationist" is problematic, but I am using it here in the sense of "making common cause with" and not in the sense of tailoring Christian faith to fit the norms of secular culture. When the term accommodationist is understood in this way, one can recognize that through the centuries Christian discipleship has been lived in dialogue and partnership with the social and political institutions of secular societies. Theologians as varied as Thomas Aquinas, Francisco de Vitoria, and Karl Barth witnessed to this in different ways, as did activists such as George Fox, Dorothy Day, Oscar Romero, Martin Luther King Jr., and Ella Baker. Indeed, in his conversations with Romand Coles, Hauerwas acknowledges that the radical democracy practiced by people like Baker and King has the capacity to feed the political imagination so that it is shaped by the gospel.[48] The hazards and compromises lie, therefore, not in the political forms that Christians adopt but rather in the manner through which Christians give witness to the gospel. Historically, the language of rights has been one of the vehicles through which the distinctiveness of Christian witness to the gospel has been embodied. Its use has not been unambiguously positive. It ought not to be promoted as the only language through which Christians engage in ethico-political debate. Nor should it be viewed as anything other than what it is—namely, a provisional and limited, though dynamic, ethical language through which the vulnerable can (sometimes) be protected from the worst excesses of worldly empires.

Conclusion

There is no doubt that the combined force of these political, philosophical, and theological criticisms of human rights represents a fundamental challenge. The gradual erosion of the initial international consensus on human rights is worrying, especially since many of the early non-Western champions are now skeptics. There are many reasons why this initial commitment to universal human rights fragmented. Some, as discussed in chapter 1, relate to the political opportunism and hypocrisy of states, and to the partiality and double standards of the international institutions. Others, however, can be interpreted in a more positive light, as indicators of a desire to transform the discourse by ridding it of its colonial baggage. The recognition that humanistic narratives can oppress as well as liberate has been hard won and should not be forgotten in any "revisioning" process. Any renewal of the discourse cannot merely repeat the philosophical assumptions that have been so seriously and consistently criticized from so many quarters. Nor can theologians simply appropriate and extend these now strained philosophical categories, or assume that the politics of accommodation is without its dangers. In the forthcoming chapters, I focus on what I have already described as the main pillars of human rights discourse—namely, the nature of personhood, the structure of moral truth, and the role of the community. I draw on the critiques discussed in this chapter to develop an account of human rights that has political efficacy, philosophical credibility, and theological resonance. It is easy for advocates to ignore the critics of human rights discourse. We ignore these criticisms at our peril not only because many are valid but also because they can provide the seeds of much-needed reform.

Notes

1. G. Elijah Dann, "Conclusion: Philosophy, Religion, and Religious Belief After Rorty," in *An Ethics for Today: Finding Common Ground between Philosophy and Religion*, by Richard Rorty (New York: Columbia University Press, 2008), 27–76.

2. See Michael Perry, *Toward a Theory of Human Rights: Religion, Law, Courts* (Cambridge: Cambridge University Press, 2007).

3. Francesca Klug, *Values for a Godless Age* (London: Penguin, 2000), 10–12. In "Religious Pluralism and Human Rights," she describes the title as "the worst judged title in history" and clarifies that her intention is not to argue that it is a secular concept but rather that rights should be understood not primarily as legal entitlements but as ethical values for a diverse society. See Klug, "Religious Pluralism and Human Rights: Problems and Opportunities," in *Rights and Righteousness: Perspectives on Religious Pluralism and Human Rights*, ed. David Tombs, 31–40 (Belfast: Northern Ireland Human Rights Commission in Association with Irish School of Ecumenics, Trinity College Dublin, 2010), 34.

4. See, for example, David Novak, "God and Human Rights in a Secular Society: A Biblical-Talmudic Perspective," in *Does Human Rights Need God?*, ed. Elizabeth M. Bucar and Barbra Barnett, 48–57 (Grand Rapids, MI: Eerdmans, 2005); and Khaled Abou El Fadl, "Islam and the Challenge of Democratic Commitment," in *Does Human Rights Need God?*, ed. Elizabeth M. Bucar and Barbra Barnett, 58–103 (Grand Rapids, MI: Eerdmans, 2005).

5. Perry, *Toward a Theory of Human Rights*, 5.

6. Ibid., 12.

7. He mentions those of Asher Maoz, "Can Judaism Serve as a Source of Human Rights?" *Heidelberg Journal of International Law* 64 (2004): 677–721; and Michael Lerner, "Jesus the Jew," *Tikkun*, May–June 2004, 33–37, both of whom discuss the issue from a Jewish perspective; and, from an Islamic perspective, Khaled Abou El Fadl ("Islam and the Challenge of Democratic Commitment") and John Mikhail, "Islamic Rationalism and the Foundation of Human Rights," *Pluralism and Law. Proceedings of the 20th IVR Congress*, edited by Arend Soeteman, Global Problems 3 (March 2005): 61–70; Georgetown Public Law Research Paper No. 777026. Available at SSRN: http://ssrn.com/abstract=777026.

8. Max Stackhouse, "Why Human Rights Needs God: A Christian Perspective," in *Does Human Rights Need God?* ed. Elizabeth M. Bucar and Barbra Barnett, 25–40 (Grand Rapids, MI: Eerdmans, 2005); and Nicholas Wolterstorff, *Justice: Rights and Wrongs* (Princeton, NJ: Princeton University Press, 2008).

9. Wolterstorff, *Justice*, 325–41; and Perry, *Toward a Theory of Human Rights*, 18–26.

10. Wolterstorff, *Justice*, 393.

11. Michael Ignatieff, *Human Rights as Politics and Idolatry* (Princeton, NJ: Princeton University Press, 2001), 106.

12. Benedetto Croce, "The Rights of Man and the Present Historical Situation," in *Human Rights Comments and Interpretations*, a UNESCO Symposium edited with an introduction by Jacques Maritain (London: Allan Wingate, 1949), 94.

13. Jacques Maritain, Introduction to ibid., 9.

14. Ignatieff, *Human Rights as Politics and Idolatry*, 106.

15. David Hollenbach, "A Communitarian Reconstruction of Human Rights: Contributions from the Catholic Tradition," in *Catholicism and Liberalism, Contributions to American Public Philosophy*, ed. Bruce Douglass and David Hollenbach, 127–50 (Cambridge: Cambridge University Press, 1994), 138; Stephen Angle, *Human Rights and Chinese Thought* (Cambridge: Cambridge University Press, 2002), esp. chaps. 4, 5, and 6; and Martha Nussbaum, "Compassion: The Basic Social Emotion," *Social Philosophy and Policy* 13, no. 1 (Winter 1996): 27–58.

16. Richard Rorty, "Human Rights, Rationality, and Sentimentality," in *On Human Rights: The Oxford Amnesty Lectures*, ed. Stephen Shute and Susan Hurley, 112–34 (Oxford: Basic Books, 1993).

17. For a recent discussion of the approach that argues for ethical realism and for the existence of certain rights from a humanistic standpoint, see Ronald Dworkin, *Religion without God* (Cambridge MA: Harvard University Press, 2013).

18. "Declaration of the Rights of Man and of the Citizen," printed in *The Ethics of World Religions and Human Rights*, ed., Hans Küng and Jurgen Moltmann, *Concilium*, no. 2 (1990): 3–5.

19. Quoted in Bernard Plongeron in "Anathema or Dialogue? Christian Reactions to the Declarations of the Rights of Man in the United States and Europe in the Eighteenth Century," in *The Church and the Rights of Man*, ed. A Muller and Norbert Greinacher, eds., *Concilium*, no. 12 (1979): 1–16.

20. Gregory XVI, *Mirari vos*, in *The Papal Encyclicals 1740–1878*, ed. Claudia Carlen, vol. 1 (Pasadena, CA: Pierian Press, 1990), 198.

21. See, in particular, Leo Strauss, *Natural Right and History* (Chicago: University of Chicago Press, 1953); and *The Political Philosophy of Hobbes: Its Basis and Its Genesis* (Chicago: University of Chicago Press, 1952). Strauss argued that the enlightenment philosophers beginning with Hobbes and Locke were the first to use the term "natural right." See also the work of Michel Villey, for whom the concept of subjective rights constituted a revolutionary idea that developed from the voluntarism of William of Ockham. See, in particular, Villey, "La genèse du droit subjectif chez Guillaume d'Occam," *Archives de philospphie du droit* 9 (1964): 97–127. See also Eugene Kamenka, "The Anatomy of an Idea," in *Human Rights*, ed. Eugene Kamenka and Alice Erh-Soon Tay, 1–12 (Port Melbourne: Edward Arnold, 1978).

22. Roger Ruston, *Human Rights and the Image of God* (London: SCM Press, 2004); Brian Tierney, *The Idea of Natural Rights: Studies in Natural Rights, Natural Law, and Church Law, 1150–1625* (Atlanta: Scholars Press, 1997); and John Witte Jr., *The Reformation of Rights: Law, Religion and Human Rights in Early Modern Calvinism* (Cambridge: Cambridge University Press, 2007).

23. Alasdair MacIntyre, *After Virtue: A Study in Moral Theory* (London: Duckworth, 1981), 69.

24. Tierney, *Idea of Natural Rights*, 43–77.

25. Ibid., 54.

26. Ibid., 57, quoting *Decretum Gratiani . . . una cum glossis* (Venice, 1600), C. 16 q.3 *dictum post*, c.15.

27. Maurice Cranston, *Human Rights Today* (London: Ampersand Books, 1962).

28. Tierney, *Idea of Natural Rights*, 75, quoting J. Hoffmans, ed., *Les Quodlibets onze-quartoze de Godefroid de Fontaines, Les Philosophe Belges* 4, Louvain 1924, 105.

29. Ibid., 74.

30. Witte, *Reformation of Rights*, 35.

31. Ibid.

32. John Yoder, *For the Nations: Essays Evangelical and Public* (Eugene OR: Wipf and Stock Publishers, 2002), 103–8; and Yoder, *The Priestly Kingdom* (Notre Dame, IN: University of Notre Dame Press, 1984), 72.

33. Joan Lockwood O'Donovan, "Historical Prolegomena to a Theological Review of 'Human Rights,'" *Studies in Christian Ethics* 9, no. 2 (1996): 54, doi:10.1177 /095394689600900205.

34. Oliver O'Donovan, *The Desire of the Nations: Rediscovering the Roots of Political Theology* (Cambridge: Cambridge University Press, 1996), 248.

35. O'Donovan, "Historical Prolegomena," 55.

36. Ibid.

37. Wolterstorff, *Justice*, 319n10.

38. Tierney, *Idea of Natural Rights*, 340.

39. Ruston, *Human Rights and the Image of God*, 215. In particular, see chaps. 11–15 for a comprehensive rebuttal of this view that Locke was the prototypical liberal individualist. Ruston traces the dominance of this interpretation, especially in the American academy, to Strauss. See note 135.

40. For a discussion of this point, see John Milbank, *Theology and Social Theory: Beyond Secular Reason* (Cambridge MA: Blackwell, 1990), chaps. 1 and 2. See also O'Donovan, *Desire of the Nations*, 275.

41. I agree with much of Jeffrey Stout's analysis in chapter 5 of *Democracy and Tradition* (Princeton, NJ: Princeton University Press, 2004), believing it to be the most accurate rendering of Stanley Hauerwas's position. Of note is Hauerwas's response in *Performing the Faith: Bonhoeffer and the Practice of Non-Violence* (Ada, MI: Brazos Press, 2004).

42. William T. Cavanaugh, *Theopolitical Imagination* (London: Continuum, 2002), 6.

43. Jonathan Glover, *Humanity: A Moral History* (New Haven, CT: Yale University Press, 2001).

44. Stanley Hauerwas, *After Christendom?: How the Church Is to Behave if Freedom, Justice, and a Christian Nation Are Bad Ideas* (Nashville: Abingdon Press, 1991), 35.

45. Stanley Hauerwas, *A Community of Character: Toward a Constructive Christian Social Ethic* (Notre Dame, IN: University of Notre Dame Press, 1981), 2.

46. Hauerwas, *After Christendom*, 58, 68.

47. Even within these traditions, perhaps with the exception of some ascetic movements, some accommodations to and alliances with secular political concerns were and are evident.

48. Stanley Hauerwas and Romand Coles, *Christianity, Democracy, and the Radical Ordinary Conversations between a Radical Democrat and a Christian* (Eugene, OR: Cascade Books, 2008).

3

Ethical Formations

Constructing the Subject of Human Rights

How are we to understand the human, the subject of human rights? This question has long preoccupied philosophers and theologians and has predated the modern human rights movement by centuries. In one sense the answer to this question is deceptively simple. We all know of what we speak when we speak about the human person. Indeed, human rights discourse has built its advocacy on the rhetorical and symbolic appeal of this idea of "the human person" and on the conviction that human beings share a nature that is essentially and fundamentally the same whether one is a *dalit* living in the slums of Bangalore or a member of the landowning elite in Argentina. Conventional interpretations of the UN Declaration of Human Rights also reinforce this view and assume that the Declaration is both dependent on and promotes a concept of a universal human nature as the basis of human rights.[1] Yet this rhetorical device obscures the fact that fundamental questions have been raised about this traditional way of grounding human rights. In particular, feminist and postcolonial commentators  have argued that the ostensible clarity about the fundamental nature of human beings hides a myriad of debates about the purpose of human life, about the natural features of the human identity, about the structuring of life in community, and about the meaning of the body. Human rights politics has, for the most part, ignored these disputes and has proceeded on the basis that it is possible to speak of the human in abstract terms and

70

to build an account of universal human rights from that sta
The previous chapter has shown the limitations of this appr
grounding of human rights and has suggested that this conce
of the subject of human rights needs to be rethought. Drawing on Michel
Foucault's insight, that our normative concepts bear the indelible marks of
their formative cultural contexts, chapter 1 underscores the limitations of
this traditional account of the subject and argues that human rights politics
would be more convincing if it abandoned its reliance on this predetermined, prediscursive fixed definition of the human.

In this chapter I ask what it would take to "change the subject" of human rights discourse and, following on from that, what human rights
politics would look like if it were grounded in the concrete experiences
of situated individuals rather than, as currently is the case, in a reified and
idealized concept of human nature. I begin by arguing that this need to
rethink the subject is not driven by some theoretical agenda but rather by
an ethical imperative that is committed to developing a more dynamic and
therefore inclusive understanding of the subject. I argue that human rights
politics currently functions with an inadequate conceptualization of what
is natural for human beings. In particular, I note that its understanding of
human nature is replete with hidden assumptions about what is natural for
human beings. Moreover, these assumptions have functioned to exclude
certain persons from participation in the polity and, even more seriously,
from being able to live lives that accord with their respective understandings of human flourishing. I illustrate this by discussing how feminism has
questioned these traditional assumptions about what is natural for human
beings—how it has, in effect, "troubled the natural." I suggest that it has
done this in a fundamental way, by questioning the presumptions that
gender is binary, that heterosexuality is normative, and that the meaning
of embodiment is transhistorical. Through feminism we came to be aware
of the constructedness of the assumptions on which we have built our
ethical frameworks. However, in this context feminism is regarded as just
one of the many prisms through which we can see this constructedness.
In the second section I address the issue of how human rights can develop
an account of the subject that goes beyond both the prediscursive category
of the human inherent in liberalism and the unending subject-in-process
of poststructuralism.[2] In this context I argue that any attempt to reconstruct the human must address what Gayatri Chakravorty Spivak calls "the

burden of representation," and must confront the ethical challenges associated with attempting to render visible the experiences of those who, heretofore, have been both unseen and excluded. I argue that human rights discourse must begin to develop an account of subjectivity that is open to differences not yet articulated, and that it must pursue a double strategy that aims to both speak with and on behalf of the marginalized while at the same time retaining a critical attitude toward its own entitlement to do so. In the final section I draw on the postcolonial theologies of Kwok Pui-lan, Mercy Amba Oduyoye, Agbonkhiameghe Orobator, and others to better understand the challenges associated with conceiving human subjectivity today. One of the points made consistently by postcolonial theologians is that a key first step in this process will involve attending more directly to the material as well as to the discursive dimensions of subjectivity. Whereas traditional human rights discourse began with a claim of ontological sameness which subsequently fragmented as the radical particularity of human life began to be understood, a renewed discourse must start from another place, that is, from the bonds of difference rather than the bonds of sameness. Will we still be able to say that we have certain rights by virtue of our humanity? My answer to this question is yes. However, this "yes" is a hesitant and complicated one because of the need to be attuned to the ethical challenges involved in representing the other and to the moral complexity of the phrase "by virtue of our humanity." Moreover, it will require particular attention to the hazard involved in using this phrase, given the exclusions and injustices that continue to be perpetrated precisely on that basis.

Troubling the Natural

One of the central contributions of feminism has been that it has exposed hidden assumptions about gender in traditional philosophical and theological discourse about the human subject. For more than four decades, feminists have questioned the manner in which human experience has been construed and represented in these discourses. Feminism has had a particular concern with the way in which the experience of being a body has been understood to shape one's experience of oneself and of the world that one inhabits. Once feminists began to articulate the distinctiveness of women's experiences, they also provoked a radical questioning of what had heretofore been regarded as the natural and settled contours of human identity. Thus, not only did the feminist critique insist on the significance of attending to the gendered dimensions of human experience but, perhaps more importantly, it "troubled what is natural" by rejecting the divinely sanctioned assumptions about the body and embodiment that shore up patriarchal social relations.[3] The feminist critique has for the most part ignored the language of human rights, perhaps assuming that its gender-neutral and inclusive language implies that it has managed to avoid or transcend the patriarchal assumptions of its philosophy of origin. However, I argue that although human rights discourse has begun to appreciate the significance of the gendering of the subject, it has not yet come to terms with the implications of the more fundamental feminist critique of the anthropological basis on which the discourse is based.

Constructing Sexual Difference

Once feminists began to inquire into the nature of gender, the meaning of the body was opened up to reexamination. Feminism, especially in its early phases, was essentially a protest against the idea that biology is destiny. As a result, it inevitably raised some difficult questions about what it means to be a body, and especially in a sexually differentiated body. Following on from such reflection, feminists also began to question how and to what extent the governing ideologies of gender and gender relations have affected the ways in which the body is conceptualized. In the West, the dominant form of feminism has been liberal. Taking their cue from Simone de Beauvoir's claim that "one is not born, rather one becomes a woman," liberal feminists have argued that the body can be transcended and that the individual can choose the meaning and significance of his or her embodiment, even against the dominant cultural interpretations. At the heart of the liberal analysis is a distinction between biological givens and the social articulation of those givens, with liberal feminists acknowledging the constructed nature of gender norms but insisting, too, that they can be transcended. What liberal feminism leaves intact, however, is the assumption that there is a clear and unambiguous distinction between biology and culture, between the body and its cultural elaboration, between sex and gender. The body is thus regarded as the material upon which society inscribes particular meanings, albeit meanings that can be

Postmodern questions assumption of clear biological givens

oppressive. But, although oppressive, such interpretations can be refused, reinterpreted, and transcended.

Postmodern feminists, by contrast, have questioned this assumption that there is a clear distinction between biological "givens" and the cultural elaborations of these biological givens. As Judith Butler has famously asked, "how is a feminist critic to assess the scientific discourses that purport to establish such facts for us" since they too are the products of preexisting assumptions about the nature of sex and gender and about the relationship between the two?[4] Butler has led this line of argument, suggesting that feminism has also wrongly accepted the established patriarchal construction of the natural world in which gender is assumed to be dichotomous.[5] She argues that we believe the world to be divided into two genders because this is what we expect. Moreover, not only do we construct two genders because we look for them, we also construct an account of the two distinct sexes because that, too, is what we expect to find. Butler challenges in a radical way this assumption that gender is binary and that sexual difference falls naturally and biologically along dualistic lines.[6]

Blurred line not B&W

The assumption that sexual difference follows a natural dualistic pattern is clearly incorrect, and, although most societies are familiar with the experiences of individuals and groups who fall outside this supposed natural categorization, the fiction of sexual dualism persists. The presence of transsexual and intersex individuals confirms that the existing categorizations are too narrowly defined and that biological identity is often blurred or indeterminate. Such is the force of the normative notion of human morphology that most societies regard these bodily forms as dysmorphic, as deviations from the norm, to be rectified through hormonal and surgical intervention, usually in infancy. In Western countries, sex is assigned, or sometimes reassigned, with surgeons speaking of uncovering the true biological identity (either male or female), but not of constructing it. The assumption is that an individual must be either male or female and have the corresponding masculine or feminine traits. Those whose bodies are different are remade and corrected, shaped according to the normative conceptualization of sex and gender as binary.[7]

In West sex assigned, must be Male or Female

In the West, this issue is medicalized. In other parts of the world, those who do not conform to established biological dualism are often exoticized. *Hirjas* (now an institutionalized third gender caste in India), *naddles* (among the Navajo Indians of North America), and *muxe* (among the

Other cultures

Mexican Zapotecs) are all examples of groups of people who take up ambiguous or indeterminate positions vis-à-vis traditional gender norms and, even more significantly, who don't conform to the traditional biological categorizations. Their ambivalent biological status also confirms that the biology that is taken to underlie gender identity and on which our assumption of gender dichotomy is based is more complex and multifarious than most societies are willing to acknowledge. Patricia Beattie Jung and Aana Marie Vigen consider the theological implications of this position in their groundbreaking *God, Science, Sex, Gender: An Interdisciplinary Approach to Christian Ethics.* They note that the emergence of a multiplex concept of gender among biologists, reinforced by the analyses of gender emerging from the social sciences and humanities, challenges the dimorphic accounts of gender complementarity that many regard as axiomatic and, one might add, that ground the traditional understanding of the person.[8] Indeed, for Butler, the body is neither irrelevant nor all determining. Rather, the body is constructed as we speak, "bodies materialise within a field in which they are bound, formed and deformed by 'a set of enforced criteria of intelligibility' as they are given meaning, and as they assume the matter of their significance."[9] Within this context, religion plays a crucial role in maintaining and policing the traditional lines of demarcation between the two genders, and especially between the two sexes. Moreover, most scientific, medical, psychological, and theological discourses both assume and reinscribe the normative account of the human body, a normative account that is based, as we have seen, in exclusion and idealization.

In challenging gender essentialism, Butler also questions the heteronormativity of philosophical and theological discourse, including that of human rights. For Butler, gender is not natural but performative—that is, made and remade through repeated performance rather than through conformity to a particular set of biological or cultural factors. Her conceptualization of gender subverts conventional binaries of both gender and sexuality and in so doing calls into question assumptions about the complementarity of "the sexes" and the normativity of heterosexuality. In her analysis, "the univocity of sex, the internal coherence of gender, and the binary framework of both sex and gender are considered throughout as regulatory fictions that consolidate and naturalize the convergent power regimes of masculine and heterosexist oppression."[10] Compulsory heterosexuality has shaped the Western imaginary to a profound degree. Rooted in a reading of the body that has essentialized sexual difference and sacralized complementarity, this most basic of assumptions has been the axis upon which the nature of human identity has been inscribed and from which all normative claims about human life have been developed. Alternative ways of narrating identity and of articulating desire have tended to be erased or negated, criminalized, or pathologized.[11] And, although human rights categories are now marshaled in support of civil and political rights for gay, lesbian, transsexual, and bisexual persons, the discourse continues to be anchored in gender binarism and heteronormativity.

Inscribing the Body

Assumptions about the meaning of embodiment have also undergone a comparable interrogation. Indeed, much in the way that normative assumptions about sex and gender have been problematized, so too have traditional beliefs about the relationship between the body and behavioral norms been called into question. Feminist and postcolonial critiques have been particularly important in drawing attention to the manner in which the body itself is enmeshed in culture, and in demonstrating that it is through the inscriptions of culture that the matter of the body is formed and acquires significance. It is futile, therefore, to speak of the meaning of bodiliness per se, as though it were a natural and transhistorical category. Rather, we can attend to the meaning of the body only by interrogating the assumptions that shape our conceptualizations of bodiliness in our own specific cultural and historical contexts. Feminism has taught us that constructivism goes all the way down and that we can only hope to understand the meaning of embodiment within the context of the specific ideologies, institutions, and cultures that construct it and that supply the interpretive lens through which it is recognized and understood. The meaning ascribed to the body, including the gendered body, has varied widely, both historically and culturally. There is no simple transcultural or universal understanding of bodiliness, nor of gendered bodiliness. Nor is there one specific way in which the body shapes human identity. Rather, the meaning of embodiment is constructed through the multiple lenses of interpretation through which the highly differentiated experiences of being in a body are constituted.

One example of the way in which the meaning of gendered bodiliness is thus shaped will suffice. When one puts the spotlight on the cultural context of the West, and more specifically of contemporary Europe, one is struck by the degree to which we are fixated on sexuality, and by the extent to which the meaning of the body is interpreted primarily through the lens of sexuality. Indeed, this is the case not only in the secular but also in the religious domain and is something that Foucault saw clearly. He argued that, for the last two centuries at least, we have tended to regard sex as "that which holds the key to our essential selves." In speaking about sex, we believe that we are enunciating the core of our identities, getting to grips with the fundamentals of our selves. As a consequence, we have privileged the sexual meaning of our bodies to the exclusion of almost every other meaning. The gradual sexualization of childhood is evidence of the manner in which this sexual frame has come to dominate the interpretive lens of Western cultures. However, not only have we privileged a sexual interpretation of bodiliness but within this sexual interpretation we have also privileged sexual pleasure. Everywhere we turn in contemporary Western culture, we are confronted with a commodification of sex in which sexual pleasure is represented as holding the key to the true meaning of bodiliness. Moreover, Western feminism has played its part in this since one of its responses to the cultural denigration of the female body has focused on the revalidation of the female body and of sexual pleasure.

The merits or otherwise of this aspect of Western culture are not at issue here. The purpose is to establish that the meaning of "being or having a body" is culturally constructed and to suggest that discourses that aspire to be either universalist or transnational will need to attend to this. In the field of human rights, this is especially pertinent since many of the most intractable and disputed issues revolve around the moral significance of embodiment. The debate about whether female genital cutting amounts to a violation of human rights is one example of a debate in which different culturally specific norms of embodiment collide. The frame of reference of much of the debate about female genital cutting has been in relation to the body as first and foremost the site of sexual meaning, specifically sexual pleasure. Yet this has a peculiarly Western resonance and is rarely, if ever, the lens through which the women in whose cultures female genital cutting is practiced construct the issue. Cultural and religious traditions embed the dynamics of sexuality differently and therefore articulate the meaning of the body and the practice of cutting that body according to a variety of frames of reference. There are a host of different meanings accorded the practice of genital cutting among those cultures in which it is practiced. Commenting on the practice, Leslye Amede Obiora notes that this idea that circumcision attenuates sexual desire is only one of the many beliefs that must be enumerated in any adequate characterization of female genital cutting and must be contextualized within what she describes as "the wide panoply of African constructions of female sexuality."[12] She, like many African feminists, is critical of Western feminists who have focused almost exclusively on interpreting genital cutting through the lens of the sexual body, as though this captures the essential meaning of the practice. Obiora argues that the idea that the essential meaning of female genital cutting can be captured is contradicted by the fact that this act, which many regard as cruel and inhuman (and a violation of Article 5 of the UN Declaration that no one shall be subjected to torture or to cruel, inhuman, or degrading treatment or punishment), is at the same time embraced in some cultures as a technology of the body that is "as integral to the scaffolding network of equilibrating values."[13] Fuambai Ahmadu's discussion of the ritual of genital cutting in terms of how it celebrates women's preeminent roles in history and society is one such example of how the multiple meanings of such practices are expressed, thereby confirming Obiora's point that efforts to construe it exclusively according to one frame of reference are inappropriate.[14] That this issue has dominated Western feminism's engagement with non-Western, particularly African, culture—despite many African feminists insisting that economic survival is of more immediate concern—further exemplifies the tendency in the West to understand the body primarily through its sexual aspects.[15] The point here is not to debate the ethics of genital cutting. Rather, it is to suggest that our conversations about human rights and specifically the meaning of embodiment will be nothing other than "the dialogue of the deaf" unless, first and foremost, we develop an awareness of the multiple constructions and interpretations of being or having a body. To say that we are concerned about the same thing—the meaning of embodiment—simply misses the point. Embodiment, the fact of being in a body, has had radically different meanings and resonances cross-culturally. However, the naturalization of these constructions within different cultures and religious traditions means that we are often blind to alternative ways of viewing and valuing the body.

Meyda Yeğenoğlu's analysis of what she calls "the sartorial fabrication of the Muslim woman's body" raises similar issues about how the body is understood and argues that we must question the presumptions of paradigms that conceive of the subject in terms of the primacy of the mind and the concomitant assumption of the body's naturalness and precultural status.[16] She, too, is critical of discourses that speak of the natural body or that assume that the meaning of embodiment can be understood directly from its biological markers since, as she argues, such naturalized constructions neutralize and universalize the specificity of different bodies.[17] For example, Yeğenoğlu argues that if veiling can be seen as a specific practice of marking and disciplining the body in accordance with cultural requirements, then so too can unveiling, and she draws on Fanon's classic text *A Dying Colonialism* to reinforce her point that it is through culture that we make, remake, transform, and interpret the body.[18] A colleague is fond of reminding me of a conversation between the great missionary anthropologist Maurice Leenhardt and one of his Melanesian converts on New Caledonia which brilliantly illustrates this point. Suggesting that Christianity must have brought the people a sense of the spiritual, Leenhardt received the reply, "Oh, no, we always had that; what you brought us was the body."[19] In breaking the body–nature continuum, the new world view revealed a cultural construction of the body that was alien to the indigenous culture. The missionary could only engage with the culture he encountered through the lens of the Western philosophical imaginary that separates spirit and matter. Thus, he inscribed onto Melanesian culture a separation that could not be apprehended within the existing Melanesian framework. As the reply suggests, the effect of hearing the Christian message was utterly unanticipated by the missionary since it disclosed to him that what he took for granted as the natural order was more likely to be a construct of his own cultural heritage rather than a viewpoint that is universally shared. The ethical writings of Isabel Apawo Phiri, Meng Yanling, Rose Wu, and Anne Dondapati Allen also confirm that this diversity of cultural interpretations of embodiment is also visible within the Christian tradition.[20] These diverse interpretations of a category that has for so long been both naturalized and universalized inevitably leads one to question

traditional assumptions about the body and its relation to the construction of the subject.

"What are the cultural contours of the notion of the human at work here?"[21] This is a critical question for human rights discourse as it seeks to establish the conditions that will allow all human beings to flourish. Once we recognize that even our most fundamental assumptions about embodiment and about sexual identity are premised on naturalized cultural constructions and on exclusionary norms, then we will need to begin to think critically about the many other ways in which the human has been constructed. Human rights politics has assumed that we know the fundamentals of the human, and that traditional articulations merely need to be modified in order to remedy earlier patterns of exclusion. It has also proceeded on the basis that already established values need simply to be extended to the newly included groups of people. However, the experiences of transsexual and intersex individuals caution against such easy conclusions and challenge us to avoid simplistic descriptions of human nature. Furthermore, the recognition that the corporeality of the body is always already inscribed with cultural interpretations means that we can no longer presume that human rights norms can simply be read from what are regarded as the natural contours of the body. We are only beginning to understand that our concept of the human is a construct, and to learn to be attentive to the manner in which the traditional construction excluded those who ought to have been protected. It would therefore be premature to assume that human rights discourse can speak confidently about the nature of the subject, or that its normative assumptions have been cleansed of their exclusionary practices, or that we can once again ground human rights on an albeit new but still fixed and predetermined concept of the human.

Concept of human is a construct

Rendering Visible, Rendering Vocal

The preceding discussion of feminism has illustrated that our operative concept of the person is replete with assumptions that have generated fixed categories and normative claims. The dualistic metaphysic of the Western philosophical imaginary has shaped the understanding of personhood in fundamental ways, drawing, as it does, on dichotomies between spirit/matter, transcendent/immanent, and culture/nature. Within human rights discourse, this Western concept of person has, for the most part, defined the entire field of vision even though other cultural and religious traditions conceptualize the person differently, as is demonstrated by the encounter between Leenhardt and the unnamed Melanesian. Intercultural and interreligious conversations, especially between East and West, have shown that a significant degree of cross-cultural understanding can be achieved, although the difficulties and complexities of such a task cannot be underestimated. For more than six decades, human rights discourse has attempted to respect, engage with, and build upon the diversity of cultural and religious world views. However, what the foregoing feminist analysis has indicated is that the process of doing so may be far more complex than we could have ever imagined. Indeed, those elements that seem self-evident and natural in one world may be precisely the dimensions that are impenetrable and incomprehensible in another. Analyses coming from different disciplines have shown that many of the most fundamental differences among cultures and traditions rest on differences in respect of how the person is conceptualized. Heretofore, human rights discourse has privileged the Western model of the subject and, within that framework, has attempted to accommodate other cultural perspectives. However, such an approach is no longer adequate to the complexity of the task of building an inclusive and globally resonant politics of human rights. Rather, the prospect of developing new, more inclusive and flexible models of the subject depends on our ability to see our existing understandings for what they are—that is, naturalized social constructions.

The Burden of Representation

We have already discussed the way in which particular conceptualizations of the subject have the effect of erasing differences in the name of a putative universality and have argued that human rights discourse must address this central problem if it is to establish its credibility as a language with global resonance. The task, therefore, is a complex one: to determine how the subject can be configured so as to resist the erasure of difference while simultaneously establishing a position from which the subject can narrate her identity and articulate an account of the good life. The first step in this process requires that the anthropological essentialism of human rights discourse be disrupted and requires that the genealogy of the modern subject be investigated. The preceding section is just one illustration of the kind of genealogical work that still needs to be done. A further step involves an interrogation of the limits of representation and in particular a consideration of the ethical challenges that human rights faces as it seeks to speak of and for the other.

Gayatri Chakravorty Spivak's work is both chastening and illuminating in this regard. In her seminal essay "Can the Subaltern Speak?" the depth of the challenge of speaking of or speaking for, of representing or mediating, "the other" is laid bare.[22] Spivak's essay asked a radical question of those who, like herself, were seeking to break away from the narratives and perspectives of the elites and ensure that the voices of those who have been marginalized because of their class, caste, gender, race, language, or culture could be heard.[23] The central concern of Spivak and her colleagues in subaltern studies has been to write history from the underside and in so doing to restore the agency of the ordinary people. While sharing this commitment to those on the margins, Spivak is not as confident as others that it is possible to speak for "the subaltern." With the term "subaltern," Spivak draws attention to those people whose experiences and actions are incomprehensible within the dominant discourse, those who are "in the space of difference" and on account of a failure of recognition are both unrepresented and unrepresentable.[24] In her essay, Spivak argues that it is impossible for subalterns to speak without appropriating the dominant language or modes of representation and that it is impossible for those who seek to speak about or for subalterns to do so adequately. Commenting on Spivak's challenge, Partha Chatterjee noted that subaltern history had successfully shown that the "man" or the "citizen" who was the sovereign subject of bourgeois history writing was in truth only the elite but that Spivak had added a further challenge when she asked why it was necessary now to clothe the subaltern in the costume of the sovereign subject. Chatterjee continued, after this seminal essay, the critical question was no longer "what is the true form of the subaltern?" Rather, it had become, "how is the subaltern represented?" where to represent meant both to "present again" and also "stand in place of." In short, Chatterjee conceded, both the subjects and the methods underwent change.[25]

Spivak's approach to the problem of representation is highly relevant to human rights discourse, but it has not thus far had the impact that it ought. She is critical of discourses that pay lip service to the power differentials between those who speak for others and those they represent, and she concludes that in most academic contexts today, the practice of problematizing the role of the investigator "remains a meaningless piety."[26] Even those theorists who are renowned for this critical attitude—namely, Michel Foucault, Gilles Deleuze, and Félix Guattari—are criticized for failing to understand how they, too, reproduce the erasure of marginalized subjects even as they believe that they are rendering them visible. She argues that although they resist speaking for the oppressed, they nonetheless "turn away from the dynamics of representation" that ought to inform their difficult intellectual (elitist?) role in rendering visible the concrete experiences of the oppressed. In short, they fail to be burdened by the problems of representation, and she contrasts what Drucilla Cornell calls "this almost willed naïveté" with other deconstructive processes that acknowledge their dependence on representational schemas and their linguistic underpinnings.[27]

If Foucault and Deleuze "retreat before the messiness of the politics of representation," then a more ethical approach requires that the burden of representation be assumed and the inevitability of the epistemic violence inherent in all representation be acknowledged.[28] For Spivak, the key is to understand that "we" are not representing "them"—that is, those who are radically outside, such as the subsistence farmers, the tribals, the zero workers in the streets—but rather that "we" are learning to "re-present ourselves."[29] Spivak does not think that all benevolent attempts to represent the interests of the other are doomed, although she is rightly cautious about the echo of earlier civilizing projects. Rather, as Rita Birla argues, "in asking us to re-present ourselves, Spivak asks us to supplement the benevolent intention of 'speaking for' with an ethics of responsibility— in the sense of cultivating a capacity to respond to and be responsive to the other, without demanding resemblance as the basis of recognition."[30] Those involved in the discourses of advocacy, including the discourse of human rights, cannot proceed as though we are not ourselves caught up in the politics of representation. Rather, we must accept the burden of representation—that is, the ethical responsibilities associated with the privilege of speaking of, or speaking for, the other.

In her Oxford Amnesty lecture in 2001, Spivak develops her analysis of this burden of representation in the context of the politics of human rights.[31] She recognizes that the history of human rights has been an ambivalent one, and she argues that human rights politics can have a future if, but *only* if, it can be "sutured into the torn cultural fabric of responsibility."[32] The torn cultural fabric of responsibility of which she speaks is the responsibility associated with the privilege of representation; it requires a commitment that we will engage in an ongoing interrogation of the assumptions we carry about the nature of, and justifications for, human rights. Human rights advocates are thus inserted into the field of representation not as dispensers of rights but rather as persons whose entitlement to represent affects the way we understand human rights. Indeed, it is only when we grapple with and deconstruct our own hierarchical sense of entitlement that we can engage with human rights politics in an ethical manner or, to use Spivak's characterization, that we will have sutured human rights to an ethics of responsibility. Moreover, this process of self-interrogation is facilitated by the presence of the subaltern: "by remaining what those of us enabled to represent cannot represent precisely because of our enablement, [the subaltern] forces us to see the limits of our definition of the human and, with the asymmetries, our view of the inequalities that also make us see the subaltern as in need of us to right wrongs, as we are the ones who grasp the meaning of those wrongs." We are forced, in other words, to address the question "who is the 'we' in the representation of how they have been wronged?"[33]

The question must therefore become "how can we speak with (not for) the other, and especially with those who have long been marginalized?" In Spivak's analysis, our ethical responsibility begins with the recognition that the human is first and foremost a being-in-relation and with the acknowledgment that traditional accounts of the demands of relationship have tended to underestimate, even ignore, the alterity of the other. Spivak draws on Emmanuel Levinas to insist that it is only when we truly appreciate the alterity of the other that we can begin to understand the demands of relationship and the responsibilities associated with being in a position to speak with or for the other.[34] "To be born human is to be born angled towards an other and others. To account for this, the human being presupposes the quite-other: This is the bottom line of being-human as being-in-the-ethical-relation. By definition we cannot—no self can—reach the quite-other. . . . This is the founding gap in all act or talk, most especially in acts or talk that we understand to be closest to the ethical—the historical and political. We must somehow try to supplement the gap."[35] Traditional human rights discourse has tried to supplement this gap by downplaying the alterity of the other and emphasizing the commonalities among people. However, as Spivak and others have shown, such an approach is no longer adequate since it inevitably reinscribes existing inequalities even as it tries to avoid doing so. A renewed discourse of human rights will need to think differently about how this gap can be supplemented. Taking its cue from Spivak, it may need to begin in solidarity with the alterity of the other, and with an appreciation that the other is what she calls "the quite-other." It will most importantly, however, need to proceed with a determination to accept the ethical burdens associated with the privilege of speaking on behalf of or with an other.

[handwritten margin note: solidarity with alterity of the other]

[handwritten margin note: accept ethical burdens]

Tracing the Itinerary of Silence

Human rights discourse can no longer ignore the ethical responsibilities associated with rendering visible the experiences of those who are both unseen and excluded. Nor can such responsibilities be regarded as ancillary to the core work of advocacy but rather must be acknowledged as integral to that project. The critical question, then, is how human rights discourse can address this gap between the privileged world of advocacy and the world of those who are "in the space of difference" since it is only on that basis that human rights advocates can speak with those who are marginalized and can be mediators on their behalf as they attempt to secure their rights. This is an immense and complex task, one in which the symbiotic nature of the relationship between "the representer" and "the represented" must be acknowledged. Indeed, every one of us is simultaneously the representer and the represented. Thus, attention must be given to the processes by which the other is constituted while simultaneously interrogating the ambiguous position of human rights advocates in the dominant culture. Western intellectual production is, after all, bound up with its imperialist economic interests, and the asymmetry between these different worlds is very clear. What may not be so clear is the extent to which this asymmetry may have affected the politics of human rights and especially the extent to which we can understand the values that are at stake when these different world views collide. Spivak's infamous discussion of *sati* (widow burning/self-immolation) captures well the itinerary of silence that results from this asymmetry. *Sati* was a critical site of contest between Hindu traditionalists and British colonialists, one in which, as in so many other political contexts, the bodies of women became emblematic of the values that were at stake for each group.[36] In India "the abolition of this rite by the British has been generally understood as a case of 'White men saving brown women from brown men,'" while "against this is the Indian nativist argument, a parody for the nostalgia for lost origins: 'The women actually wanted to die.'"[37] Throughout the decades-long ideological battle and among the endless analyses, the voices of the women themselves were silent and silenced. Moreover, that silencing was so profound that the voices are now impossible to recover. According to Spivak, the two competing discourses of imperialism and traditional patriarchalism have functioned to legitimize each other while at the same time ensuring that "one never encounters the testimony of the women's voice-consciousness."[38] Colonialists, nativists, feminists, human rights advocates, and indigenous elites have all projected certain motivations onto the *sati*, have each claimed to represent her interests, even as the *suttee* herself is silent. In fact the *satis'* voices are now irretrievable because of the subsequent debates that have played out over their bodies, in the course of which their silencing has been completed. In this context, there is no way to hear this subaltern: she cannot speak. All attempts at retrieval are futile. Thus, as we interrogate the mechanics of this discourse of silencing, we begin to see just how hazardous the process of representation can be. It is only when we are prepared to accept that we can be complicit in the silencing of the subaltern that we can begin to address our own blind spots and attend to the ideological formation of our own discourses.

It is imperative, therefore, that we in the West unlearn our conviction that we are entitled and able to speak for the marginalized. This will be a challenge since much of the academic and political debate about human rights is based on this presumption. Unlearning our entitlement to speak will not necessarily result in an enforced silence, however, but will require a different way of engaging in this multilayered conversation, one in which the asymmetries of power and entitlement are acknowledged and addressed. In recent decades human rights politics has begun to attend more closely to the manner in which its Western biases have, for the most part, established the parameters of the discourse. We have begun to realize that our representations of the other have been articulated through the lens of empire and established through the dynamics of colonialism. We cannot forget, either, that colonialism has been the vehicle through which millions across the globe came to hear the language of human rights for the first time.

In many respects it is inevitable that we construct the other according to our own presuppositions about the meaning of the body, or about the nature of agency, or about the imperatives of freedom. We see life through a certain prism and find it difficult to do otherwise. But the process of noting the hazards and failures of representation is itself an important step in the "unlearning" process since it reinforces the realization that not everything in one culture can be appropriated or understood through the categories of another. It is, however, only one step on a long journey that will require human rights discourse to attend to the mechanics of its constitution of "the other" while also interrogating its own complicity in the creation of subordinate cultures and subaltern groups. Human rights politics will therefore have to live with the ambiguity of speaking with the subaltern while also accepting the precarious nature of its own facility to speak. Moreover, it will need to continue to trace the itineraries of silence even as it attempts to represent the other. How can those whose experiences have been erased be rendered visible in human rights discourse? How can those who have traditionally been silenced be enabled to articulate their own interests and desires? These continue to be the most pressing questions for human rights politics as it seeks to remedy its earlier failures and in so doing be a voice with, rather than for, the voiceless.

Ethical Formations: Conceiving the Bonds of Difference

This chapter is concerned with how the subject of human rights is constructed, and it makes the case that human rights discourse needs to think differently about how subjectivity is understood. I argue that human rights discourse needs to develop a more dynamic and inclusive understanding of the subject, suggesting that its operative model is premised on an inadequate conceptualization of what is natural for human beings. I illustrated this point by discussing how feminism has problematized many of the most basic of our assumptions about what is natural for human beings, including the presumption that gender is binary, that heterosexuality is normative, and that the meaning of embodiment is transcultural and transhistorical. I suggest that human rights discourse must adapt its conceptualization of subjectivity to take account of the fact that many of our presumptions about what is natural cannot simply be "read from the body" but rather are better understood as naturalized social constructions.

Following that, I argue that any new understanding of subjectivity must avoid both the reification of essentialism and the destabilization of post-structuralism. Outlining what I think are the critical next steps in developing this new way of thinking about the subject, I suggest that human rights discourse must accept the ethical burden associated with the privilege of representing the other, and in particular must attend to the itinerary of silence that inevitably accompanies any normative discourse. In this final section, I draw attention to what some of the disqualified voices are currently saying about how they understand the nature of their subjectivity, and I consider the extent to which these newly emerging constructions challenge existing ones. As always, the aim is not to dismiss certain constructions of subjectivity or to prefer one account over another but to re-affirm the point that the manner in which we understand our subjectivity is intimately connected with and dependent on our respective world views and not a consequence of a universal account of human nature. Thus, our key concern can no longer be whether our concept of the subject is true or accurate but must be how carefully we represent the diverse ways in which subjects construct their self-understandings, how closely we listen for the voices of those whose cultures have been delegitimized, and how diligently we seek out the experiences of those whose absence we have not yet noted. Understood in this way, the subject of human rights is no longer an abstraction of a universalist discourse but rather a situated individual whose fate is inextricably linked with the futures of situated others.

Hearing the Disqualified Voices

Among the hundreds of books and articles that have recently been published on the subject of human rights, one in particular stands out: David Hollenbach's edited collection *Refugee Rights, Ethics, Advocacy and Africa*. It alone includes, as a central component of its analysis, the voice of Abebe Feyissa, an Ethiopian who has lived in a refugee camp for sixteen years and who reflects on the long-term effects of that experience.[39] It would be wrong to universalize from one individual's experience or to valorize particular experiences at the expense of policy and other forms of analysis. Nonetheless, its inclusion among the voices of other human rights activists and advocates is an important reminder of the direction in which human rights discourse needs to proceed, and its uniqueness in the literature is a sign of how far we still have to go in this regard. Human rights can only function as a voice with the voiceless, as a framework of advocacy, when it names the silences and enables previously disqualified voices to be heard.

What are those whose voices have previously been disqualified saying about how they understand their subjectivity? What are the critical elements that shape their identities? How far do these elements challenge the model of subjectivity that is operative within human rights discourse? The task of analyzing these discussions is an interpretive one that also carries the burdens of representation, of which we have already spoken. But the diversity and complexity of these voices makes this interpretative task an onerous one. In this context, I focus on the voices of Christian ethicists who are writing from and with the perspectives of the marginalized. Drawing on a range of theologians, I discuss just one dimension of such experiences, which continues to be neglected by the dominant discourse on subjectivity, which challenges traditional conceptualizations, and for which human rights makes little provision. The dimension in question is the material—specifically, the economic—dimension of experience that, when its role in the construction of subjectivity is dealt with appropriately, provides an important counterpoint to the classic account of the subject. In this regard, one can see very clearly how subaltern voices challenge, moderate, and transform the dominant discourse in fundamental ways. Indeed, it both illustrates and confirms the fact that subjectivity is constructed in and through the fabric of cultures and the technologies of power. Important as these voices are, however, it must be remembered that perspectives such as these are merely illustrative, since certain marginalized voices are only beginning to be heard while others have, as yet, had no hearing.

The inadequacies of the traditional liberal conceptualization of the subject have already been rehearsed. We now know that we cannot speak of a natural, universal subject, or of normative claims that can simply and unambiguously be read from the nature of the person. Rather, we acknowledge that there are multiple constructions of the subject, each shaped by assumptions about embodiment, agency, and destiny, and each constructed in the context of particular historical, social, and cultural circumstances. Recent analyses of subjectivity have therefore rightly focused on the manner in which the subject is discursively constituted. This has been an important development that has allowed previously neglected historical and cultural differences to be recognized. However, what continues to be neglected is the seminal role that economic factors play in conceptualizations of subjectivity. Indeed, one could go so far as to say that it constitutes a major blind spot in human rights discourse, one that allows the classical tradition to ignore its ongoing complicity in the silencing of the subaltern, and one that enables human rights advocates to neglect the impact of our unacknowledged privilege.[40] Yet, as Kwok Pui-lan, Mercy Amba Oduyoye, Jean-Marc Éla, Agbonkhiameghe Orobator, and a host of other postcolonial theologians demonstrate, the discursive aspects of culture cannot be separated from their material conditions.[41] For example, Felix Wilfred's *Asian Public Theology* engages in an extensive discussion of how the overlapping categories of caste, family background, and economic circumstances reinforce the exclusionary impact of "each other," and reinforce that the impact of the economic factors cannot be neglected.[42] Indeed, in the present circumstances of global capitalism, as these analyses insist, it is the economic factors above all that may determine the extent to which the subject can articulate her commitments, desires, and needs—that is, can construct her identity.

Yet human rights discourse rarely attends to this critical factor in its philosophizing on the nature of the subject. Although it has begun to acknowledge that cultural and religious factors play a seminal role in how subjectivity is understood, it remains silent on the economic ones. Maria Mies's classic study of the lacemakers of Narsapur, India, provides the kind of analysis we need if we are to understand the complexity and distinctiveness of the processes of subject construction.[43] In particular, it highlights the fact that subjectivity is shaped not only through cultural and religious norms but also through the socioeconomic spheres of production. Mies's study focuses on the household industry of lace making that produces luxury goods for the West and that is now a permanent part of the capitalist system in Andhra Pradesh. Of significance for our discussion is how the economic and cultural-religious ideologies combine to create an account of their identities among the women lacemakers. The women are defined, and define themselves, as "non-working housewives," and their work is regarded as leisure time activity. By functioning within this patriarchal ideology of the housewife, and by obeying the rules of *purdah* and seclusion, the women not only reinforce oppressive patriarchal norms but they also support a form of economic growth that results in their own pauperization. In Mies's discussion one can see the complex interaction of economic, cultural, religious, and other ideologies through which the woman is constructed as subject and through which she constructs herself. In this context one can see that the economic factors play a central, not an ancillary, role in the creation and maintenance of that identity. Mies's analysis is instructive in this regard since it cautions against neglecting the material dimensions of cultural production and subject formation—a point made consistently by those who speak "with" the marginalized. Classic human rights discourse is, of course, concerned about the social justice dimensions of the circumstances in which the women of Narsapur find themselves, and the focus on economic rights in the UN Declaration is a reflection of this. However, what even the post–UN Declaration discourse has failed to appreciate is that economic circumstances have an impact not only on the concrete conditions of these women's lives but perhaps more fundamentally on how the women construct their subjectivities, on how they determine their expressed desires and interests, and on how they articulate their imagined futures. Indeed, this neglect of the formative influence of material circumstances in the construction of the subject may account for the inability to accept the legitimacy of certain ways of life that deviate from Western life choices. Moreover, it requires that attention be given not only to the material conditions through which the subjectivity of the marginalized is constructed but also to the impact that Western economic privilege has had on the manner in which the idealized subject of human rights has traditionally been understood. With this attention to the material conditions through which the subject is formed comes a realization that, for many people worldwide, some of the classic elements of subjectivity have little resonance. The issue of autonomy is an interesting case in point. As has already been noted, traditional human rights discourse is premised on a model of subjectivity that has its roots in the Western philosophical tradition and in which the concept of autonomy is central. Autonomy plays a critical role in classic explanations of why human beings are due respect. Margaret Farley summarizes the Kantian account of the significance of autonomy thus:

> Kant argued that every human being is absolutely valuable as an end in itself. Persons are ends in a radical sense (not simply as the last in a series of means) because they are autonomous. They are autonomous because of their rationality—more specifically, because of their capacity to recognize in

and by themselves what counts as a moral obligation and to resolve to act in accordance with it or not. Autonomy is, therefore, that feature of persons whereby they are not solely determined in their actions by causes external to their own reason and will, not even by their own desires and inclinations. Negatively free (undetermined, uncoerced) in this sense, persons can recognize their own law (reason "legislates" for itself); they are thereby also positively free (self-governing) to determine the meaning of their own lives in an ultimate (moral) sense. This is the basis of human dignity.[44]

A person's autonomy is thus the ground of her dignity and the basis on which individuals can claim human rights. Farley goes on to discuss the various feminist and communitarian critiques of this conceptualization of autonomy, noting in particular "its formalism, its indifference to human vulnerability and its delusion of a self-generating self," and subsequently makes an argument about the need to temper this understanding of autonomy with a sense of the comparable importance of relationality.[45] While I have no quarrel with Farley's argument about the need to revisit the way in which respect for persons is grounded, one wonders whether her rearticulated account of autonomy has the universal resonance that she assumes. Furthermore, one wonders if an account of why human beings are due respect might not also be made on the basis of human vulnerability. Human frailty is, after all, as much a feature of human experience as is autonomy. Indeed, human vulnerability may be precisely the basis on which the obligation to respect all persons can be most effectively grounded in this age of global capitalism. James Keenan's compelling discussion of how suffering can create solidarity suggests that this approach has potential.[46] The more one encounters the material realities through which millions of persons worldwide construct their subjectivities, the greater is the distance from the language of autonomy, rationality, and freedom. This is not to suggest that those who live with poverty, violence, and degradation have no sense of autonomy. Rather, the point is that there are other ways of grounding the respect which individuals are due, and that the shared experience of human vulnerability may be an equally compelling way of so doing. Thus, for some, autonomy is the anchor of their subjectivity; for others, it is vulnerability. Rosi Braidotti suggests something similar with her insistence that codependence should replace recognition as the basis for a new ethic.[47] The dignity of the person can be established in multiple ways. We do not need to establish the bonds of sameness but rather can build a more persuasive discourse of human rights from the bonds of difference. However, it is only when we can hear those who have heretofore been silent and silenced that we can begin to have the kinds of conversations we need about the grounding of human dignity. As Kwok Pui-lan reminds us, "we cannot understand ourselves without listening to others, especially to those we have oppressed or have the potential to oppress. Such critical engagement is the beginning of solidarity."[48]

Resisting Foreclosure

What, therefore, can human beings be said to share? This chapter argues that this and other comparable questions need to be recast in order to take account of the manner in which subjectivity is differently constructed in and through concrete historical circumstances. It is through the interaction of the cultural, religious, economic, and political dimensions of experience that the contours of personhood are established and accounts of what is "natural" for human beings are determined. Since these material circumstances and their interactions vary widely, it is to be expected that there are manifold and conflicting constructions of the nature and purpose of human life. This, therefore, is the context of understanding in which the language of personhood can be posited and through which discussions about commonalities can be pursued. Thus, it is the situated rather than the abstract individual who ought to form the centerpiece of human rights discourse.[49] A new paradigm can then be constructed around the specificity of human life, and this new paradigm will then have the capacity to become a platform on which one can build an, albeit provisional and revisable, account of what human beings share, and from which one can begin to articulate an ethic that will guarantee the flourishing of these situated human beings. This is the basis on which a renewed discourse of human rights can be developed. It is a framework in which the language of personhood can be retained, although its tenor must be recast.

Alongside the constructive task of narrating the human and of delineating her rights, human rights politics must also be engaged in a constant interrogation of the nature of the discourse through which the human is represented, noting the silences and absences and making space for the emergence of new voices. Human rights discourse can no longer ignore the contradictions in its own position where it both attempts to speak with the oppressed while continuing to be uncritical about the historical role that Western intellectuals and human rights advocates have played in the construction of normative accounts of personhood. Indeed, it is essential that we recognize that this is the double bind of all human rights advocacy, that even as we aspire to speak with and on behalf of the marginalized, we must interrogate the nature of the enterprise on which we have embarked. An adaptation of George Steiner's idea of making "a wager on the meaning of meaning" may be helpful in this context.[50] Steiner's wager is that, notwithstanding this radical dislocation, one can nonetheless hold one's nerve not by reiterating the old certainties but rather by pushing oneself, to use Seamus Heaney's words, "beyond the range you thought you'd settled for."[51] Similarly, in the context of how human rights claims are grounded, it may be possible to acknowledge how little we know about what we have traditionally described as "human nature" even as we work toward establishing the material conditions for human well-being. We may have to push ourselves to continue to use the language of personhood while at the same time acknowledging that our understanding of the "marks of humanness" has been, until recently, the product of colonial gestures that have shaped "the other" according to Western assumptions. Indeed, it may even be feasible to continue to use the metaphor of human nature while also recognizing that such an abstraction is itself the product of a particular philosophical imaginary and can only be properly appreciated within that context.

Traditional human rights discourse has been built on the assumption that one can speak abstractly about the nature of the human subject and that there are certain marks of the human that are self-evident, that can be read from the nature of persons, and that are universal and transhistorical. Although the persuasive power of this rhetorical claim cannot be overstated, as we have seen, it has serious limitations. A renewed discourse of human rights will need to find other ways to capture the obligating features traditionally associated with this appeal to human nature and in so doing find new ways to establish the significant rhetorical effect that the concept of human nature has traditionally had. However, given what has been said about the importance of placing the experiences of situated individuals at the core of a renewed human rights discourse, it is recognized that no one rhetorical device, metaphor, or narrative can today perform this function.

double bind

marks of humanness product colonial gesture

Indeed, it will be important to understand that human rights discourse will need multiple ways of talking about the obligations that flow from these more dynamic models of subjectivity for which I argue. Thus, in addition to drawing on the perspectives of those who have traditionally been marginalized, human rights discourse will also need to learn how other philosophical frameworks and lifeworlds express the obligating features of what we in the West have called human nature. It is likely that we will discover that there are many rhetorical devices to draw upon that will facilitate a more nuanced approach to the ambiguities of human rights discourse. Many years ago, for example, Gayatri Spivak recommended adopting "practices of strategic essentialism" as a way of naming the commonalities among situated individuals while also remaining vigilant about the exclusionary potential of such language. This is an approach that has also been adopted by some feminists as a way of recognizing the differences among women while also retaining the ability to speak in generic terms about women's experience. These and other rhetorical devices may hold some potential for human rights discourse as it tries to navigate its complex ethical project, and literary and other imaginative devices are likely to be as central to this enterprise as philosophical ones. The key, however, is that we recognize that our objective is not to generate a better or more accurate account of human nature or of the human person but rather to gain a better understanding of what precisely we are doing when we use this language of human nature or personhood. "How might we encounter the difference that calls our grids of intelligibility into question without trying to foreclose the challenge that the difference delivers? What might it mean to live with the anxiety of that challenge, to feel the surety of one's epistemological and ontological anchor go, but to be willing, in the name of the human, to allow the human to be other than what it is traditionally assumed to be?"[52] These questions go to the heart of the ethical challenge facing human rights discourse. Addressing that challenge hinges on being able to develop an account of the person who is open to rearticulation and contestation, who is cognizant of the manifold ways in which subjectivity is constructed and established. We can no longer hope for a discourse that is grounded in the presumption of sameness. Rather, our concern must be to engender solidarity through the bonds of difference and promote coalitions of concern among all those who are committed to establishing the material conditions through which the well-being of all persons

is guaranteed. As she reflects on the challenges posed by these questions, Judith Butler suggests that we must make a choice between two alternative and mutually exclusive approaches to living with the ambiguity of difference. She describes them as the violent and the nonviolent responses. "The violent response is the one that does not ask [who are you?], and does not seek to know. It wants to shore up what it knows, to expunge what threatens it with not-knowing, what forces it to consider the presuppositions of its world, its contingency, its malleability." The nonviolent response "lives with its unknowingness . . . in the face of the Other, since sustaining the bond that the question opens is finally more valuable than knowing in advance what holds us in common."[53]

Human rights discourse must walk a fine line when it speaks about the affinities that persons share. It need not eschew all talk about what we hold in common. What is essential, however, is that human rights discourse accepts the ethical burden associated with the privilege of speaking for and with the other, and that it remains constantly vigilant about the itinerary of silence that is an inevitable feature of its normative framework.

Notes

1. Johannes Morsink argues in chapter 2 of *Inherent Human Rights* that this is the underlying philosophy of the preamble and first article. However, he also concedes that the extensive discussions in the Third Committee about the phrase "by nature," together with its eventual exclusion from the text, suggest that there were a variety of views among the drafters about how human rights ought to be grounded. He nonetheless makes the case for what he calls a metaphysics of inherence as the basis of human rights, and he argues that many of the drafters meant the inherence claim literally and not just symbolically.

2. This is a paraphrasing of Kwok Pui-lan's comment when she notes that postcolonial feminist theology must aim to go beyond both the universalist female subject of liberal feminism and the unending subject-in-process of poststructuralism. Kwok, *Postcolonial Imagination and Feminist Theology* (London: SCM-Canterbury Press, 2005), 144.

3. This is Maura Ryan's description in her introduction to *A Just and True Love: Feminism at the Frontiers of Theological Ethics; Essays in Honor of Margaret A. Farley* (Notre Dame, IN: University of Notre Dame Press 2007), 3.

4. Judith Butler, *Gender Trouble: Feminism and the Subversion of Identity* (New York: Routledge, 1990), 9.

5. It is interesting to note that even classics like Elizabeth Spelman's *Inessential Woman: Problems of Exclusion in Feminist Thought* (Boston: Beacon Press, 1988), although focused on the differences among women, do not question the binary nature of gender.

6. Judith Butler, *Undoing Gender* (New York: Routledge, 2004).

7. Judith Butler discusses the complex and tragic story of David Reimer in "Doing Justice to Someone: Sex Reassignment and Allegories of Transsexuality," in ibid., 57–74. David Peter Reimer (1965–2004) was a Canadian man born biologically male but raised female following medical advice and surgical intervention. He transitioned to living as a male at age fifteen but committed suicide at age thirty-nine, having suffered severe depression for many years.

8. Patricia Beattie Jung and Aana Marie Vigen, with John Anderson, eds., *God, Science, Sex, Gender: An Interdisciplinary Approach to Christian Ethics* (Urbana: University of Illinois Press, 2010), 8.

9. Susan Frank Parsons, *The Ethics of Gender* (Oxford: Blackwell, 2002), 76.

10. Butler, *Gender Trouble*, 33.

11. Kate Rudy's *Sex and the Church: Gender Homosexuality and the Transformation of Christian Ethics* (Boston: Beacon Press, 1997) develops this point in relation to the normative force of theological categories.

12. L. Amede Obiora, "Bridges and Barricades: Rethinking Polemics and Intransigence in the Campaign against Female Circumcision," *Case Western Reserve Law Review* 47, no. 2 (Winter 1997): 277–387.

13. Ibid.

14. Fuambai Ahmadu, "Rites and Wrongs: An Insider/Outsider Reflects on Power and Excision," in *Female "Circumcision" in Africa: Culture, Controversy and Change*, ed. Bettina Shell-Duncan and Ylva Hernlund, 305–7 (Boulder, CO: Lynne Reiner, 2000).

15. This point is made by Mercy Amba Oduyoye in "Christianity and African Culture," *International Review of Mission* 84 (1995): 86–87.

16. Meyda Yeğenoğlu, "Sartorial Fabric-ations: Enlightenment and Western Feminism," in *Postcolonialism, Feminism and Religious Discourse*, ed. Laura E Donaldson and Kwok Pui-lan, 82–99 (New York: Routledge, 2002).

17. Ibid., 92.

18. Ibid., 95; and Frantz Fanon, *A Dying Colonialism*, trans. Haakon Chevalier (New York: Grove Weidenfeld, 1965), 58–59.

19. My colleague John May acknowledges Theodor Ahrens, who brought this to his attention in an unpublished manuscript, "'Was ihr uns gebracht habt ist der Körper.' Erwägungen zur Frage, was Missionswissenschaft zur Erkenntnis Gottes beiträgt," 13–17, drawing on Maurice Leenhardt, *Do Kamo: La personne et le mythe dans le monde mélanésien* (1947; repr., Paris: Gallimard, 1971). May discusses this in

Transcendence and Violence: The Encounter of Buddhist, Christian, and Primal Traditions (New York: Continuum, 2003), 45, 57–58; and in Linda Hogan and John May, "Gender and Culture as Dimensions of Bodiliness," in *Bodiliness and Human Dignity, An Intercultural Approach*, ed. Harm Goris, 45–61 (Münster: LIT, 2006).

20. See Isabel Apawo Phiri, "HIV/AIDS: An African Theological Response in Mission," in *Hope Abundant: Third World and Indigenous Women's Theology*, ed. Kwok Pui-lan, 219–28 (Maryknoll, NY: Orbis, 2010); Meng Yanling, "Women, Faith and Marriage: A Feminist Look at the Challenges for Women," in *Hope Abundant: Third World and Indigenous Women's Theology*, ed. Kwok Pui-lan (Maryknoll, NY: Orbis, 2010), 229–40; Rose Wu, "A Story of Its Own Name: Hong Kong's *Tongzhi* Culture and Movement," in *Off the Menu Asian and Asian North American Women's Religion and Theology*, ed., Rita Nakashima Brock, Jing Ha Kim, Kwok Pui-lan, and Seung Ai Yang, 275–92 (Louisville, KY: Westminster John Knox Press, 2007); and Anne Dondapati Allen, "No Garlic Please, We Are Indian: Reconstructing the De-eroticized Indian Woman," in *Off the Menu: Asian and Asian North American Women's Religion and Theology*, edited by Rita Nakashima Brock, Jing Ha Kim, Kwok Pui-lan, and Seung Ai Yang, 183–96 (Knoxville, KY: Westminster John Knox Press, 2007).

21. Butler, *Undoing Gender*, 24.

22. Gayatri Chakravorty Spivak, "Can the Subaltern Speak?" in *Can the Subaltern Speak? Reflections on the History of an Idea*, ed. Rosalind C. Morris, 237–91 (New York: Columbia University Press, 2010). The original essay was published in Cary Nelson and Lawrence Grossberg, eds., *Marxism and the Interpretations of Cultures* (Urbana: University of Illinois, 1988).

23. Subaltern studies emerged in the early 1980s initially as a series of journal articles published by Oxford University Press in India. Its early focus was how the history of India was told and its concern was to retake history for the marginalized and to challenge the dominance of imperial history. The historian Ranajit Guha is regarded as the founder of the field of study. Other key theorists include Dipesh Chakrabarty, Partha Chatterjee, and Gayatri Chakravorty Spivak. The journal *Subaltern Studies*, published by Oxford University Press since 1982, is the best source of this material. Although begun in India, subaltern studies has evolved and made an impact, especially in Latin America (and to a lesser extent in West Africa), where the complexities of postcolonial subject formation are also of central concern.

24. See Gayatri Chakravorty Spivak, "In Response: Looking Back, Looking Forward," in *Can the Subaltern Speak?*, ed. Morris, 227–36, at 233.

25. Partha Chatterjee, "Reflections on 'Can the Subaltern Speak?'" in *Can the Subaltern Speak?*, ed. Morris, 81–86, at 83.

26. Gayatri Chakravorty Spivak, "Can the Subaltern Speak?," in *Can the Subaltern Speak?*, ed. Morris, 237–91, at 237.

27. Drucilla Cornell, "The Ethical Affirmation of Human Rights: Gayatri Spivak's Intervention," in *Can the Subaltern Speak?*, ed. Morris, 100–116, at 103–4. The deconstruction she has in mind is that of Derrida.

28. This is Rita Birla's phrase in "Postcolonial Studies: Now That's History," in *Can the Subaltern Speak?*, ed. Morris, 87–99, at 92.

29. Spivak, "Can the Subaltern Speak?," 259. "Tribals" refers to the many different groups of tribal peoples who live across India, and who generally are marginalized, without education, and with poor living standards. A "zero worker" is a contract worker who has a zero-hour contract and therefore has no guarantee of work from week to week but is obliged to be available for work and to take whatever random hours are given.

30. Birla, "Postcolonial Studies," 93.

31. Gayatri Chakravorty Spivak, "Righting Wrongs," in *Human Rights, Human Wrongs*, ed. Nicholas Owen, 164–227 (Oxford: Oxford University Press, 2002).

32. Ibid., 202.

33. Cornell, "Ethical Affirmation," 108, commenting on Spivak's "Righting Wrongs."

34. Spivak has a complicated articulation of the alterity of subordinate cultures in which the contradictory impulses of incorporation/appropriation and exclusion are acknowledged.

35. Spivak, "A Moral Dilemma," in *What Happens to History: The Renewal of Ethics in Contemporary Thought*, ed. Howard Marchitello, 215–36 (New York: Routledge, 2001), 215–16.

36. The work of postcolonial feminists throughout the world has drawn attention to the manner in which women's bodies inevitably become the site of contestation between colonialists and traditionalists. Mercy Amba Oduyoye's *Daughters of Anowa: African Women and Patriarchy* (Maryknoll, NY: Orbis, 1995) makes this argument in respect of sexuality, as does Kwok Pui-lan's "Unbinding Our Feet: Saving Brown Women and Feminist Religious Discourse," in *Postcolonialism, Feminism and Religious Discourse*, ed. Laura Donaldson and Kwok Pui-lan, 62–81 (New York: Routledge, 2001), in relation to the practice of foot-binding in China.

37. Spivak, "Can the Subaltern Speak?" 268.

38. Ibid.

39. Abebe Feyissa with Rebecca Horn, "There Is More Than One Way of Dying: An Ethiopian Perspective on the Effects of Long-Term Stays in Refugee Camps," in *Refugee Rights, Ethics, Advocacy and Africa*, ed. David Hollenbach, 13–26 (Washington, DC: Georgetown University Press, 2008).

40. It is important to note that, as discussed earlier, significant progress was made, particularly during the twentieth century, in terms of recognizing the importance of the economic conditions in which people live. This was given prominence in the UN Declaration with the enumeration of economic and social rights, and was copper-fastened in the 1966 International Covenant on Economic, Social and Cultural Rights. However, I am suggesting that—this progress notwithstanding—there remains within human rights discourse a failure to appreciate the depth of the impact that material conditions have on the construction of subjectivity— something that the case of the lace-makers in Narsapur, India, illustrates.

41. See especially Kwok, *Postcolonial Imagination and Feminist Theology*, 150– 67; Oduyoye, *Daughters of Anowa*, chaps. 4, 7, and 9; Jean-Marc Éla, *My Faith as an African* (Maryknoll, NY: Orbis, 1988); and Agbonkhiameghe Orobator, *Theology Brewed in an African Pot* (Maryknoll, NY: Orbis, 2008).

42. Felix Wilfred, *Asian Public Theology: Critical Concerns in Challenging Times* (Dehli: ISPCK, 2010), esp. chaps. 4, 8, and 9.

43. Maria Mies, *The Lacemakers of Narsapur: Indian Housewives Produce for the World Market* (London: Zed Books, 1982).

44. Margaret Farley, "A Feminist Version of Respect for Persons," *Journal of Feminist Studies in Religion* 9, no. 1–2 (Spring–Fall 1993): 183–98.

45. Ibid., 188.

46. James Keenan, "Impasse and Solidarity in Theological Ethics," *Catholic Theological Society of America Proceedings* 64 (2009): 1–14.

47. Rosi Braidotti, *Transpositions: On Nomadic Ethics* (Cambridge, UK: Polity Press, 2006), 132.

48. Kwok, *Postcolonial Imagination*, 60.

49. Seyla Benhabib uses the terminology of "the concrete other."

50. George Steiner, *Real Presences: Is There Anything in What We Say?* (London: Faber & Faber, 1989), 4.

51. Seamus Heaney, "Squarings, xxxix," from *Seeing Things*, reprinted in *Opened Ground: Poems 1966–1996* (London: Faber & Faber, 1998), 383.

52. Butler, *Undoing Gender*, 35.

53. Ibid. Butler is summarizing Adriana Cavarero's *Relating Narratives: Storytelling and Selfhood* (London: Routledge, 2000), 20–29 and 87–92, who in turn is paraphrasing Hannah Arendt.

4

Building Discursive Bridges

Situated Knowledge, Embedded Universalism,
Plural Foundations

Nothing captures the ambiguity of human rights more acutely than its claim to universality, which is both the basis of its potency and the condition of its vulnerability. Its claim to be grounded in universal values that are underpinned by an objective moral order is deeply embedded in the legacy of its philosophical origins. Yet, notwithstanding this philosophical heritage, this claim is belied by the nature of the political contestation that has accompanied its development. Chapters 1 and 2 discuss the complicated history and contradictory impulses of human rights discourse through an analysis of its political, philosophical, and theological development. Thus, politically, human rights discourse can either be interpreted as being relentlessly Western or understood as an evolving language of shared value; philosophically, it can be regarded either as a discourse of enlightenment universalism or as an insurrectionary praxis;[1] and theologically, it can either be understood to be necessarily grounded in a theistic framework or read as the language of values for a godless age.[2] In each case, the claim to universality is significant for the manner in which these debates have evolved. Moreover, it is often the decisive factor as advocates and critics marshal their respective arguments either in support of or against the politics of human rights. In many respects, one might conclude that human rights discourse has entered a cul-de-sac, with universalists and relativists each defending opposite sides of the same epistemological model, without any hope of a rapprochement.

In this chapter I take a step back from these much-discussed debates to ask what kind of universality is appropriate and necessary for the pursuit of human rights today. This, I suggest, is a critical question that tends to be overlooked as advocates and critics do battle over the putative universality and objectivity of human rights claims. I defend a form of universalism but argue that this crucial category needs to be recalibrated to take account of what we have come to understand about the nature of moral knowledge and its apprehension. The form of universalism I defend, therefore, is not grounded in one single philosophical or theological framework; is not discerned through a form of decontextualized or abstract reasoning; is not oriented toward the development of a neutral normative regime; and does not expect that disputes over particular human rights will be resolved through declarations of their universality. Moreover, remembering Aristotle's important insight, it recognizes that ethics is not an exact science, and it acknowledges that one cannot expect the same degree of precision and certitude from morality as might be expected, for example, from mathematics.[3] The form of universalism I defend is grounded in the conviction that all our knowledge of the world is situated; that the universalist convictions we articulate are inevitably embedded in the cultural values through which they are expressed; that the justifications we marshal are contingent on the frameworks through which they are intelligible; that the foundations on which human rights are based must allow for a plurality of philosophical, religious, and cultural world views; and that the universalism to which we aspire can only emerge and be confirmed through multiple, inclusive, tradition-thick, cross-cultural conversations.

In Chapters 1 and 2, I argue that human rights discourse will only be credible if it can deal with the legitimate concerns of communitarian, feminist, and postcolonial scholars who are critical of its abstract universalism. I suggested that human rights discourse must abandon the illusion that it derives from a form of abstract reasoning that is discernible independently from the social matrices in which it is exercised. Human rights discourse can no longer be conceived as a set of normative ethical principles that can be grasped by the individual drawing conclusions that are objectively and universally true and independent of the cultural, historical, and religious

[handwritten margin notes: "Ethics Not an exact Science" / "Knowledge in the world is situated" / "Foundations of the HR must be plural"]

context she inhabits. Rather, a renewed discourse of human rights must build on the conviction that the norms of rationality are enmeshed in lived traditions of enquiry and that, as a consequence, our expectations of what we are claiming when we assert that human rights are objective and universal need to be rethought. In this chapter, I discuss this issue of the kind of moral knowledge and the form of universalism on which human rights discourse can depend, and I propose that it is more appropriate and credible to reconceptualize human rights as a form of situated knowledge and as a version of an embedded universalism. I illustrate this philosophical point by drawing on one particular aspect of the history of human rights.

Following on from this conviction that human rights discourse can only be credible if it embraces its embedded character, I argue that the classical approach to the issue of the foundations of and justifications for human rights must also be rethought. In this section, I defend the idea of a plurality of approaches to the question of foundations and argue that human rights discourse and politics will become more durable if the many and diverse forms of their justification can be harnessed. Then I consider the form that this deliberation and debate might take so that human rights can become the genuinely global language of moral evaluation to which it aspires. Ultimately, this approach is consensus based, and is grounded in the conviction that, notwithstanding the contingencies of moral discernment and the exclusionary functions of power, human beings do have the capacity to engage in meaningful cross-cultural, inclusive dialogue about how human dignity can be protected and human flourishing be promoted. I end with a discussion of some of the risks associated with abandoning the strong universalist, objectivist claims that have traditionally been associated with human rights and that, I have argued, have no place in the contemporary discourse.

HR discourse more durable if diverse forms are harnessed

Situated Knowledge, Embedded Universalism

There is no doubt that many of the claims relating to the universality and objectivity of human rights will need to be revised if this argument about the nature of the moral knowledge and the forms of rationality on which we can depend is accepted. Notwithstanding the discomfort and uncertainty that may be created, however, it is important that we acknowledge that our political and ethical reasoning is contingent and historically shaped, and it is essential that we articulate an account of human rights that is grounded therein. Many human rights advocates worry that if they set aside their strong universalist claims or if they abandon their dependence on the rhetoric of assertion and declaration, then the ethical and political force of human rights will be lost. Moreover, they take comfort in the ostensible clarity that comes with these assertions and declarations of the universality of human rights. Contrary to that view, I think that the ethical and political force of human rights claims is undermined, rather than reinforced, when we fail to acknowledge that human rights discourse began as a particular historical and cultural expression of value that, over time and through its persuasive appeal, acquired and continues to acquire a global influence and attraction. We are creatures of tradition and history. Our expressions of value, our accounts of the good life, our apprehension of the virtues, our practical reasoning about how to live a dignified life— these and all our other deeply held convictions emerge from the communities we inhabit and become our own through the world views we encounter and through the narratives we construct and reconstruct. This contingent character of our understanding, especially of our moral understanding, is at the heart of how we must begin to think about the ethics and politics of human rights.

Inevitably, in this context, the question of relativism is raised, with human rights advocates expressing the concern that once the contingency of moral knowledge is conceded, then there is no firm ground on which to stand and from where the truth of human rights claims can be established. However, although understandable, I believe that such an anxiety reveals a basic misunderstanding about the nature of truth and justification in ethics. In making this judgment I am in agreement with the conclusion drawn by writers as diverse as Jeffrey Stout, Stanley Hauerwas, Gianni Vattimo, and Kwok Pui-lan, who—each for very different reasons—insist that we must give up this unhealthy obsession with the idea of absolute truth in ethics and make peace with the reality that our ethical discourse is constructed and narrated through the cultural and religious worlds that we inhabit. We can recognize that rationality is contingent and that justification is always contextual without also endorsing a relativist position in respect to truth. Indeed, within the field of philosophical and theological ethics there have been a host of different attempts to establish ethical frameworks that are simultaneously realist in respect to truth while also holding a contextualist account of justification. Within this context, the approach that I find most appealing is the modest pragmatism of Jeffrey Stout, in large part because of his determination, as he describes it, to dig truth-talk "out of the bog where philosophies have sunk" and to ensure instead that truth-talk be considered on "the solid ground of actual language use . . . [and that it be made sense] 'in terms of an empirically oriented linguistic theory.'"[4]

Stout's insistence that we attend to the distinctions between adjudication, justification, and truth is important for my approach to human rights. He is rightly critical of the manner in which these distinctions have been ignored in contemporary ethical and political discourse and suggests that the failure to make adequate and appropriate distinctions has led to a situation where we seem to be faced with a choice between "two package deals, one of which is metaphysically realist with respect to truth, anticontextualist with respect to justification, and cosmopolitan with respect to rights and obligations, the other being metaphysically antirealist with respect to truth, contextualist with respect to justification and parochial with respect to rights and obligations."[5] Stout rejects this characterization of the field of ethics and instead sets about picking apart the ties that bind realism to anticontextualism, arguing that the assumption that they are necessarily of a piece is itself the result of the conflation of a series of distinctions that need to be more carefully delineated.

The account Stout gives of the ways in which we adjudicate among ethical claims and justify our positions to one another allows for a degree of durability to be attributed to such processes while at the same time allowing for the recognition that these conclusions are ultimately provisional and therefore must be open to change.[6] Stout is adamant that the possibility of adjudication among values or practices in particular cases of conflict is itself no guarantee that adjudication will be possible in all cases. This is because the possibility of adjudication is itself dependent on a degree of kinship in respect of world views or of commensurability in respect of certain values or of some other form of comparability that would make the practice of adjudication meaningful. Moralities are embedded in situated, historical communities, and moral conflicts come in many different guises. Adjudication is only possible where there is a basis for believing that the terms of comparison are meaningful. Moreover, such adjudication will not be of the kind that involves evaluating discrete moralities according to their conformity to abstract ethical norms. Rather, as Stout argues, the process

adjudication is cross-contextual

of adjudication in ethics functions according to a different model; that is, it takes different forms, proceeds on an ad hoc basis, and trusts "that whatever uniformities there are will necessarily turn up locally among the similarities obtaining to the case at hand."[7] Adjudication in ethics is, in other words, cross-contextual.

Since justifications are essentially answers to why questions, they, too, are inevitably context dependent "first because conversational context determines the question to which a justification counts as an answer and thus the sort of information being requested; second, because conversational context determines a justification's audience; and third, because a justification's success can be appraised only in relation to its audience, including their relevant reasons for doubting and the commitments they are entitled to accept."[8] Thus, in justifying our ethical positions to one another, we must explain why we believe we are correct in holding the view we do, for example, on the equality of men and women, but we should do so in a manner that conveys something about the moral framework out of which we are speaking and acting and which we hope will be intelligible and convincing to the other. Especially on important ethical and political issues, the justifications we give will inevitably draw heavily on the core values we espouse and on the moral worlds we inhabit. Justifications that are essentially abstract or that are focused purely on procedure are therefore unlikely to convince since the answer to a why question is such that it must be a bridge between the world of the one who is asking the why question and that of the one who is providing the explanation.[9]

That our adjudications and justifications are context dependent is evident. However, as Stout argues, one can acknowledge this fact without automatically adopting a relativist position in respect to moral truth. I agree with Stout that the prospect of adjudicating a moral conflict between two different groups depends to a significant degree on the nature of the contextual moralities and discursive practices of the different groups that are in conflict. I also agree that whether one is justified in holding a particular moral position also depends on the extent to which it is intelligible and persuasive within the moral framework within which it is articulated. In both these respects, one must concede relativity in adjudication and in justification. Yet relativity in these contexts can coexist with a moral realism—that is, with a confidence that the distinction between good and evil is a meaningful one in the moral context and that we must strive to reflect and embody this in our codes and practices. Stout, correctly in my view, retains the inferential, acceptance, equivalence, and cautionary uses of the language of truth and demonstrates that many of the ordinary ethical uses of the term "truth" are covered by such notions and therefore not undermined by the contextualist epistemology that is being defended here.[10] The correspondence use, however, is a different matter, and in this context Stout goes quite some way with Richard Rorty, arguing that this focus on defining truth in terms of a correspondence to some metaphysical reality has no explanatory value at all and certainly has no place in the discussion about truth in ethics. I believe that there is merit in this assessment. Indeed, it has a particular resonance when one observes and analyzes the most intractable debates in ethics, where one can see that this issue of "correspondence to reality" is rarely what is at stake when people engage with each other on their respective views and when they claim that their respective positions are true.

The most consistent and enduring framework through which the correspondence use of truth has been promoted has been through the language of correspondence to or conformity with the moral law. Of course, the language of moral law or moral order is itself an imaginative construct, essentially a way of expressing the conviction that the way we treat one another matters, that human beings have an inherent dignity, that our social order and political structures must function to promote this dignity, and that those who are especially vulnerable must be the focus of particular concern and protection. Within the Christian tradition, the language of the moral law, and especially of the natural law, has been deployed to convey the belief that the difference between good and evil is a meaningful one, and that human beings—frail and flawed though we are—have an obligation to strive in all our decisions and actions to do good and to avoid evil. Moreover, when Christians and adherents of other religious traditions consider what is required by that moral law, they refer to sacred texts and traditions, to classic narratives of moral heroism and exemplary practice, and to a repository of core principles, values, and virtues all expressed through the languages, metaphors, and practices of theological traditions.

When we speak about the truth of our ethical positions, we tend to engage in inferential, acceptance, equivalence, and cautionary uses of the term. If we engage in metaphysical uses, then we do so in the sense that they express something fundamental about our religious world view and the ethical commitments required by that world view. Typically, metaphysical uses also imply that we believe that such claims have a purchase that is wider than the contexts from which they have originated. The question, therefore, is whether the universalist impulses and aspirations of such claims can be defended while their embedded character is also acknowledged.

Although not a Rortian, I am inclined to believe that, in the field of ethics, the claim that "truth is that which corresponds to reality" is of little use because it is circular. And it is circular because it is we—flawed human beings—who ultimately communicate the account of "reality" to which our concept of truth conforms. As such, our articulations of the truth are inevitably flawed, fractured, and provisional. Moreover, notwithstanding the fact that they have tended to dominate the philosophical agenda, these metaphysical concerns do not capture what is at stake when the major ethical issues of the day are being discussed. In political and ethical debate, particularly on the most intractable issues, the critical concerns relate to whether and how different views of the good life can be accommodated and whether and how particular proposals protect or undermine the dignity of the most vulnerable. If the language of correspondence to reality is meaningful at all, it has a function as a rhetorical device that underwrites and reinforces one's conviction that a particular course of action is the right one, that it is the course of action that allows for the most humane, just, or loving outcome. Indeed, if it has any value at all, it is only as a synonym for the different ways in which we describe the ground of our most fundamental values. The moral realism on which finite human beings can depend is not such that it corresponds to some abstract and universalist set of norms or principles. Rather, this moral realism is a fractured realism. It is a realism that is based on an acknowledgment that, while our identities are shaped by the material and discursive conditions of our lives, and while the ethical judgments we make are inevitably shaped by the historical and religious contexts of our moral formation, we can nonetheless strive to embody the virtues and excellences that we have come to believe reflect the best that human beings can be.

When we situate human rights discourse within this kind of epistemological framework, then we come to understand that it is not a global version of public reason. Rather, it is a form of situated knowledge, a particular manifestation of an embedded universalism. Thus, human rights norms are better understood in terms of being particular or local expressions of universalist claims that over time and as a result of the persuasiveness of their appeal have evolved into a global moral language. In fact, I would suggest that in addition to being more credible philosophically, this characterization of human rights norms is also far more accurate historically. Moreover, as I show in the following discussion, the history of human rights displays the trajectory of its evolution from local to global very clearly. We can see this pattern both in relation to the concept of human rights itself and in relation to different specific human rights claims, each of which went through a developmental process that included first a declaration, then the appropriation and inculturation of that initial rights claim in a different cultural context, and then the rearticulation of that original claim in a different form and often with a radically different emphasis.

The transformation of human rights discourse from one that was dominated by a concern for individual liberty to a far more expansive one that is also concerned with the economic, social, and cultural interests of individuals and communities provides an excellent example of this trajectory. It illustrates the point that human rights discourse is a form of situated knowledge that over time and through the persuasiveness of its embedded universalist claims has gained a global appeal and resonance. Through the twentieth century, the traditional focus on individual liberty (itself a mark of the Western context from which modern human rights theory emerged) was gradually replaced by a broader and more extensive account of human rights encapsulated in the language of second- and third-generation rights. This process has involved defining new rights as well as extending the conventional scope of the claimants of rights to include groups as well as individuals. The primacy traditionally accorded civil and political rights has thus been superseded by a commitment to a more extensive set of rights that are understood to be indivisible. As a result, democratic governments can no longer simply point to the existence of a free press or to the right to free association as evidence of their commitment to human rights but rather must recognize that access to adequate shelter, health care, and social services is an integral part of that commitment. These newly articulated rights have embodied in a particular way the concerns of individuals and groups who had been traditionally excluded from the ambit of rights or for whom, because of their material situation, first-generation rights had not been especially meaningful. They have been significant, too, because they have extended the concept of right into areas

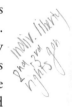

of human interest that had not originally been envisaged to be within its remit.

It is clear, especially from the debates during the third session of the Commission, that this idea that individuals are entitled to socially provided goods, services, and opportunities such as food, shelter, health care, social security, and education represented a significant challenge to the conventional Western conceptualization of rights. Although delegates from the United States and Britain reluctantly accepted their inclusion in the Declaration, they continued to regard these rights as having lesser status than civil and political rights. For example, Charles Dukes, Lord Dukeston, a British delegate, articulated a view still widely held that "economic and social rights and social security rested primarily on the affirmation of the freedom of speech and free association . . . [and that] human rights developed primarily through the recognition of freedom of speech."[11] Nonetheless, despite the hesitations of some, the Declaration marked an important point of departure. Not only did it mention economic, social, and cultural rights among the fundamental rights to which all individuals have a claim, it also included, in Article 28, the right "to a social and international order in which these rights and freedoms can be fully realised." The Declaration's recognition of the individual's right to full development is also significant in this regard, particularly because it recognizes the formative role of community in its elaboration of what this "full development" entails. And, although none of these initiatives on its own constituted a major break with the then dominant Western understanding of human rights, taken together they constitute an important stage in the ongoing transformation of rights talk. Of significance for the point I want to make is the fact that it was the non-Western and newly independent nations who were crucial to the articulation and promotion of second- and third-generation rights. In particular, it was the countries in the Latin American socialist tradition, together with the USSR and later the former colonies, that really pushed for the inclusion and retention of these economic, social, and cultural rights in the Declaration. Moreover, these rights were only on the agenda in the first place because they were included both in the Inter-American text and in the Panamanian submission, both of which served as blueprints for the first draft of the Declaration. In addition, they were retained because of the vigilance of the same delegates as well as on the insistence of China.[12] Once included, however, their significance was recognized by delegates from many different quarters who began to realize that without minimum economic and social guarantees, civil and political rights are meaningless.[13]

Cold War politics stalled the development of the covenantal portion of the international bill of rights for many years. However, the stalemate was eventually broken by the former colonies, many of whom, in the intervening years, had used human rights discourse to further their own political aspirations. Although they did not achieve much in terms of consensus, the decades of political maneuvering in advance of the establishment of the covenants nonetheless raised the profile of the newly established rights. The eventual promulgation, in 1966, of the twin covenants, one on civil and political rights the other on economic, social, and cultural rights, signaled yet another step in the transition from the traditional Western discourse dominated by civil and political rights. Even the Covenant on Civil and Political Rights departed from its strong individualistic tone and recognized the importance of ethnic, linguistic, and religious identities. Additionally, the Covenant on Economic, Social and Cultural Rights also pressed ahead into new territory by elaborating on these recently established rights in great detail. Over the next decade, in an effort to minimize the damage caused by the fragmentation of the Declaration into two covenants, many advocates directed their attention to promoting the idea of the indivisibility of all human rights. Thus, in 1968, during the International Conference on Human Rights in Teheran, the delegates declared that "since human rights and fundamental freedoms are indivisible, the full realisation of civil and political rights, without the enjoyment of economic, social and cultural rights is impossible."[14] The covenants are noteworthy, too, in that they mark the beginning of the formal recognition of what would later become known as third-generation rights, which represented a further step in the development of human rights discourse.

In this evolution one can see the trajectory that human rights discourse has followed: emerging from a particular context, articulating universalist claims, and then being adopted and appropriated by other situated communities who then developed it in ways unanticipated by the originators. The transformations have been radical and organic, not superficial. As a result of the particular transformation discussed here, for example, we now no longer conceive of human rights primarily in terms of individual liberties. Rather, they have been reconceived in such a way as to expand their remit into the domain of cultural, social, and economic rights, thereby

[Handwritten margin notes: "Twin covenants"; "Impossible to enjoy civil & political rights without economic, social & cultural"; "3rd gen rights"; "No longer see HR primarily as of individual"]

Certain groups have right to maintain their autonomy

ensuring that the formal claim to civil and political liberty is given real force. In addition, the gradual acceptance of the idea that certain groups have the right to maintain their autonomy in matters relating to institutional and local affairs, including culture, religion, education, and health, shifts the center of gravity considerably.[15] The substantive issues raised by these transformations are not our concern here. Rather, the purpose is to highlight the significance that the development of second- and third-generation rights has had in the evolution of the discourse. Through this example, one can discern a trajectory that is also evident in relation to other aspects of human rights discourse: a Western expression of a core value acquires a degree of international standing, finds a resonance with other contextual articulations of value, and, through this interaction, not only forges a consensus but in the process transforms the original value. It is recognized that the initial articulation of the claim emerges from within a moral tradition and reflects the values and commitments of that tradition. It is a form of situated knowledge, but insofar as it expresses a value that is believed to have global resonance, it is also an expression of an embedded universalism. It is a mistake, therefore, to characterize such expressions of value as merely local since all such expressions of value are ultimately local and contextual. They are, rather, contextual expressions of value in which are embedded universal aspirations. In fact, the history of human rights is replete with instances of the kind of interaction exemplified in the development of second- and third-generation rights. In reading the historical record, one can see that human rights claims are not, in the end, grounded in an abstract or universal conceptualization of rationality but rather emerge from the complex interactions of multiple situated communities who, drawing on their own expressions of value, articulate claims that they believe to have universal purchase. Human rights norms express the settled consensus as it is currently. Moreover, as we engage in deliberation on human rights claims, we aim for a consensus on the importance of certain values, all the time aware that in this consensus building we are shaped by the cultural and historical limitations of our moral languages, our moral traditions, and our moral imaginations. The issue at stake, therefore, is not ethical relativism but rather ethical pluralism as it is constituted and produced in different concrete situations, often with significant power differentials.[16]

Ethical pluralism

The issue of how these power differentials can be mitigated and how such discourses can be structured to ensure that vulnerable individuals and marginalized communities can have a voice is a vexed and complex issue that is particularly problematic because many of the factors that create marginalization and vulnerability are overlapping and mutually reinforcing, something that is highlighted by Axel Honneth and by Tariq Modood and Jan Dobbernack.[17] Thus, cultural, ethnic, linguistic, racial, religious, and economic factors may converge to make meaningful participation in a pluralist discourse difficult if not impossible. It is only when we deal with these power differentials head on by developing robust and inclusive public strategies to address these embedded, historic, and institutional biases that a meaningful pluralist discourse of the kind I am promoting will be possible.

Plural Foundations, Diverse Moral Frameworks

I have argued that the history of human rights is properly understood as an embedded discourse of value that, over time and through a series of interactions that has involved both colonialism and consensus building, has emerged as a moral language with global appeal. Admittedly, traditional human rights theory has been conceptualized somewhat differently, as a universal language, grounded in transcendent norms, and apprehended through a form of abstract reasoning. My argument, however, is that such a conceptualization is flawed not only because it misreads the philosophical nature of human rights discourse but also because it ignores its historical trajectory. This redescription of human rights discourse as situated knowledge and as embedded universalism allows us to think differently about its epistemological nature. It is also significant for the manner in which the issue of its foundations is understood.

Although the question of the grounding of human rights has long preoccupied philosophers and theologians, the debate has been reignited in recent years and in the process has become even more intractable. Behind the contemporary manifestation of the debate is the enduring question of how human rights claims are grounded. In the current debate, however, the discussion revolves around an expanded set of propositions regarding the question of foundations, including whether the idea of human rights must be premised on a particular religious or metaphysical claim; whether human rights can be grounded on a concept or a justification that all human beings can reasonably be said to share; whether the focus on foundations should be jettisoned in favor of a version of positivism, constructivism, or pragmatism; or whether the discourse can function with a plurality of accounts of its grounding.

It is clear from the discussion thus far that I do not believe that a recalibrated human rights discourse can be grounded in one single metaphysical theory, whether it is theistic or secular. Nor, given my argument about the contingent character of rationality and the contextual nature of justification, do I expect that some universal, shared account of the grounding of human rights will emerge. The question, therefore, is whether the discussion of foundations should be dismissed completely, regarded as indicative of an earlier, now-failed philosophical project, or whether the quest for foundations should continue. Within this context there is a growing body of opinion which suggests that the traditional debate about foundations should and can be ignored in the pursuit of a viable politics of human rights. In this vein, Michael Ignatieff argues that human rights politics can be successfully sustained without choosing from among the options of fixed, contingent, or plural foundations. He recommends abandoning the discussion about foundations altogether, insisting that human rights politics will be more durable if we focus not on the issue of its grounding but rather "on what such rights actually *do* for human beings."[18] He refutes the claim that human rights categories can survive different and even contradictory explanations of how they are grounded. Since such claims are believed to be true by those who hold them, and since they are controversial to those who don't, Ignatieff believes that a multiplicity of accounts of how human rights are grounded is "likely to fragment the commitment to the practical responsibilities entailed, rather than strengthening them."[19]

The idea that we should forego the debate about foundations is also made by Jack Donnelly, who argues that the almost universal consensus on the existence of human rights today means that the problem of foundations can be relegated to the margins.[20] His account of this international agreement incorporates what he insists is a striking cross-cultural consensus on many issues and upon which much of today's human rights activism is based. He acknowledges that this global activism does not provide a philosophical basis for human rights claims. Yet he believes that it does mitigate, even if it doesn't refute, what he calls the logically impeccable arguments of cultural relativists.[21] However, Donnelly's stance is ambiguous and ultimately fails to satisfy. He argues for a foundationless discourse, yet in the background is an anthropological claim about the moral nature of human beings. He accepts that the arguments of cultural relativists are persuasive, yet he puts his faith instead in the consensus and aspirations of human rights activists. In addition, he acknowledges that this consensus is often very shallow and frequently undermined in practice, yet it remains a cornerstone of his confidence in human rights politics. Moreover, in an extraordinarily counterintuitive move, he holds that a majoritarian consensus ought to be binding on dissenting minorities. In drawing the parameters of the debate as he has, Donnelly translates the problem of foundations from a philosophical question into a political one. And, although his particular resolution of the issue is not convincing, in transforming the question from a philosophical to a political one, Donnelly invites a broadening of the discussion about foundations to include a focus on the function they play within human rights discourse and politics.

Ronald Dworkin also follows the political route. He agrees with Alasdair MacIntyre that the existence of human rights cannot be demonstrated, although against MacIntyre, he argues that it does not follow from this that they cannot in fact be claimed. He proposes a modest constructivist approach to human rights that locates the reason for positing the existence of human rights in "our habits of thought and political convictions," habits that are cemented "at a level so deep that we cannot coherently deny that supposition."[22] No doubt, to the philosophical or theological realist, the location of human rights categories on this contingent and historical premise appears to weaken it considerably. However, following from his refutation of the persuasiveness of naturalist arguments, he claims that human rights have force not because they are grounded in human nature or in the structure of reality but rather because we now have a robust body of international human rights law that establishes those rights. But what if this body of law loses its power? Will human rights values lose theirs too? For Dworkin, although such questions signal potential difficulties, he is convinced that human rights values are now so deeply ingrained in our politics and theory that they will not come undone. Human rights can thus coherently be thought of as constructed rather than natural, as deriving their force from the now extant legal apparatus rather than from any underlying sense of shared human dignity or of universal moral knowledge. They can thus be foundationless but no less compelling for that.

Whereas for Donnelly the idea of a foundationless discourse is in some respects an admission of defeat, for Dworkin it is a feature of its constructed nature. For Rorty it has merit because it facilitates the defense and development of human rights values while allowing for a refutation of the representationalist view of language upon which the discourse has traditionally been based.[23] As is discussed in chapter 1, Rorty rejects the idea that human rights norms must be grounded in some kind of metaphysical foundation and dismisses as a fallacy the desire to "find something stable, which will serve as a criterion for judging the transitory products of our transitory time."[24] He believes that the historical conditions in which a human rights culture emerged have significance both in terms of their content and in terms of their appeal. He claims that since the Enlightenment, Americans and Europeans have created a human rights culture on the basis of security and sympathy. Our security consists in establishing "conditions of life sufficiently risk-free as to make one's difference from others inessential to one's self respect, one's sense of worth." Our sympathy entails "the ability to put one's self in another's shoes to perceive the Other as a fellow human being."[25] Indeed, Rorty's account of this extension of sympathy can be understood in terms of the globalization of the virtue of compassion.[26] Therefore, the much-vaunted international consensus on human rights is, according to Rorty, the product of this gradual extension of both security and sympathy. In this context, for Rorty, the pursuit of foundations is both a distraction and a cul-de-sac. It adds nothing to the persuasive appeal of the discourse and has nothing to contribute in the politics of implementation. Security and sympathy rather than agreement on foundations hold the key to a viable and vibrant discourse of human rights.

By contrast, however, the eminent historian of human rights Johannes Morsink is scathing in his criticism of theorists who abandon the metaphysical foundations of human rights while retaining a commitment to the politics. He refutes Ignatieff's pragmatic approach and rejects the constructivism of Donnelly, Dworkin, and Thomas Pogge.[27] He is insistent that the idea of human rights can *only* be grounded on the twin pillars of metaphysical and epistemic universality. Moreover, he argues that a close textual reading of the text of the UN Declaration and the debates leading up to its promulgation supports his conclusion. While I take issue with

the strong version of Morsink's argument, there is merit in his belief that the success of human rights politics depends on a shared belief in the dignity of human beings. Morsink calls this the doctrine of simple inherence and argues that human rights advocates ought to support and defend this doctrine, which he suggests aims to take a middle position "between the full-blown essentialism Rorty rightly rejects and the total constructivism he ends up recommending when he tells us that 'If we work together, we can make ourselves into whatever we are clever and courageous enough to imagine ourselves becoming.'"[28] I believe that Morsink's intuition is correct when he says that human rights discourse inevitably invokes and implies the conviction that human beings have a dignity and worth. I agree that this conviction was regularly and explicitly expressed throughout the various stages of the adoption debate; however, I take issue with Morsink's apparent insistence that a belief in the dignity of human beings (Morsink's doctrine of inherence) inevitably commits one to a metaphysical and epistemic universality.

Human rights politics is ultimately underwritten by a belief in the dignity of each person, and Morsink is correct when he draws attention to this. In this work, I argue for an approach that simultaneously defends human dignity while rejecting essentialism. Human dignity is understood as a summative term that holds together the fundamental human rights that, I argue, can be understood in terms of a particularly compelling form of embedded universalism that has acquired an extraordinary persuasive appeal, and whose grounding can be supported by a plurality of moral frameworks. In chapter 6, through a discussion of torture, I demonstrate how this nonfoundationalist, antiessentialist approach can act as a powerful basis on which to defend human dignity. However, I believe that Morsink fails to see that there are many different ways of defending the dignity of human beings, or at least he seems not to accept the legitimacy of other ways of accounting for this dignity. As a result, he conceives the grounding of human rights too narrowly, as seen particularly in his insistence that the doctrine of inherence necessitates a commitment to certain ontological positions. His criticism of those who argue for human rights but without this ontological commitment is derisory, describing them as "philosophical free-riders who want the benefits of human rights talk without making the ontological theory our theory considers necessary for a clear understanding of what a human right is."[29] What Morsink seems to refuse to countenance is that other philosophical and religious traditions may have entirely different ways of describing what is at stake with human rights discourse, may have alternative ways of thinking about the relationship between abstract propositions (like the inherent dignity of human beings) and political norms, and, indeed, may not even convey ethical values through a language of abstraction at all. Morsink seems to be reluctant to grant that different moral languages and world views can adopt, appropriate, and develop the language of human rights from very different vantage points, of which the vantage of enlightenment universalism is just one. Although he is acutely aware of the tremendous significance of the non-Western nations' contributions to the flourishing of the discourse, he seems to imply that these contributions were supported by a form of latent enlightenment liberalism.[30] And while this may be true of the drafters of the Declaration—namely, the elite, mostly Western educated diplomats and philosophers who represented the different nations during the drafting—this has not been the dominant dynamic in respect of the grounding of human rights in this pluralist world.

Consider, briefly, the early decades of the twentieth century, during which the idea of human rights was beginning to gain worldwide currency. In Russia during the 1917 revolution, millions of workers and peasants together with political reformers took to the streets demanding basic political and economic rights. In India and in many African and Asian colonies, the idea of human rights was pivotal in the development of the concept of self-determination. Women's groups, political reformers, and nongovernmental organizations from Indonesia, the Philippines, Korea, and China of that period adopted the language of human rights too. Moreover, it was the voices of indigenous groups, the colonials, and the religious minorities from around the globe, the vast majority of whom expressed their interests in terms of the language of human rights, who made the most significant and enduring impression at the Paris Peace Conference of 1919.[31] Crucially, however, they did so in a context that was replete with discussions about the dependencies, attachments, narratives, and practices that shape the individual and her sense of flourishing. There was no coherence in respect of ontology, epistemology, or metaphysics. There was, however, a shared ethical and political commitment. A century of appropriation and transformation later and the distance between global human rights discourse and the foundations that Morsink regards as crucial has increased further. It is not that the language of inherent human dignity or of universal human rights has receded, since obviously it has not. Rather, it is supported, rendered intelligible, mediated, and adapted in and through a myriad of different world views and traditions. The global appeal of human rights discourse has not begotten either an ontological or an epistemic convergence. It has nonetheless become a language around which the world's manifold world views, with their plural foundations, can cohere.[32]

In her insightful analysis of this issue, Grace Kao characterizes the debate about foundations as being divided among theorists who are either minimalist or maximalist, and in the end she opts for an approach that she describes as straddling the minimalist-maximalist divide.[33] Thus, she attempts to carve out a space for the kind of justification "that could fit between the minimalist and maximalist poles—a justification that is neither theory-thin (as in the extremes of minimalism) nor invariably religious (as the maximalists insist it must be) but nevertheless premised on an underlying commitment to the real moral worth of human beings."[34] While there is much in this conclusion with which I agree, I believe that Kao is misguided in her search for *a* justification, as if the viability of human rights discourse depends on one justification that will be meaningful and resonant throughout the globe. Surely what the history of human rights has shown us is that it has endured because it has been receptive to the many different justifications. Indeed, the diversity and creativity of the human intellect and imagination has been consistently on display through the discourse of human rights as communities worldwide attempt to explain why, from their particular vantage points, human rights should be respected. The answer to the question of how to explain the foundations of human rights must therefore be a pluralist one. The political theorist Amy Gutman, also makes the case for a pluralist approach to the issue on the basis that "several foundations . . . taken together, are likely to be agreeable to more people than any single foundation, and no single foundation has a monopoly on reasonable claims to be made in its favour."[35] It is an approach that combines a refusal to attach final significance to any one set of foundations, with a pragmatic endorsement of whatever rationale that particular traditions find to be useful. Thomas Pogge adopts a similar view, holding that the transition from the language of natural rights to human rights has allowed the contemporary discourse to avoid the metaphysical and metaethical baggage of its earlier incarnation. As a result, he argues,

"the potential appeal of the select moral demands is thereby broadened in that these demands are made accessible also to those who reject all variants of moral realism—who believe, for instance that the special moral status of all human beings rests on nothing more than our own profound moral commitment and determination that human beings ought to have that status."[36]

This idea of plural foundations underlying a set of agreed principles aims to reconcile the prospect of agreement on human rights values with the recognition of the diversity of moral traditions and world views. In some respects this model may seem to mirror the liberal ideal of a neutral public square, with comprehensive doctrines relegated to the background culture. However, the relationship that I am proposing between human rights discourse and its plural foundations is a very different one to that envisaged by John Rawls in his *Political Liberalism* and in *The Law of Peoples*. Rather than a globalized version of public reason, I envisage a discourse in which the languages, metaphors, and images of comprehensive doctrines are deployed rather than excluded, a discourse that not only acknowledges but also celebrates the undeniable reality that there are many different, sometimes conflicting ways of accounting for why human beings can be said to have human rights.[37]

Building Discursive Bridges

The approach to human rights that I advocate is grounded in an appreciation of the integrity of the distinct moral and religious traditions and seeks to build discursive bridges across these traditions in the expectation that a durable and global consensus on shared values can be established and in the hope that this in turn will be given practical expression through concrete legal protections. At its core is the conviction that the most persuasive answers to serious moral questions will only be found in the interactions between the diverse situated ethical traditions that characterize the moral landscape. While there are many different moral languages and categories through which this consensus can be pursued, there is no doubt that the discourse of human rights continues to hold a privileged place in this endeavor. Its appeal is neither formal nor top-down.[38] Rather, it has gained traction as it has been adopted by and developed in diverse communities worldwide, both in place of and alongside other moral languages. In recent decades it has become ever more evident that, in addition to the genuine pluralism that characterizes human moral experience, another impulse encapsulated in the language of human rights can be discerned, one that expresses a desire to articulate shared values and to generate moral consensus on fundamental human concerns. Nor are these two impulses—the one toward moral pluralism, the other toward shared values—necessarily contradictory. As I argue throughout this chapter, it is possible to acknowledge that there are many ways to conceptualize the good life and that there are many routes to human flourishing while also keeping faith with human rights. Indeed, I would suggest that one of the reasons why human rights discourse has maintained its grip on the moral imagination of contemporaries is precisely because it can accommodate much of the pluralism present in this complex moral world. Particularly if we bracket the juridical component of "rights talk" for the moment, we can agree with Sumner Twiss that human rights discourse is, in fact, "the expression of a set of important overlapping moral expectations to which different cultures hold themselves and others accountable."[39] The process of articulating these overlapping moral expectations is a complex one, to which we now turn our attention, and although much has been achieved, I do not wish to imply that this de facto though limited consensus provides an adequate response to the moral challenges of value pluralism. Rather, it is simply a sufficiently durable site from which to begin our deliberations. The existing consensus is simply the starting point and not the end of the discussion.

Much in the way that humanitarian law has developed, I believe that an incremental consensus on human rights norms can be generated on the basis of what Kwame Appiah calls "incompletely theorised agreements"[40]—that is, through processes that defend and promote human rights but without committing participants to any specific high doctrine or to any particular metaphysical or epistemological position. This model is already evident, to a limited extent, in current human rights discourse and, as I have demonstrated, is also present throughout its history. Its appeal is that it allows for the richness of the moral languages, metaphors, and images of comprehensive doctrines to be deployed in the articulation of the specifics of such a consensus. The model is premised on the conviction that an authentic and sustainable agreement on human rights can only emerge through multiple, inclusive, tradition-thick, cross-cultural, multireligious engagement and dialogue. The critical questions are what shape this deliberation and

dialogue should take in order that human rights discourse can become a genuinely global language of moral principle and evaluation, and what it will take to create the spaces in which such dialogue can take place.

Traditional Christian ethics, together with the liberal political theory that accompanied its global progress, allowed for a confidence that human beings knew what Christians were doing when we spoke about shared values in the pursuit of a shared future. In the past people confidently spoke in terms of the truth of the Christian message and of what William Temple called the great world fellowship of Christians. Today, however, we are more nervous of this kind of language and are more hesitant about the idea of shared values in the pursuit of a shared future, notwithstanding the irony of the fact that our respective futures are more closely tied today than at any other time in history. Whether and how agreement can be found, either on the shared values or on the legal protections that flow from such values, is therefore a crucial question. How can we ensure that human rights discourse does not simply replicate the failures of the great civilizing projects of the past, including the recent past? What role will the different religions play in this process? On what basis will Christianity play a role? Will the secularist assumptions of Western liberalism frame how "the public square" is conceptualized, thereby according religion a private but not public role? And even if the public square is acknowledged as religiously plural rather than neutral (in both its global and manifold local manifestations), will the different religions have the capacity to engage in the kind of dialogue and debate that will necessarily precede any articulation of a shared future based on shared values? Will they be prepared to cede their previously privileged speaking positions and engage in the deliberative politics of a pluralist public square? These are critical questions for human rights as we try to envision its possibilities as an ethical discourse, and as we leave behind the reductive, faux universalism of previous centuries.

I have argued throughout that if human rights discourse expects to achieve a global resonance, then it will need to engage with the manifold moral traditions, including religious traditions that are flourishing worldwide. Contrary to the earlier assumptions of liberalism, social and technological progress has not led people to abandon what were regarded as the naïve superstitions of faith. Rather, around the globe we see a resurgence of religious faith in its many manifestations, and with this one can discern a renewed visibility for the moral languages and traditions of the different

[handwritten margin note: for HR to achieve global resonance must engage w/ manifold]

religions. For this reason it is essential that the religions, in their formal and informal expressions, are among the conversation partners as we attempt to develop an intercultural and cross-cultural dialogue on shared values and human rights. It is important to enter a caveat here, one that is fully explored in the next chapter: that in foregrounding the role of communities and traditions, we must give due recognition to the fact that communities are heterogeneous, and that all traditions are evolving and internally diverse. Therefore, the task of generating a multireligious, cross-cultural dialogue on human rights, on the foundations, values, and concrete norms thereof, is a complicated one. Given that a great deal of modern human rights philosophy has been premised on the avoidance of engagement with all comprehensive doctrines, including but not limited to religious ones, the model that I propose challenges the traditional modes of engagement in this sphere. Certainly, some significant progress has already been made, particularly in the last four decades. However, even when the indigenous traditions of religious and moral communities have been successfully engaged, the context has often been of a grudging acceptance of their involvement rather than of a principled commitment to a multireligious and intercultural discourse. Today, we cannot ignore religion. Nor can we fail to harness the moral categories through which millions of people articulate their commitments, values, and aspirations. The success of human rights discourse will depend on its ability to resonate with the languages through which people express their fundamental values, and on its determination to build discursive, practical, and imaginative bridges across religious and cultural boundaries.

In this regard, there is much to learn from colleagues working in the fields of comparative theology, including comparative religious ethics, and of interreligious dialogue. Reflection on this issue of interreligious and cross-cultural communication has been extensive, and a host of comparative approaches and hermeneutical practices have been evolved in order to support the process of such communication. These processes have, in different ways, attended to the textual, doctrinal, ritual, and ethical dimensions of such communication. One of the things that distinguishes the sphere of human rights from these other interreligious contexts of dialogue is that the human rights context has to engage humanistic and other non-religious comprehensive doctrines as well as religious ones. Therefore, although there is much from which to draw, since this classical interreligious

communication has tended not to extend to include secular perspectives, its limitations must be acknowledged. Notwithstanding the limitations, however, these long-standing though fragmentary forms of cross-cultural and interreligious communication provide critical points of learning as we strive to develop a durable consensus on human rights. Three points in particular are worth highlighting: (1) interreligious and cross-cultural engagement on human rights must be multidimensional, multimethodological, and multidisciplinary; (2) it must deal with the genealogical issue of power and its impact on the formation and processes of interreligious and cross-cultural communication; and (3) it must guard against easy resolutions that are based on naïve comparisons and superficial complementarities.

3 key points [handwritten margin note]

Multidimensional, Multimethodological, and Multidisciplinary Discourse

The experience of interreligious dialogue over many centuries, but especially since the 1960s, confirms that engagement of this kind will only be fruitful if it is pursued in a manner that is multidimensional, multimethodological, and multidisciplinary.[41] It must engage the cultural and religious worlds in their many dimensions, including their interpersonal, academic, and communitarian expressions, and with the guiding institutions of faith and politics. Significant intercultural and interreligious understanding on human rights has already been achieved through the interpersonal and academic routes. Yet there is a danger that such dialogue will remain elitist and will fail to have an enduring impact on the political and contextual debates about specific human rights. For this reason, the faith communities, particularly in their formal dimensions, as well as the guiding institutions of culture and religion must also be engaged in what Francis Clooney calls "deep learning across borders."[42] Within this context it will be important to ensure that the diversity of views within religious and moral communities is visible—a topic that is discussed in the next chapter. At this point, however, it is important simply to note that a multidimensional approach to interreligious dialogue on human rights should go some way to ensuring that religious and political leaders can no longer ignore the serious consequences of failure in this regard while at the same time allowing for alternative and dissenting voices to have a formative role in the debate.

The impact of this deep religious and cultural pluralism on our global and local conversations about human rights cannot be underestimated, and as a result the dialogue in which we engage will need also to be multimethodological and multidisciplinary. Religiously derived assumptions about the nature and structuring of human dignity are deeply rooted in the sacred texts and doctrines of different religious traditions and find expression not only in the norms that determine social roles but also in what Pierre Bourdieu calls the *habitus*—that is, in the dispositions that are inculcated, structured, durable, and generative.[43] Thus, structuring meaningful communication across cultural and religious boundaries will require the employment of a host of methodological and disciplinary approaches. The methodologies of comparative theology, comparative ethics, and comparative religious ethics will be crucial to this task, as will approaches from the theology of religions and from the discipline of interreligious studies. Moreover, the manner in which the textual, doctrinal, ritual, and ethical discourses are intertwined in these historical, living traditions suggests that we will need to learn the practices of comparative and interreligious reading, scriptural reasoning, and interreligious hermeneutics as we seek to build consensus on human rights. Nor should engagement of this kind be limited to conversation. If we are to gain a more comprehensive understanding of what is at stake in these discourses, then we must also experience the religious and cultural worlds of others by sharing in the material as well as the intellectual dimensions of their traditions through ritual and worship, through their contemplative pathways, and, where possible, through their forms of social action.

Discourse That Attends to the Politics of Power

Interreligious and intercultural dialogue is frequently idealized and is assumed to proceed in a space apart from the normalizing functions of power relations. However, there can be no refuge from the discursive effects of power. Just as liberal human rights discourse has had to acknowledge that its assumed neutrality has in actuality obscured the power differentials of participants, so too have the processes of interreligious and intercultural dialogue functioned in this way. Indeed, the all-too-evident disparity of speaking positions in intercultural dialogue means that, without sensitivity to the politics of cross-cultural discourse, this pathway will merely replicate existing problems by relegating them to a different sphere. Through the works of Karl-Otto Apel and Jürgen Habermas we have become attuned to the difficulties attendant on the development of ethical forms of discourse, and a more detailed discussion of this point follows in the next chapter when we focus more specifically on the role of moral communities in the construction of a shared ethic based on human rights. Notwithstanding its limitations, Habermas's theory of communicative action is particularly important as one seeks to develop processes that will facilitate structured communication among equal citizens in the pursuit of mutual understanding.[44] Alongside these important philosophical interrogations, however, are the no-less-important reflections on the ethics of discourse that emerge from the practice of intercultural and interreligious dialogues themselves.

Sharing Values: A Hermeneutics for Global Ethics is a recent example of a set of reflections on the ethics of dialogue that has itself arisen from extensive and extended conversations among people who have been at the forefront of intercultural and interreligious conversations on the issue of shared values for many decades.[45] This particular volume is the result of the Care and Compassion: Methodologies in Sharing Values across Cultures and Religions conference held in Nairobi in 2009, where the ethical challenges associated with cross-cultural and interreligious communication were discussed. The report from the working group whose task was to consider the difficulties of "balancing power relations, and inducing a real transformation" is illuminating, particularly since its conclusions are based on the experience of decades of involvement in these kinds of conversations.[46] Focusing on "how the dynamics of power relations affect interreligious dialogue, especially in relation to values and ethical concerns," the working group notes that a widespread "hermeneutics of suspicion" tends to be at work. From the group members' extensive experience, they concluded that "interreligious dialogue is distorted by huge differentials in the power wielded by different parties to the dialogue," but they also noted that, since the dynamics of power is diffuse, diverse, and sometimes contradictory, the impact is often difficult to discern.

This working party draws attention to the fact that disparities of economic resources can distort or even prevent interreligious dialogue, but it also notes that in contexts of gross inequality, "dialogue may be an essential means for addressing basic needs and finding ways for different religious communities to address such needs cooperatively." They recognize that the need for interreligious dialogue "may be even more urgent in situations of conflict and violence, particularly where religious sentiments are manipulated to sharpen the conflict and polarise communities from one another." In these contexts they insist that interreligious dialogue needs to keep in mind "the social structures that subordinate some parties to the interests of those in power." The group also draws attention to the fact that imbalances of power may thwart dialogue not only on the level of economic or political power but also in terms of religious power. They note that religious leaders in many countries refuse to allow their exercise of power to be scrutinized or criticized, and, as a result, dialogue is very difficult because cultural practices do not permit any criticism of religious authority. They also caution that interreligious dialogue can also be a cover for oppression and may be manipulated in accordance with the interests of the powerful. The government of President Suharto in Indonesia is given as an example of a context in which government-sponsored interreligious dialogue functioned to legitimize the status quo and was, as they suggest, "a ritual practice intended to strengthen *a habitus* of social inequality."[47]

If it is to have a role in the articulation of a renewed ethic of human rights, then interreligious and cross-cultural dialogue will need to find ways to address the dynamics of power that inevitably shape its processes and practices. Power relations within religious communities, among different traditions, and exercised in diverse cultural and geographical contexts all have an impact on the shape of our cross-cultural conversations and on the prospects for those conversations to be successful. Indeed, our aspirations for consensus on shared values and on basic human rights will come to nothing unless we learn from the experiences of past dialogues and on that basis develop forms of dialogue that are both ethical and transformative.

In order that a dialogue is both ethical and transformative, one must attend directly to the issue of the power differentials that inevitably feature between and among participants in dialogue. It is clear that there must be some structural protections to ensure that vulnerable persons and marginalized communities can fully participate in such dialogue. Although philosophical and psychoanalytic perspectives on power and how it is exercised in the social realm are relevant and important to this discussion, so too are discussions about the practical steps that need to be taken to facilitate meaningful participation and to mitigate, insofar as is possible, historic and embedded discrimination and marginalization. In this context it becomes important both to build capacity within marginalized communities and to challenge the hidden biases within the dominant culture that often serve to manufacture consent. In terms of strengthening the capacities of marginalized communities, grassroots education, empowerment, and leadership training are vital if such communities are to gain a meaningful voice in such dialogue. Education is also likely to involve and necessitate research, particularly when the prejudices of the dominant society need to be challenged. Empirical research that can refute inherited biases, disseminate concealed information, and aid in the construction of alternative narratives can be a vital part of this essential educational process. In this context, it is important to note that this kind of dynamic may also be happening within the community since, as is discussed in chapter 5, communities themselves are also the products of such discursive power. Thus, the processes that are relevant to the practice of ensuring that marginalized groups have a voice are also relevant to the internal dynamics of the marginalized communities themselves.

Structural power asymmetries are multidimensional and must be addressed in a systemic and multigenerational manner. However, there is also much that can be done in the short term. Thus, in addition to building capacity among marginalized groups and vulnerable individuals, it is incumbent on the state to ensure that there are also structural protections in place. Therefore, in each dialogue the process of defining the issue to be addressed must be done collaboratively; tokenism must be avoided; the practicalities of the dialogue must be worked out in a cooperative manner; the economic, social, and cultural differences in terms of the price of participation must be acknowledged and addressed; and the framework for dealing with conflict must be devised jointly and trusted by all. In fact, there has been significant progress in developing and implementing structural protections of this kind over the last three decades. This is particularly the case in countries where there has been a sustained focus on addressing cultural and religious differences in the context of multiculturalism. In the United Kingdom and across the European Union as well as in the United States and Canada, there have been a host of national, transnational, and local processes in which such dialogues have been pursued and from which we have learned a great deal both about how deeply embedded and malign power differentials between and within communities can be and about the importance of developing robust, nuanced, and dynamic strategies for dealing with them.[48]

Discourse That Proceeds from an Acknowledgment of the Depth of Difference

At the core of the pursuit of such interreligious and intercultural communication is the conviction that the manifold expressions of faith can form the basis of agreement on human rights. Notwithstanding this conviction, even when we discern complementarities among the different religious and moral traditions, it is likely that these affinities will be contested and that other readings of the various traditions will stress incommensurability and dissonance. However, interreligious ethics cannot shy away from these areas of dissonance and ambiguity. Durable communication of this sort must be premised on the recognition that the categories through which we construct and interpret our experiences are contextual. I argue this point in chapter 3 in relation to the category of embodiment, insisting that the meanings ascribed to the body have varied widely, both historically and culturally, and suggesting that we can only hope to understand these multiple meanings in the context of the specific ideologies, institutions, and cultures through which these meanings are constructed. This discussion of embodiment illustrated the broader point that the categories through which we construct and interpret our experiences are contextually shaped and that cross-cultural and interreligious dialogue must also pay attention to these multiple constructions of human experience. Nor are these radical differences limited to such categories as embodiment or subjectivity, where the marks of tradition are highly visible. The point also holds in relation to many of the fundamental theological categories that ground and structure our intercultural and interreligious conversations, including how the individual and community are understood to relate; how the relationship between the sacred and secular is conceptualized; and how what we in the West call the public and the private domains are distinguished. For example, Felix Wilfred questions whether the concept of "the public sphere" with which most Western theological and ethical analysis engages can have resonance in societies in which political participation is impeded by authoritarianism or immiserization. However, even Wilfred's critique itself assumes a construal of public versus private that has evolved from Western political arrangements and that may not, in fact, translate.[49]

In his groundbreaking study in comparative ethics twenty years ago, Lee Yearley analyzed the virtue of courage in the writings of both Aquinas and Mencius and observed that he was trying to chart "similarities within differences and differences within similarities."[50] What I am suggesting, however, is that the differences may be far more profound than we have heretofore understood. Indeed, the experience of interreligious and comparative theology has revealed that any complementarities that do appear to exist will only be discovered through painstaking, deep learning. It will be the practitioners and scholars "who have entered deeply into religious traditions other than their own and who are also conceptually equipped to reflect on their experience in such a way that they can mediate one tradition's convictions to their own and others," a necessary first step in the building of bridges.[51] Commenting on such matters, Jean Porter concludes that "the claim that all moral traditions share a fundamental core, which amounts to a universally valid morality, appears to me to be defensible only if the core in question is described at such a high level of generality as to be virtually empty, and even then, it is difficult to arrive at a statement of principles that would be universally acceptable."[52] While I have some sympathy with this conclusion, I believe that it is, in fact, too early to tell whether this is the case. The reality is that, until relatively recently, we have not attempted to acquire the deep learning of other traditions that is the necessary starting point of any cross-cultural conversation. Nor, until even more recently, have we attended to the cultural dynamics of power in any serious way. Moreover, it was not until postcolonial, feminist, liberationist, and other marginalized voices began to be vocal that there has been access to the enculturated and alternative versions of the world's many moral and religious traditions. In short, although the task is complex and immense, there are reasons to be hopeful that we now have some sense of how we ought to proceed.

In all this, Joseph Raz's comment rings true when he notes that "tension is an inevitable concomitant of accepting the truth of value-pluralism." It is "a tension without stability, without a definite resting point of reconciliation of the two perspectives, the one recognising the validity of competing values and the one hostile to them." He continues, "there is no point of equilibrium, no single balance which is correct and could prevail to bring the two perspectives together. One is forever moving from one to the other from time to time."[53] The ambiguities inherent in this moral condition of ours are immense and, as Raz suggests, will not be easily reconciled. Our interreligious and cross-cultural dialogue must aim to be a transformative one not merely dedicated to learning from the other but also aiming to re-shape our interactions and deliver meaningful consensus on human rights. However, we cannot wait until we have found the formulae for transformative dialogue; rather, we must continue to engage in such dialogue, aware that even as we do it we are only learning how to do so. In this regard we are, in the words of John D'Arcy May, constructing the life raft while we are being tossed about on the sea. Such is the urgency of the task that it must be undertaken.

Notes

1. Upendra Baxi, *The Future of Human Rights*, 3rd ed. (Oxford: Oxford University Press, 2008), 19.

2. This is Francesca Klug's characterization, which I discuss in chapter 2.

3. Aristotle, *Nicomachean Ethics*, 1.3. 1-4, 1094b.

4. The phrase "modest pragmatism" is one that Stout uses of his own position. He does not demur, however, from David Fergusson's characterization of his (Stout's) position as realist in *Community, Liberalism and Christian Ethics* (Cambridge: Cambridge University Press, 1998) 101. Jeffrey Stout, *Blessed Are the Organized: Grassroots Democracy in America* (Princeton, NJ: Princeton University Press, 2010), 253 and 255.

5. Stout, *Blessed Are the Organized*, 247.

6. Stout's discussion of these distinctions draws heavily on Robert Brandom, especially his classic *Making It Explicit: Reasoning, Representing, and Discursive Commitment* (Cambridge, MA: Harvard University Press, 1994).

7. Stout, *Blessed Are the Organized*, 230.

8. Ibid., 235.

9. The classic argument for the procedural approach to justification in the debate about basic justice is Rawls's idea of public reason, the limitations of which in the context of human rights will be discussed later.

10. Stout, *Blessed Are the Organized*, 249.

11. E/CN./SR.42/I4/15, quoted in Johannes Morsink, *The United Nations Declaration of Human Rights: Origins, Drafting and Intent* (Philadelphia: University of Pennsylvania Press, 1999), 223.

12. For a detailed discussion of the exchanges during the various drafting phases, see ibid., chap. 6.

13. Morsink even goes so far as to argue that the traditional distinction between the old civil and political rights and the new economic, social, and cultural ones did not exist for the great majority of the drafters. Rather, in the minds of most delegates "all the human rights in the Declaration were cut from the same moral cloth." Ibid., 1191. While there is evidence that this is the case for a number of the drafters, the arguments of the British and French delegates in particular suggests that they were reluctant to regard economic, cultural, and social rights in the same way as civil and political rights.

14. Proclamation of Teheran on Human Rights, May 13, 1968, in UN Document A/CONF.32/41, quoted in Paul Gordon Lauren, *The Evolution of International Human Rights: Visions Seen* (Philadelphia: University of Pennsylvania Press, 1998), 350n99.

15. The issue of the extent to which group and individual rights can be harmonized continues to be debated.

16. This is Kwok Pui-lan's characterization of the nature of religious pluralism today. However, I have adapted her text because I believe that it captures very well the core ethical issue in human rights discourse. See Kwok, Pui-lan, *Postcolonial Imagination and Feminist Theology* (London: SCM-Canterbury Press, 2005), 204.

17. Axel Honneth, *The I in We: Studies in the Theory of Recognition* (Cambridge, UK: Polity Press, 2012); and Tariq Modood and Jan Dobbernack, "Accepting Multiple Differences: The Challenge of Double Accommodation," in *Tolerance, Intolerance and Respect. Hard to Accept?* ed. Jan Dobbernack and Tariq Modood, 186–207 (Basingstoke, UK: Palgrave MacMillan, 2013).

18. Ignatieff, *Human Rights as Politics and Idolatry* (Princeton, NJ: Princeton University Press, 2001), 54.

19. Ibid. However, there is an inconsistency in his position because later he suggests that human agency is the common experience that can support human rights, but he refuses to accept that this concept of human agency is itself built on a particular understanding of human nature.

20. Although he discusses this approach in many different places, this analysis is based on Jack Donnelly's position in *Universal Human Rights Theory and Practice* (Ithaca, NY: Cornell University Press, 1989), 23–27, and on Michael Freeman's engagement with the argument in *Human Rights: An Interdisciplinary Approach* (Cambridge, UK: Polity Press, 2002).

21. In a strange move that appears to contradict his "foundationless human rights" position, he claims elsewhere that ultimately the origins of human rights can be found in the nature of the person. Freeman, *Human Rights*, 502.

22. Ronald Dworkin, *Taking Rights Seriously* (London: Duckworth Press, 1977), 290.

23. Richard Rorty, "Response to Appiah," in *Globalising Rights: The Oxford Amnesty Lectures, 1999*, ed. Matthew Gibney, 233–37 (Oxford: Oxford University Press, 2003), 235.

24. Richard Rorty, *Philosophy and Social Hope* (London: Penguin, 1999), 3, 4, 5.

25. Richard Rorty, "Human Rights, Rationality and Sentimentality," in *On Human Rights: The Oxford Amnesty Lectures*, ed. Stephen Shute and Susan Hurley, 112–34 (Oxford: Basic Books, 1993), 128. While I have some sympathy with Rorty's argument about the crucial role that security and sympathy have played in the creation of a human rights culture, I think that he is incorrect when he locates its center in "America and Europe" since it is evident that these experiences and impulses are present and promoted in many different cultures and communities worldwide.

26. This is my characterization, not Rorty's.

27. See Johannes Morsink, *Inherent Human Rights: Philosophical Roots of the Universal Declaration* (Philadelphia: University of Pennsylvania Press, 2009), especially the introduction and chapters 1 and 4, where he refutes the positions of Ignatieff, Pogge, and Donnelly, respectively.

28. Morsink, *Inherent Human Rights*, 38, quoting Rorty's Amnesty lecture "Human Rights, Rationality and Sentimentality," 121.

29. Morsink, *Inherent Human Rights*, 26.

30. Indeed, Morsink has contributed more than most to the retrieval of the role of the non-Western nations in the development of the UN Declaration.

31. E. J. Dillon, *The Inside Story of the Peace Conference* (New York: Harper & Brothers, 1920), 4–6.

32. Some theorists describe this feature of human rights discourse in terms of its "thinness." However, I think the term seems to imply a level of abstraction and disconnection against which I have been arguing. Instead I prefer to think of the global appeal of human rights in terms of an embedded universalism that grew as it encountered comparable, although differently expressed, moral convictions.

33. Grace Kao, *Grounding Human Rights in a Pluralist World* (Washington, DC: Georgetown University Press, 2011).

34. Ibid., 153.

35. Gutman quoted in Ignatieff, *Human Rights as Politics and Idolatry*, xviii.

36. Thomas Pogge, *World Poverty and Human Rights* (Malden, MA: Blackwell, 2002), 57.

37. For a fuller discussion of this point, see Linda Hogan, "Religion and Public Reason in the Global Politics of Human Rights," in *Religious Voices in Public*

Places, ed. Nigel Biggar and Linda Hogan, 216–31 (Oxford: Oxford University Press, 2009).

38. In contrast to the "global ethic" project, which, while it shares many of the values and aspirations of human rights language, remains a discourse of the academy and has not "gone local" in any meaningful way.

39. Sumner Twiss's paraphrase of Michael Walzer's discussion of the components of a moral minimalism in *Thick and Thin*, 17–18, found in Sumner Twiss and Bruce Grelle, "Human Rights and Comparative Religious Ethics," *Annual of the Society of Christian Ethics* (1995): 33.

40. K. Anthony Appiah developing the position of the American legal philosopher Carl Sunstein in "Grounding Human Rights," in *Human Rights as Politics and Idolatry*, edited by Michael Ignatieff, 101–16 (Princeton, NJ: Princeton University Press, 2001), 108.

41. This conclusion is drawn from my general reading in the field of interreligious dialogue over many years. I have learned a great deal from my colleague John D'Arcy May, particularly from his *After Pluralism: Towards an Interreligious Ethic* (Münster: LIT Verlag, 2000), as well as from the writings of David Burrell, Catherine Cornille, Gavin D'Costa, Perry Schmidt-Leukel, and Keith Ward.

42. Francis X. Clooney, *Comparative Theology, Deep Learning across Religious Borders*, (Malden, MA: Wiley-Blackwell, 2010).

43. See, for example, Pierre Bourdieu, *Distinction: A Social Critique of the Judgment of Taste* (Cambridge, MA: Harvard University Press, 1984).

44. Habermas's model of "the ideal speech situation" on which "discourse is immunised against repression and inequality in a special way" is important but flawed. See Jürgen Habermas, *Theory of Communicative Action*, vol. 1, trans. Thomas McCarthy (Cambridge, MA: Polity Press, 1984), 25 and following.

45. Ariane Hentsch Cisneros and Shanta Premawardhana, eds. *Sharing Values: A Hermeneutics for Global Ethics* (Geneva: Globethics.net, Series No. 4, 2011), www.globethics.net/documents/4289936/13403236/GlobalSeries_4_SharingVal ues_text.pdf/6162b4a5-5cd2-4af6-bdc5-70699b69d923.

46. "Balancing Power Relations, Inducing a Real Transformation" is the title of the fourth working group. Its commentary is found in ibid., 394–404.

47. This paragraph is a summary of the deliberations of the working party, in ibid.

48. Among the vast literature, a number of works are notable, including Jan Dobbernack and Tariq Modood, *Tolerance, Intolerance and Respect: Hard to Accept?* (Basingstoke, UK: Palgrave MacMillan, 2013); Stout, *Blessed Are the Organized*; and Anna Triandafyllidou, Tariq Modood, and Nasar Meer, *European Multiculturalisms: Cultural, Religious and Ethnic Challenges* (Edinburgh, UK: Edinburgh University Press, 2012).

49. This comment of Wilfred's was made at a conference entitled *From World Mission to Interreligious Witness*, Irish School of Ecumenics, Trinity College Dublin, June 2010. Some of the papers have been published in a special issue of *Concilium*, no. 1 (2011). The paper to which Wilfred was reacting is Will Storrar, "Religion and Theology in Public Life: From World Mission to a Public Paradigm of Interreligious Witness," an unpublished work.

50. Lee Yearley, *Mencius and Aquinas: Theories of Virtue and Conceptions of Courage* (Albany: State University of New York, 1990), 3.

51. John May and Linda Hogan, "Visioning Ecumenics as Intercultural, Interreligious and Public Theology," in *From World Mission to Interreligious Witness*, edited by Felix Wilfred, Solange Lefebvre, Norbert Hintersteiner, and Linda Hogan, 70–84. *Concilium* Special Issue, no. 1 (2011). This point is made by John May.

52. Jean Porter, "The Search for a Global Ethic," *Theological Studies* 62 (2001): 120.

53. Joseph Raz, *Ethics in the Public Domain: Essays in the Morality of Law and Politics* (Oxford, UK: Clarendon Press, 1994), 165.

5

Resisting Culturalist
Frameworks

Porous Communities, Constructed Traditions

Human rights politics has long since recognized that it must address the question of culture, and in particular that it must address the issue of the role that communities and traditions should have in the development of a moral framework that aspires to a global reach. The approach that I advocate throughout this book is one that grants a seminal role to distinct moral and religious traditions, and that seeks to build discursive bridges across these traditions in the expectation that a durable global consensus on shared values can be established and in the hope that this in turn will be given practical expression through concrete legal protections. In chapter 4 I argue that such an approach can continue to underwrite the universality of human rights claims but with important clarifications about how universality is understood. Thus, the universalism to which human rights discourse can legitimately aspire is grounded in the recognition that our ethical knowledge is a form of situated knowledge, and that these universalist convictions are irrevocably embedded in the cultural values through which they are expressed. It is also accepted that the ethical justifications that we marshal are contingent on the conceptual frameworks through which they are intelligible and that the universalism to which we aspire can only emerge and be confirmed through multiple, inclusive, tradition-thick, cross-cultural conversations. Chapter 4 argues that a renewed human rights ethic must be built not on a set of false abstractions but rather on a framework that recognizes the contingent character of all ethical understanding, insisting that by proceeding in this manner, its ethical and political force would be restored.

The fact of ethical pluralism must therefore be our starting point as we rearticulate a conceptual framework for human rights. Of course human beings have always lived in the midst of ethical pluralism. However, the cumulative effect of centuries of colonialism and of globalization means that its impact and significance is qualitatively different today. Indeed, as we consider the contemporary context of ethical pluralism, Charles Taylor's analysis of the changed nature of religious pluralism is particularly illuminating. In *A Secular Age*, Taylor insists that one of the distinctive features of late modernity is its secularity, the core of which is a significant change in our idea of what it means to believe. In relation to the pluralism of religion, he writes that the critical factor globally today is that "belief in God is no longer axiomatic . . . [that] there are alternatives."[1] Thus, believers and unbelievers alike live with the fact of religious pluralism and have to cope both with its theological significance and, importantly for our purposes, with its ethical and political ramifications. In effect, late moderns inhabit a global context that contains different milieu, "within each of which the default option may be different from others, although the dwellers within each are very aware of the options favoured by the others, and cannot just dismiss them as an inexplicable exotic error."[2] We hold fast to our own religious beliefs and ethical values, live alongside those whose beliefs and values are equally deeply held, and live in political contexts that, in the main, promote a culture of respect and tolerance. What is distinctive about contemporary pluralism according to Taylor, therefore, is that it shapes the whole context of understanding in which our "moral, spiritual and religious experience and search takes place."[3] It is not just one factor among others. Rather, it is *the* determinative feature of late modernity.[4]

My focus thus far in this book has been to explain how a credible discourse of human rights can be constructed in the midst of this defining pluralism. Chapter 3 pursues this in relation to the ethical subject, the "who" of human rights, whereas chapter 4 focuses on the nature of moral value and values. In this chapter, I now turn my attention to the sites of this pluralism—that is, to the cultures, communities, and traditions in which this ethical diversity is manifested. My concern is to clarify the role that these situated cultures, communities, and traditions can play in the articulation of a human rights ethic. While previous chapters valorize the role of situated communities, insisting that we can only engage with human rights discourse from our specific, thick, culturally embedded vantage points, in this chapter I argue that we must be mindful of the inherent limitations in such an approach. In the first section I focus on these embedded cultures, communities, and traditions and note that, as their role in the development of a human rights ethic is discussed, these categories are often idealized and essentialized. I draw on the works of feminist and post-colonial theologians and philosophers in order to develop what I regard as a more nuanced approach to these important categories. In this context, I argue for an understanding of culture in which its internal diversity is recognized, for an approach to community that can adapt to the hybridity of contemporary belonging, and for an account of tradition that is mindful of its dynamic character. Viewed in this way, these categories become partners rather than adversaries in the pursuit of a human rights agenda, since the debate is no longer between progressive human rights norms on the one hand and static cultural values on the other. Rather, I suggest the discussion can be focused on the persuasive appeal of the values being articulated. In the second section, I ask what shape an appropriate mode of engagement between these internally diverse, situated discourses (of which the human rights framework is one) might take. With Michael Walzer's work in the background, I argue that these interactions must be characterized by mutual recognition, reiteration, and immanent critique. I discuss the question of change and argue that, in the end, the case for inclusive and emancipatory politics will have to be made and remade. In the final section, I discuss some of the difficulties associated with the adoption of this approach, and acknowledge that in the end we may have to accept that there will continue to be intractable disagreement on the value or on the applicability of certain human rights. Notwithstanding this difficulty, however, I argue that the prospects for a shared commitment to human rights will only emerge through the dialogical engagement of situated, historical communities that are themselves open to internally and externally generated social criticism. Processes that seek to marginalize this kind of engagement hold no prospect at all.

Deconstructing Stereotypes

When terms like "culture," "community," and "tradition" are invoked in discussions about human rights, they tend to be idealized and essentialized, associated with homogeneity and stasis rather than with diversity and development. The following section deconstructs the most common stereotypes associated with the categories of culture, community, and tradition and demonstrates that cultures are contested, that communities are porous, and that traditions are constructed.

Contested Cultures

Ethical pluralism forms the backdrop of all of our moral debate today, with culture being regarded as the primary vehicle of that pluralism. As a result, culture is one of our central preoccupations today. In part a reaction to the ethnic and racial diversity that is a feature of most societies and nations, the category of culture has been the prism through which we pursue many of the debates about how we should live together. As with all such categories, however, the concept of culture itself is contested and is recognized to be shaped by the very discursive processes that it seeks to explain. In this context, my concern is to develop an understanding of culture that recognizes its significance and impact while also resisting essentialist interpretations. Anthropological and political theories of culture have come a long way from the time when culture was treated as a totalizing category. Edward B. Tylor's classic explanation of culture or civilization "taken in its wider ethnographic sense" as being "that complex whole which includes knowledge, belief, art, morals, custom, and any other capabilities and habits required by man as a member of society" is typical of definitions that have been criticized for the manner in which they regard culture as all-determining, as structuring the entire life-world of a society.[5] While theories of culture have evolved significantly from these classic definitions of the colonial period, and while they have been divested of the worst of their colonial heritage, nonetheless the legacy of this classical approach persists. One sees this legacy most clearly in the enduring tendency to treat cultures as distinct self-contained entities and as radically separate from one another. Implicit in this view of culture is an assumption that each culture is internally coherent and, moreover, that the beliefs and practices of each separate cultural group function to support the distinctiveness of that culture. Such an approach also proceeds with the expectation of cultural conformity in the sense that all the members of the cultural group are assumed to share the same beliefs and values, and to construct their identities and shape their behavior accordingly.

Contemporary theorists of culture have been critical of the ethnocentricism and orientalism implicit in earlier discussions and have sought to explain the role of culture in terms that do not replicate these tendencies. Moreover, since culture continues to be one of the central explanatory categories in contemporary political and ethical theory, these discussions have acquired an even greater significance. In fact, culture has had something of a renaissance in recent decades, mainly because of its importance in the debate about multiculturalism, especially as these debates have been played out in the democratic societies of the West. Ironically, however, the debate about multiculturalism has tended to reinforce some of the earlier problematic assumptions about the nature of culture and its role, particularly when it focuses on its significance for minority and non-Western groups. Multiculturalism promotes policies that have at their core a commitment to respect for the distinctive values, traditions, and practices of minority groups. It strongly resists assimilationist models of social organization and argues that the goal of an inclusive society is best pursued through policies that value cultural diversity and promote tolerance. Of course proponents of multiculturalism differ about the limits of tolerance, with disagreements usually played out in the context of disputes about gender, sexuality, and family.[6] Underlying the details of these debates, however, is the more fundamental issue of how the discourse of multiculturalism theorizes the category of culture, and in this regard it is clear that it has compounded the problems associated with classic conceptualizations of culture by promoting accounts that tend toward essentialism.

Human rights discourse has also tended to follow this trajectory and has theorized the interface between the global and local in terms of an opposition between human rights on the one hand and culture on the other. In the context of this juxtaposition, the category of culture can be either romanticized or demonized, but either way it tends to be treated in essentialist and unitary terms. Whether the cultures in question are minority ones that exist within Western democratic states or those of indigenous groups in far-flung locations, the underlying conceptualization continues to be one of cultures that are bounded and homogenous. Jacob Levy's characterization of ethnocultural identity captures this approach to culture when he explains the dynamic thus:

> Persons identify and empathize more easily with those with whom they have more in common than those with whom they have less. They rally around their fellow religionists; they seek the familiar comforts of native speakers of their native languages; they support those they see as to protect those places; they are raised in particular cultures, with particular sets of knowledge, norms and traditions, which come to seem normal and enduring. These feelings, repeated and generalized, help give rise to a world of ethnic, cultural and national loyalty, and also to a world of enduring ethnic, cultural and national variety.[7]

In this characterization, the cultural boundaries are firm and fixed; the natural affinities of people are oriented toward maintaining and perpetuating them; the allegiances of individuals are assumed to fall naturally toward their kin; and the values and practices of the members of the communities are believed to be shared and confirmed by all. In addition, culture is sometimes used as a synonym for tradition or national essence, reinforcing yet again its characterization as bounded and unitary.[8] Occasionally, too, it replaces the categories of race or ethnicity in political discourse.[9]

Critics of such characterizations of culture dispute the juxtaposition of culture and modernity and refute the notion that cultures can be thought of as homogenous and distinct. Indeed, this deconstruction of the concept of culture has gathered pace, particularly in the last two decades, and primarily in an effort to resist the cultural essentialism inherent in the multiculturalism debate. Feminist theorists in particular argue that culture cannot be conceptualized in ahistorical or apolitical terms. Rather, culture ought to be understood as "unbounded, contested, and connected to relations of power, as the product of historical influences rather than evolutionary change."[10] Critics reject essentialist accounts that treat cultures "as if they were natural givens, entities that existed in a neatly distinct world, entirely independent of our projects of distinguishing between them."[11] Crucially, according to feminist Uma Narayan, such essentialist notions of culture "eclipse the reality that the labels of designations that are currently used to demarcate or individuate particular 'cultures' themselves have a *culture → iteration of political process*

Essentialist

historical provenance, and that what they individuate or pick out as 'one culture' often changes over time."[12] Thus, the historicity of cultures must be recognized. So too must the fact that our conceptualizations of culture are iterations of political processes. Therefore, the lines of demarcation between cultures cannot be as clearly drawn as some assume, nor can the internal unity and coherence of cultural groups be assumed.[13] Rather, according to Susan Engle Merry, given that cultures include "institutional arrangements, political structures and legal regulations," and since "institutions such as laws and policing change, so too do beliefs, values and practices." As a result, it must be accepted that "cultures are not homogenous and 'pure' but produced through hybridization or creolization."[14]

Anne Phillips is not simply critical of the essentialist manner in which culture is deployed, she is also skeptical of the way it is routinely invoked as an explanation for any behavior that appears to be irrational or that might seem to run against a group's long-term interests.[15] Culture is the fallback explanation, the first port of call when we encounter behaviors that are unfamiliar. However, as is demonstrated by Phillips, the cultural element is often only one within a more complex set of factors. In some contexts it is simply not relevant to the reasons why people choose in particular ways. Phillips cites two examples where culture is invoked to explain the persistence of what are generally regarded as harmful practices but where there are equally plausible or even more plausible noncultural explanations. The first is the case of a nongovernmental organization–led campaign against female genital cutting in Senegal. In that context, Phillips argues, the practice persisted not out of ignorance of the dangers or because of the overwhelming power of custom and tradition but rather because of the recognition that daughters would be unmarriageable if they had not undergone the practice. However, when there was a guarantee that everyone would simultaneously discontinue the practice, it was abandoned. In fact, from 1997 onward, village after village collectively abandoned the practice. It was not adherence to culture that had ensured its continuation but rather a more practical concern for the economic well-being and future prospects of the young women.[16] In her analysis of this case, Phillips fails to acknowledge that the belief that these young women would be unmarriagable is itself an expression of the overwhelming power of custom and tradition and that the economic well-being and future prospects of young women are precisely tied to the futures made possible in the context of custom and tradition. Nonetheless, the example does show that there is rationality to the decision in the sense that it is a concern for economic well-being rather than adherence to custom per se that is driving the decision. Phillips draws on Didier Fassin's work on Ecuador for her second example of culture being wrongly invoked as an explanation for behavior that appears to work against the interests of the individuals involved.[17] This case relates to maternal health in which the official explanation of why indigenous rural women failed to attend maternity clinics, thereby putting their own health and that of their babies at risk, had been unambiguously cultural. A study commissioned by the Ecuadoran Ministry of Public Health concluded that women were inhibited from attending the maternal health clinics because of "cultural aspects related to their sense of modesty," and explained that "there was too big a gap between their own symbolic world and the more formal cultural system of the health service."[18] Against this, however, Fassin and Phillips insist that the women's behavior is more accurately understood in terms of "an almost banal universality of attitudes." They cite the practical difficulties the women faced in traveling to the clinics, the well-grounded anticipation of being treated with disdain once they got there, the equally well-grounded fear that they would end up having cesarean sections (there is a high reliance on cesarean section in Ecuadoran obstetrics[19]), and so on, as logical and understandable, not irrational and cultural, reasons why the women resisted attending the clinics. In both cases the cultural explanation may seem to be the obvious one, at least at first glance. The fact that culture and tradition are the "go-to" explanations in contemporary political debate on such matters further compounds the problem of an overemphasis on cultural explanations. As these two cases have shown, however, there may be other equally or even more compelling factors that explain why certain choices are made. Yet culturalist explanations are so dominant in our multicultural world that it is difficult to avoid invoking them even when behaviors can be explained in more commonly understood terms and according to values and concerns that are more widely shared.

Notwithstanding its limitations, however, the category of culture can have an explanatory value in a renewed discourse of human rights. In his work, *The Location of Culture*, Homi Bhabha develops a theory of culture that resonates with contemporary cultural formations and explains how the negotiation of cultural identity is an endless process of engagement and exchange. Culture in this sense is a performative activity rather than a static entity.[20] In the postcolonial context, culture is not only a site of exchange but a liminal space in which cultural differences narrate and produce imagined constructions of cultural and national identity. Culture in a postcolonial world is characterized by ambivalence and hybridity. According to Bhabha, "the representation of difference must not be hastily read as the reflection of pre-given ethnic or cultural traits set in the fixed tablet of tradition." Rather, culture must be seen in terms of "a complex, on-going negotiation that seeks to authorize cultural hybridities that emerge in moments of historical transformation."[21] Kwok Pui-lan develops this insight in the theological context, insisting that the structuring of the world according to the language of cultural difference arises "not because there are many pre-constituted cultures existing side by side" but instead "is manufactured through particular discourses at critical moments when the status quo is questioned."[22] Within this framework, culture is the function of the discursive process of negotiation and renegotiation. It is characterized through its hybridity and cannot be defined in terms that assume a unitary form. It is dynamic and diasporic, not static and bounded, and as such can be an agent of change.

Porous Communities

In many respects, developments associated with the idea of community have followed a similar trajectory to those of culture. In contemporary ethical debate, the renewed focus on the concept of community has tended to be deployed as a counterweight to what is regarded as the atomism and individualism of modern societies. In that sense, therefore, the language of community is used to evoke an idealized earlier era in which identities were fixed, social roles were clear, and belonging was unambiguous and singular. Interestingly, the communitarian philosophies of the 1980s have had a comparable impact on the concept of community that scholars of multiculturalism have had on the notion of culture. So, in the same way that the language of multiculturalism served to reinforce an overly static understanding of culture, communitarianism has similarly reinforced an overly separatist idea of community. Identity politics has also contributed to this exaggeration because of the way in which it has amplified the commonalities within particular communities and drawn sharp differences between the inside and the outside.

Alongside this revalorization of the concept of community, however, critics have begun to interrogate the manner in which it is understood. Thus, in the same way that the category of culture has been deconstructed, so too the notion of community has undergone a similar process. Unsurprisingly, the work of Homi Bhabha and of Bhikhu Parekh also feature prominently in this deconstruction of the concept of a unitary community.[23] Important in this context, too, has been the work of theologians such as Bénézet Bujo and Kwok Pui-lan as well as the emerging Puerto Rican theologian Maria Teresa Davila.[24] Each critic challenges one to think differently about the classic conceptualization of community. From their different perspectives they resist accounts of communities as bounded and instead highlight the many ways in which this determinative social category is formed and reformed through discursive processes of power and privilege. Davila's focus is on processes of racialization, while Pui-lan and Bujo interrogate the processes of colonization in the construction of "imagined" communities.

Inevitably, contemporary ways of belonging are shaped by, as well as shape, the multiple ways in which identities and subjectivities are constructed today. As is argued in chapters 1 and 2, identities are constructed through a complex interaction of cultural, religious, economic, and political factors so that belonging is multiple and nomadic, not given, singular, and static. Whether one's life is lived in the midst of poverty and violence or of privilege, the subject has multiple commitments to multiple jurisdictions. From their very different speaking positions, both Gayatri Spivak and Rosi Braidotti highlight how globalization has changed irrevocably the shape of belonging. In a world that is structured "by multiple and dynamic centres of power" and in which "shifts, mutations and processes of change' are amongst its key features," Braidotti argues that we must rethink our idea of community in ways that allow for "complex allegiances and multiple forms of cultural belonging."[25] Braidotti and Spivak, as well as other postcolonial theorists, are aware of the danger associated with the language of multiple belongings and nomadic identities since it can convey a "pseudouniversal cosmopolitan bravado" that obscures the fact that in this globalized world there are "qualitatively different degrees of access and entitlement to power."[26] The multiple jurisdictions of one's affiliation may be sites of violence, exclusion, and marginalization. Moreover, one's mobility may be restricted or, alternatively, it may be forced and unchosen.[27]

Thus, as we rethink the nature of belonging within the context of "this logic of multiplying differences" we cannot ignore "the centuries-old forms of sexism, racism and anthropocentric arrogance" that, as Braidotti notes, seem to be "miraculously unscathed" by these new conditions of subjectivity and of belonging.[28]

multiple belongings

The motifs of multiple belonging and of dual belonging are also prominent in reflections on how people engage with religion today. There is no doubt that the nomadism of which Braidotti speaks is also a feature of contemporary religious practice, especially in the West. It can take many forms. Claude Geffré draws attention to a form of multiple belonging that he characterizes as generating a religious bricolage, and that he criticizes heavily as being typical of the "spontaneous syncretism" of Westerners.[29] Catherine Cornille, however, believes that this way of belonging to religious communities is more accurately described as a form of no belonging rather than of multiple belonging since there is no anchoring in any particular community.[30] Such theorists contrast this form of religious nomadism (which is harshly criticized) with a form of double belonging that is regarded as a legitimate way of inhabiting religious communities and that is acknowledged to be an increasingly chosen expression of the religious impulse. Peter Phan provides an interesting analysis of the form of multiple or dual religious belonging that is positively regarded. His work is focused particularly on the experiences of practitioners who started from a Christian commitment and "relentlessly endeavoured to combine, in their own life, their Christian commitment and another faith experience."[31] And while Phan's discussion is focused on exemplary or well-known figures, he acknowledges, as do other theorists, that there has been a significant growth in the numbers of individuals worldwide whose religious quest has led them to embrace this form of dual or double belonging and whose bilingualism, or even multilingualism, is changing the shape of belonging and having an impact on the nature of community.[32]

Not only has the manner in which individuals belong to communities (including religious communities) changed but, in addition and in part because of this pattern of multiple belonging, the boundaries between communities—religious and secular—are also becoming more porous. The hyphenated identities that are a feature of multiethnic societies and that are prevalent also among many contemporary religious believers not only facilitate but also generate a substantial degree of exchange between ethnic, racial, religious, and cultural communities. Of course, there have always been significant points of intersection between religious and cultural communities through history. However, the speed, intensity, and proximity of the exchange today have meant that such interaction is as unavoidable as it is constant. As Hans Ucko comments, since "most of the major traditions today have had the experience of being cultural 'hosts' to other religious traditions and of being 'hosted' by cultures shaped by religious traditions other than their own," therefore "the identities of religious communities and of individuals within them are never static, but fluid and dynamic."[33]

The boundaries between the communities are neither fixed nor solid but rather are permeable and porous. Moreover, just as Braidotti and Bhabha insist that the social and political landscape has been irrevocably transformed through the changing shape of belonging, so too, argues Perry Schmidt-Leukel, has the religious landscape. Such is the significance of this emerging global interreligious encounter, according to Schmidt-Leukel, that it "might be compared to an interstellar exchange" in which "a range of new and unexpected phenomena occur, among which is the possibility not only of penetrating and understanding another religious universe but of seeing our own world through the others' eyes."[34] In such a context, therefore, one can hope that the encounters between and among communities will become occasions of development and change rather than moments of retrenchment and refusal.

Constructed Traditions

The language of tradition, even more than that of culture and community, evokes images of an inheritance that, as described by Seamus Heaney, are

> upright, rudimentary, unshiftably planked
> In the long long ago, . . .
> cargoed with
> Its own dumb, tongue-and-groove worthiness
> An un-get-roundable weight[35]

Yet whether we are considering secular or religious traditions, we must be aware that they will be radically misconstrued if they are characterized in terms that are unchanging and timeless. Traditions—secular and religious—are dynamic and evolving. The products of discursive processes, traditions are historically constructed and internally diverse. Consider, for example, the Roman Catholic moral tradition, which is frequently characterized as unchanging. The historian John Noonan has demonstrated that this idea of a fixed and unchanging moral tradition is a fiction. In fact, he characterizes the Catholic Church's moral tradition thus: what was forbidden became lawful (the cases of usury and marriage); what was permissible became unlawful (the case of slavery); what was required became forbidden (the persecution of heretics).[36]

So whether one examines the Roman Catholic Church's tradition on marriage, on divorce, on abortion, on slavery, on conscientious objection to war, or on religious freedom, one encounters an always evolving, often inconsistent, and occasionally contradictory body of thought. Christianity's engagement with the notion of human rights itself provides an excellent illustration of this dynamic. Historical studies confirm that there is significant internal diversity on the matter of whether human rights language has any place in the Christian vocabulary. The Roman Catholic Church was vocally hostile to human rights from the time this language was adopted by the revolutionaries of the late eighteenth century right up until 1963, with the promulgation of *Pacem in Terris*. The churches of the reformed tradition, by contrast, played a seminal role in articulating and promoting certain fundamental rights, although this support fragmented somewhat over the centuries, so that one now has pockets of resistance to the very idea of human rights. In Northern Ireland, for example, one can see this dynamic at play in the various submissions to the Human Rights Commission on the Bill of Rights. The Caleb Foundation, in its response to the Human Rights Commission's request for submissions on a Bill of Rights, commented on the claim that all human beings possess an inalienable dignity, writing "put simply we do not believe any such thing. Man does not have inherent dignity but is possessed of 'Total Depravity.' Consequently, freedom, justice and peace in the world do not flow from mankind, rather mankind, without restraint, would naturally tend to bondage, injustice and war."[37] In contrast, although it expressed serious reservations about certain aspects of the Draft Charter of Fundamental Rights of the European Union, the Catholic Commission of Bishops' Conferences of the European Community (COMECE), in its formal response to the draft charter, confirmed that "protecting the fundamental rights of citizens in relation to the European Union, its institutions and its agencies is an important initiative to which COMECE attaches great value."[38]

There is a double irony here. In the first place, although some of the most vocal contemporary Christian critics of human rights belong to some churches of the reformed tradition, particularly in the United States, many of the central tenets of liberalism, of democratic organization, and of individual political rights were articulated and developed by the Christian reformers. One only has to think about many of the fundamental political rights to see how central the churches of the reformed tradition were in their development—for example, the origins of the right to live in a state in which there is no established religion and the right to freely exercise one's religious beliefs, the origins of the value of tolerance, freedom of conscience, and of speech—each of these rights was developed in response to the religious reforms of the sixteenth century and was given political expression by Christian reformers. The second irony is that although the Roman Catholic Church now uses the idiom of human rights consistently in its political and social ethics, there was a time when it expressed hostility to the modern concept of human rights. Thus, not only did Pius VI declare that it was anathema for Catholics to accept the 1789 Declaration of the Rights of Man and of the Citizen, saying "this equality, this liberty, so highly exalted by the National Assembly, have then as their only result the overthrow of the Catholic religion," but Gregory XVI's 1832 encyclical *Mirari vos* also strongly condemned liberalism, individualism, democracy, and freedom of conscience, of speech, and of the press.[39] Thus, in terms of the Christian denominations, we see a complicated trajectory whereby the churches have had periods of expressed hostility to human rights and periods of support. In fact, at each stage in the development of human rights thinking there were supporters and opponents within all of the Christian churches.

As this tradition on human rights demonstrates, when one brings a genealogical perspective to bear on moral traditions, one discovers that previously unquestioned positions have frequently been abandoned and substantial innovations have occurred. And not only have the conclusions about the morality of certain practices changed, but the ethical frame within which many practices are evaluated has also been transformed. Of course it would be wrong to overstate the trajectory of change in the evolution of this and other moral traditions because it is precisely as *tradition* that they evolve. Nonetheless, moral traditions are best understood as discursive traditions forged through an ambiguous dynamic of continuity and change. Studies in comparative religious ethics confirm that a similar trajectory, especially in respect of morality, is evident in the other major world religions. Indeed, even as the most conservative of religious thinkers have been committed to the timelessness of certain religious truths, they also acknowledge the need to interpret the significance of these religious truths, especially in respect of moral behavior, in each particular historical context. Scholars of Islam, Hinduism, and Buddhism as well as Judaism and Christianity (and all of the manifold traditions they generated, such as Sikhism and Jainism) confirm this evolutionary nature of religious traditions, even if religious leaders often downplay its significance.

Throughout this book I argue that human rights discourse must engage with the diversity of multiple situated, historical communities, including religious communities, and must find a way to deploy their traditions and languages in support of human rights. Hand in hand with this revalorization of communities and traditions, however, must come a critical approach to these traditions—namely, one that recognizes their evolutionary nature and their internal contestation. Conversations and processes that aim at meaningful religious and cultural exchange on critical issues, such as human rights, ignore at their peril the constructedness of religious and cultural traditions. Therefore, a renewed human rights discourse must bring a genealogical perspective to bear on religious and cultural traditions. Viewed through the genealogical lens, one can see that each tradition is embedded in political processes that have involved choices between various and varying interpretations of the community's history, power struggles over the authorization and legitimation of the community's traditions, disagreements about the criteria for belonging, and debates about where the power to define the limits of the tradition resides. The space for interreligious and cross-cultural engagement on critical moral issues will inevitably be enlarged when we no longer regard religious and cultural traditions as prediscursive entities that provide a refuge from the politics of knowledge but rather when they are accepted as being the products of historical and political processes through which their distinctiveness is constructed and according to which the parameters of orthodoxy are drawn.

Accommodation and Its Limits: The Case of Religion and Gender Equality

There is probably no single place where culture and rights more visibly collide than in relation to gender norms, and more specifically in relation to a society's expectations about women's behavior. As the earlier discussions about the development of the UN Declaration of Human Rights illustrate, the articles that had a bearing on gender norms were the most hotly contested. Moreover, as the follow-up report on the fifteenth anniversary of the Beijing Conference (1995) confirms, in the year 2000 women and girls continued to experience significant vulnerabilities because of their unequal legal, economic, and social status, and especially because of cultural factors.[40] It is worth noting that in this and other such contexts, the language of culture tends to be used as a synonym for religion, resulting in the conclusion that cultural and religious norms remain critical impediments to the achievement of women's equality worldwide. Of course there are many reasons why cultural and religious norms appear to be disproportionately focused on gender. The relationship between the sexes tends to be of seminal concern for religions and cultures, with philosophies of difference or complementarity being commonplace. Gender norms are also often central to the maintenance and reproduction of the identity of the community since it is usually through the family that membership of the community is demarcated and policed. Additionally, women, more than men, tend to carry the burden of this demarcation, which is usually expressed in terms of women's special position, focusing on their role in the reproduction and nurturing of children. In this way they become the primary conduits of the culture, although ironically their special position is also the source of their inequality. The works of Nira Yuval-Davis, Haleh Afshar, Leila Ahmed, and a host of other feminist scholars have brilliantly captured this paradox of women's position specifically in the context of religious communities, highlighting the irony that it is through adherence to gender norms in which their interests are subordinated that women gain their status.[41] It is true that a century of feminist politics has transformed the extent to which women can resist these normative accounts of their role. Indeed, there are very few cultural or religious contexts wherein there is not an active debate about gender and its significance. Nonetheless, notwithstanding the impact of feminism, women continue to be assigned the role of "bearers of cultural values, carriers of traditions and symbols of the community."[42] As many case studies confirm, this is particularly true in times of change, when women frequently bear a heightened responsibility for the transmission of the community's norms and are often charged with embodying the symbolic significance of their communities, for example, by veiling or by cutting their bodies. This ongoing discussion about gender norms, therefore, is an appropriate context in which to consider the question of the extent to which cultural and religious values, especially those that conflict with human rights, can be accommodated in a given society. Specifically in this context, we are concerned not so much with the resolution of specific instances of conflict but rather with the issue of how the parameters of such accommodation can be established.

This issue has been much debated in the last two decades and has for the most part been played out in terms of the tensions between feminism and multiculturalism. Susan Moller Okin's now infamous essay "Is Multiculturalism Bad for Women?" suggested that most cultures are deeply patriarchal and that policies that promote multicultural accommodation can be detrimental to women's interests and can work to undermine women's equality. While this is not a particularly contentious point, the manner in which the argument was made led many to conclude that the values and practices associated with non-Western cultures, traditions, and religious beliefs had been particularly targeted for criticism and had been assumed to be especially offensive. Okin came to the conclusion that some women would perhaps be better off had the cultures into which they were born become extinct. This, unsurprisingly, became the lightning rod that sparked a divisive and still unresolved debate about the extent to which diverse and competing values can be accommodated, where the limits of that accommodation should be drawn and by whom.

Although contentious, Okin's essay became the catalyst for a discussion about the nature of culture, and from which a more nuanced and nonessentialist understanding of culture emerged. This has led to a growing recognition that the conflicts between cultural diversity and human rights norms (specifically gender equality, in this case) can best be addressed when the categories of culture, community, and tradition are deconstructed in the ways that have earlier been discussed. Indeed, in *Multiculturalism without Culture*, Anne Phillips takes a further step, arguing that "multiculturalism can be compatible with gender equality and women's rights so long as it dispenses with an essentialist understanding of culture."[43] The important point for our purposes, however, is that we are able to identify a way of clarifying the limits of what can be tolerated when values collide, as they inevitably will. Anne Phillips's work is particularly helpful in this regard. A key feature of Phillips's deconstruction of culture is the way in which she challenges the language of culture as constraint and refuses to accept the assumption that individuals who comply with restrictive cultural and religious norms are lacking in autonomy. Phillips argues that this belief that culture essentially incapacitates people, making it impossible for them to exercise agency, is widespread and endemic in Western societies. Indeed, she highlights the fact that this notion of "culture as constraint" is deployed both by those who wish to challenge as well as by those who wish to support multiculturalism. Thus, a common argument for multicultural accommodation—for example, to allow Muslim girls to wear headscarves in school or to allow clitoridectomy to be performed in clinical settings, "rests on the notion that membership in a cultural or religious group is involuntary, and yet significantly curtails an individual's room to manoeuvre. This being so, it is claimed, it is discriminatory to require members of minority groups to abide by rules and regulations that were dreamt up with members of the majority group in mind."[44] Ironically, the same presumption about the constraining nature of culture is also made in support of the regulation or banning of certain practices on the basis that such prohibition would protect young women from cultural pressures. The implication, according to Phillips, is that "none of the young women in question would have freely chosen to behave in this way, that they are all being coerced by their community or prevented by their culture from operating as autonomous beings."[45] Phillips challenges such an assumption, arguing that we need to move away not only from essentialist understandings of culture, as has already been suggested, but also from deterministic ones. She insists that doing so will allow us to recognize that women do act according to their own agency, even when it is limited or curtailed in important respects, and that they cannot simply be viewed as either victims or dupes of patriarchal cultures.

This question of agency goes to the heart of the issue, and rethinking the way in which women's agency is understood may allow for a more nuanced approach to identifying where the limits of accommodation may lie and, more importantly for our discussion, how they can be delineated.

This is also true in relation to individuals who belong to other minority or indigenous groups, whose cultures tend to be treated in a comparably dismissive manner. In these contexts, the apparent conflicts between human rights norms and cultural values are particularly acute when the individuals most disadvantaged by such practices make the case for the continuation of what, viewed from the outside, seem like highly discriminatory practices. Thus, one often finds women and girls insisting that they should be permitted to veil, including to wear either a niqab or burqa, or, where abortion is permitted, that they ought to be permitted to abort a female fetus on the basis of her sex.[46] The debate about how such expressed preferences should be treated has been the subject of much debate, and I do not intended to rehearse the arguments here. The proposals span the spectrum from banning such practices even when they represent the expressed wishes of women and girls on the basis that such is the coercive impact of culture that these preferences cannot be regarded as autonomous to proposing that if individuals do not accept the values of a culture, then they are, and should be, free to leave.[47] Phillips offers a more subtle approach to this dilemma with her proposal that the constraints of culture need to be treated in a manner that is similar to the way in which we have come to understand the limitations that class and gender place on our capacity for agency and autonomous choice. This is made all the more complex by the fact that class and gender positions are woven so tightly into prevailing cultural norms that it is difficult to make analytical distinctions or treat these as discrete categories.

Phillips is critical of the rather exaggerated distinction between autonomy and constraint that is a feature of discussions about the impact of culture on agency. Her understanding of autonomy is, she acknowledges, a modest one in that she takes autonomy to be "the capacity to reflect on and, within the limits of our circumstances, either to endorse or change the way we act or live—thus, in some significant sense, to make our actions and choices our *own*."[48] Thus, our choices can be neither regarded as untouched by the contexts in which they are made nor entirely determined by them. Phillips remarks that when an individual's life chances or sense of themselves is discussed in relation to how their gender or class impacts on those chances, we tend to recognize that individuals are shaped but not determined by such factors. She draws on Gerald Dworkin's work on autonomy to support this critical point that "you do not have to be the sole author of your actions to count as autonomous, and you do not have to arrive at your principles or beliefs entirely uninfluenced by anyone around you."[49] Yet the constraints of culture and religion continue to be viewed as more determining than other factors, and therefore as posing a threat to the capacities of individuals to exercise agency. The significance of Phillips's argument lies in the way it challenges the dichotomy between culture and autonomy that pervades much of the discussion about how and on what basis diverse values can be accommodated either in a particular society or in the international context. Indeed, as her detailed consideration of a range of cases demonstrates, treating the constraints of culture in ways that are analogous to those of race or class makes it possible to recognize that culture can affect an individual's life chances and can be a significant factor in the individual's experience of social exclusion. It also allows for the acknowledgment that some choices are made under pressure, whether direct or indirect, and that our capacity for agency is inevitably affected both by our learned preferences and by the extent to which we are exposed to particular ideologies or worldviews. Autonomy, therefore, cannot be thought of as "an all-or-nothing concept but is more a matter of degree," and the critical issue then becomes how and on what basis we can determine where cultural influence ends and coercion begins.[50] In this context it also becomes important to be able to identify who may be particularly vulnerable to coercion as well as how they can best be protected.

There is no doubt that individuals have different degrees of attachment to their families and their faiths as well as to their cultures and traditions. They are differently affected by the constraints of gender, class, or race and are shaped to a greater or lesser extent by the limitations a society places on their life chances by virtue of these factors. Phillips is strongly critical of approaches that conclude that an individual's agency is wholly destroyed by the constraints of culture or religion, and she argues that, although it is never easy to do so, it is imperative that we find a better way of clarifying "who is being coerced, who claims to be acting for herself but is in reality being coerced, and who is genuinely making up her own mind."[51] She argues that governments have a particular responsibility to intervene to ban or limit certain practices where individuals are being coerced, but she also recognizes that such coercion is often extremely difficult to determine and therefore accepts that intervention cannot be limited to proven or explicit cases of coercion. She also acknowledges that limiting the remedy for coercion to "the right to exit" one's culture or community is inherently flawed because the very individuals who seek to exit may not have the resources necessary to do so. Indeed, they are likely to lack the resources to exit not only because the costs of leaving may be unacceptably high but also because those most socialized into the acceptance of conditions that in other cultures would be regarded as unacceptable are often precisely those for whom an alternative life experience is unimaginable.[52] The alternatives of either regulating certain practices or allowing them to continue while providing those who no longer wish to adhere to them to exit the group are appropriate in some circumstances. Where the regulation option is pursued, it must be done in a manner that avoids cultural stereotypes and that differentiates cultural influence from coercion. Where the option to support the exit of individuals is pursued, it must do so in a way that it represents a genuine possibility of a life outside the community. The critical point for Phillips in this regard is that the discussion about establishing the limits of accommodation must be focused on the interests and rights of individuals as members of communities and not focused on the cultures or communities themselves. It is essential, therefore, that the remedies and regulations that are sought are contextually sensitive since, as I have been arguing throughout, generic solutions to context-specific problems are wholly inappropriate. In this context it becomes even more important to be able to establish a deliberative process through which society can determine where the parameters of accommodation lie. Moreover, this deliberative process must be such that the many different and divergent voices of individuals can be heard.

Reimagining Culture as a Site of Emancipatory Politics

Culture, community, and tradition tend to be invoked as a bulwark against development and change, particularly when there is disagreement in society about the applicability of certain ethical values or about the enforcement of certain moral norms. As has already been suggested, however, simplistic appeals to culture or tradition are neither warranted nor defensible since they fail to acknowledge that these categories have changed and continue to change. The focus on the specific case of gender equality highlighted the inadequacy of many contemporary discussions of culture, illustrating just how pervasive these essentialist and deterministic stereotypes of culture and religion continue to be. The first part of this chapter explains why I believe that it is imperative that we move away from essentialist understandings of culture, from unitary accounts of community and from static portrayals of tradition. I argue that due recognition must be given to the role that both history and politics have played in the construction of our current accounts of these categories, and insist that they must feature in our working definitions of culture, of community, and of tradition. Moreover, I argue that doing so will allow the inherent dynamism of these categories to emerge and to be properly acknowledged, and suggest that this can be especially helpful in conversations about their role in the promotion of human rights norms. Furthermore, I suggest that such an approach ought to facilitate the development of a different kind of conversation about the relationship between human rights norms and culture values, one in which they might be regarded as partners, rather than adversaries, in an ongoing process of ethical deliberation. Viewed in this way, culture can be repositioned as a site of emancipatory politics rather than as a place of conservatism and coercion.

The Anatomy of Change

I began this chapter by arguing that the categories of culture, community, and tradition (and, by implication, religion) tend to be inappropriately essentialized in our human rights discourse and suggesting that if we pay attention to the genealogy of these categories, we will quickly discover that they are neither static nor unitary but rather are dynamic and internally diverse. Indeed, as was illustrated in the case of gender norms, the problem with two of the most common approaches to managing cultural diversity—regulation or exit—is that they engage with cultural and religious traditions as though they are static and unitary; therefore, they run the risk of underestimating the role that internal criticism can play in the rearticulation of a culture's values or a community's identity. In addition, the exit option also fails to give due recognition to the deep attachment that many people feel to their cultures or religions. Thus the rather simplistic solution of proposing that people can leave if their beliefs of practices do not conform to the expressed marks of belonging often does not address their concerns. In the case of each of these approaches to resolving conflicts about value differences, one particular definition or interpretation of the tradition predominates, and the boundaries between belonging and not belonging are firmly drawn. Yet cultures, traditions, and communities cannot be represented thus, so in any attempt to determine where the limits of the accommodation of cultural and religious difference may lie, it is important that the presence of internal debate within cultural or religious groups be acknowledged, especially when such contestation may be focused on what might be regarded as exclusionary values or of discriminatory practices.

There can be little doubt that pluralism has changed the way in which individuals experience the cultures they inhabit. Moreover, this is the case irrespective of how clearly the boundaries of the culture are drawn or how strong is its sense of its distinctiveness. As Madhavi Sunder notes, more and more people are claiming the right to remain as members of a group but define what that cultural membership means to them in their own term. Thus, she argues, we are moving "away from imposed cultural identities towards a conception of cultural identity based on autonomy, choice and reason."[53] One can cite many examples of this more "agent-centered" approach to belonging, and many of the world's religions can be seen as interesting laboratories in which such conceptualizations of identity and belonging are being redrawn. Indeed, Sunder draws attention to feminist religious reform movements found in all the major world's religions and more recently among indigenous and native religious traditions, which have developed new interpretations of sacred texts, beliefs, and practices in which women's equality and dignity are to the fore, and which have become the centerpiece of their understanding of their religion. One could also cite the sea change that has occurred in Roman Catholicism in the last five decades. At the center, initially, was a challenge to the hierarchical magisterium's teaching on sexuality. However, this initial challenge has been transformed into a worldwide movement for reform in which large numbers of Catholics voice their often deep-seated criticisms but in the context of continuing to belong to the Church. The *We Are Church* movement expresses this posture vis-à-vis the Roman Catholic tradition very well. As Sunder argues, people determining their cultural and religious belonging for themselves, establishing the parameters of their own belonging are far less likely to exit simply because they differ with the religious or cultural authorities about the salience or persuasiveness of particular values, norms, or practices. People are therefore far more likely to challenge and critique contested values and seek to generate some momentum for change from within.

Notwithstanding this dynamism, however, existing hierarchies are likely to continue to shape and influence the community's response to proposals for change, and are likely to maintain their gatekeeping role as the guardians of the tradition and its inherited values. Feminist criticism of the gatekeeping function of established hierarchies has been especially insightful, highlighting the significance of a tradition's gatekeepers as facilitators of change, or as resisters of change, and analyzing the nature and scope of their influence.[54] Some, like Alison Jaggar, have been particularly concerned about the different ways in which the cultural gatekeepers pressure members to conform to prevailing values by imposing both formal and informal sanctions, and by severely curtailing possibilities for dialogue about the case for change. Ayelet Shachar, by contrast, focuses more on how cultural elites may be encouraged to become catalysts for change rather than agents of conservatism. In this regard, she is particularly interested in how the external protections that a state may provide for vulnerable members within a group can be used to reduce internal restrictions, thereby encouraging cultural elites to increase their "accountability and sensitivity to otherwise marginalised group members."[55] Shachar proposes a mode of engagement that she calls "transformative accommodation," which takes as its starting point an acknowledgment that the community and the state each hold significant power and authority, both formal and informal.[56] Her strategy for promoting change lies in encouraging individuals to think of their loyalties in a nonexclusive fashion. This, she believes, will minimize the likelihood of a standoff between the values held by members of bounded cultural groups and those that predominate in the societies in which they exist. In addition, it holds the possibility of facilitating the kind of internal discussions that will lead to a reexamination of the merits of certain values and practices and should also give a stronger voice to internal critics and dissenters. For Shachar as well as for Phillips, there is no necessary contradiction between the two objectives of respecting the diverse values and practices of particular cultures and also of ensuring that the life chances of vulnerable individuals are not wholly determined by the future that may be mapped out, on their behalf, by the imperatives of the tradition or the community. Rather, the key to the resolution of value conflicts lies in the manner in which these different groups to which individuals give their allegiance relate to each other.

Although we speak frequently, and often casually, about effecting change, it can be difficult to understand precisely how it is or can be achieved. Indeed, value change can be especially difficult to effect and often becomes even more so when certain values are perceived to be under threat. Kwame Anthony Appiah's consideration of moral revolutions is especially instructive in helping us to think about what might be called "the anatomy of change." In *The Honor Code*, Appiah asks the question "what can be learned about morality by exploring moral revolutions?" With the term "moral revolutions" he has in mind occasions when societies or groups underwent a fundamental change in respect of what they valued or regarded as good or right. He examines three moral revolutions in detail—namely, the end of dueling, the dissolution of foot-binding in China, and the end of the Atlantic slave trade, all in the nineteenth century, and argues that in each of these instances of radical change, there occurred a fundamental alteration in the way in which the society determined what was to be regarded as honorable. Although the language of honor may not have much purchase or salience today, all moral systems do tend to have analogous concepts and synonyms for honor, and in this regard Appiah's essential point is particularly insightful.

Appiah notes that when a society or a group undergoes a major transformation of its values and alters its sense of what is good or right in certain circumstances, it tends to do so by drawing on existing values and reinterpreting them, either by extending their remit or expanding the range of their application or by changing the grounds on which they are determined. Rarely, if ever, is there a fundamental repudiation of an existing value but rather there is an attempt to protect the existing value, albeit in a different guise, or to reinterpret its meaning and significance in light of changed circumstances or beliefs. Indeed, as his analyses demonstrate, in each of these moral revolutions, what Appiah calls "the motivating power of honor" was channeled, not challenged.[57] He acknowledges that there are many different ways in which honor can function in moral revolutions; however, he suggests that each of these instances of moral transformation teaches us something important about how change can be effected. In particular, they reveal that cultural and religious values and practices invariably invoke and depend on codes of honor that are typically being challenged long before any transformation occurs, and that these codes of honor ultimately need to be recruited to the side of change or progress if a moral transformation is to occur.[58] Moreover, as Appiah points out, notwithstanding the fact that the transformation, in a particular community's practice, may initially be experienced as unsettling and unfamiliar when existing codes of honor can be harnessed in the service of change, a moral revolution can come about with "astonishing speed."[59]

Appiah is as much concerned here with the psychology of change as he is with the morality of change. In this regard, one of his most interesting insights is that when we look closely at any of these moral revolutions, we realize that the arguments for change had been well rehearsed in the preceding decades and that the impetus for change, especially in relation to value change, has rarely come from the development of new arguments but rather from the gradual recognition of the persuasive appeal of the existing ones. In this context, the role of the internal critic is especially important.

All traditions understand the subversive and prophetic potential of the critic, and especially of the internal critic. Great innovations in cultural and religious life have come about because of the courage and determination of individuals who have challenged their inherited traditions to live up to the idealism contained therein or to dispense with the evasions and hypocrisies that may have become embedded in its practices. Walzer calls this "the subversiveness of immanence" and remarks on its significance, not only in calling into question but also in overturning certain fundamental values to which a group may hold.[60] A critical and often overlooked insight, however, is that although the story of "the critical enterprise" is usually told through the prism of what Walzer calls "the heroic moments," although, in fact, criticism is best understood as a reiterative activity in which the case for change is made again and again, in and through the language and narratives of the particular tradition.[61] This is precisely what Appiah's discussion about the role of honor confirms. A similar dynamic comes into play when diverse cultural or religious traditions encounter each other and seek ways of living together. Indeed, our contemporary society is replete with multiple strands of immanent criticism, each engaging not only with its own heritage but also with a wider social context of ethical debate. This wider context is highly significant in the search for a viable discourse of human rights. And although explicitly particularist, these immanent critiques collectively have the potential to generate significant social change.

Convergence Values

A convergence of values is more likely to arise not when we ignore our differences but rather when we come to understand that cultures express their fundamental values according to different idioms and with different emphases. Thus it is through "mutual recognition" of certain minimal standards in the midst of diversity that we can begin to recognize what, if anything, human beings hold in common.[62] The stark contrast drawn between the dynamism of human rights discourse and the conservatism of cultures is therefore wholly inappropriate. Certain cultures and religious traditions tend to portray themselves thus, but, as has been demonstrated, these portrayals are frequently disputed and criticized by members themselves. The inherent dynamism of these categories can be—indeed, needs to be—marshaled in the service of a viable human rights discourse. The debate, improvisation, and deliberation through which these traditions are constructed can enable rather than frustrate this globally resonant conversation. In this way, culture can be repositioned as a site of emancipatory politics rather than as a bulwark against change.

In chapter 4 I argue that incremental consensus on human rights can be generated on the basis of what Appiah called "incompletely theorized agreements" and suggest that an authentic and sustainable agreement on human rights can only emerge through multiple, inclusive, tradition-thick, cross-cultural, multireligious engagement and dialogue. I enumerate some of what I believe to be the most important questions to be considered in relation to the role of religion in this regard. Fundamental to this discussion, of course, is how the public square is framed, and in particular whether it is pluralist and multireligious or secular in its constitution and, as a result, whether it can grant an explicitly public role for religious voices alongside others or whether it seeks to relegate religion to the private sphere. The EMILIE project's work on multicultural citizenship in nine European countries is highly informative in this regard because it confirms that the manner in which nationhood is conceptualized, especially in terms of cultural, religious, and ethnic identities, and particularly whether and how the political orientation is geared toward cohesion or recognition, has a major impact on the manner in which it engages with difference.[63] I have argued elsewhere for a multireligious pluralist public square and suggest that if we are to deal with the intensification of the interactions of the complex social identities that characterize contemporary society, then we will need a robust deliberative politics that can reckon with the faith claims of others, whether these faith claims are religiously or humanistically derived.[64]

In that context, however, politicians and policymakers are often at a loss as to how to structure the public square to ensure that religious voices can enter this arena. In parallel, religious communities are also uncertain as to how they can participate authentically and intelligibly in public debate, particularly on contentious and contested issues. Our recent history is replete with conflicts that revolve around the difficulty of constructing a deliberative politics that can cope with the increasingly common situation in which the deeply held convictions of citizens collide and in which the contours of these conflicts of value are linked with religious belonging. Value conflicts associated with the Islamic tradition, particularly in states that are currently styled as secular but that have historically been Christian, have been especially prominent and have exposed the limitations of such political movements as feminism and multiculturalism that originally aimed at avoiding the marginalization of minorities. Martha Nussbaum's *The New Religious Intolerance: Overcoming the Politics of Fear in an Anxious Age* provides an overview, at a particular point in time—that is, the post-9/11 world—wherein, in different European countries as well as in the United States, the public presence of religious practices, symbolisms, and values has been debated and discussed with varying degrees of success and civility.[65] Such experiences in, for example, France, Switzerland, the United States, and the United Kingdom highlight some of the hazards to be avoided. They show why it is essential that there is a commitment to the exchange of ideas, in a spirit of open communication, and with a genuinely open mind on how such conflicts can be resolved. Religious and other intentional communities are alert to tokenism and are often mistrustful of participation in deliberation of this kind as a result. It is important, too, not to assume that there is a simple homogeneity of views within communities, even if community representatives claim to speak for the whole. A case in point is the rise of *Ni Putes Ni Soumises* in the suburbs of Paris, which highlighted the sexism and gender-based violence within some Muslim communities and which challenged the traditional Islamic leadership when the French polity was debating whether and how Islamic perspectives on gender equality could be given formal recognition.[66] This illustrates why the public square must be hospitable to religious voices and specifically why it is important to have mechanisms through which the heterogeneity of communities and traditions can be visible. Nor should the importance of tradition and the challenge of change be regarded as an issue only for minority groups. In fact, dominant cultures can be particularly resistant to change, especially when assumptions are so embedded in the fabric of the society that they have become naturalized.

For more than three decades now local communities and national bodies have been involved in interreligious and multicultural engagements on matters of great significance with varying degrees of success. However, even long-standing, productive, and reciprocal relationships are coming under strain from what Nussbaum calls "the politics of fear." It is thus incumbent on both political and community leaders to draw on the successes of past engagements to build a robust culture of engagement, exchange, and agreement. Religion cannot be privileged above other world views, and religiously derived values should not expect a special hearing in public debate. However, neither should the public square marginalize or problematize religious voices since the durability of our shared future depends on the continued pluralization of our public square and on our ability to deal with difference.

Cultivating the Virtues in Cross-Cultural Communication

If we are to have a viable interreligious and cross-cultural communication about the nature and scope of human rights, then the manner in which we treat cultures, communities, and traditions is of critical importance. As we embark on such communication, we may hold fast to this conviction that our world views may be complementary. However, even as we do, we will need to recognize that certain ethical values and commitments that are promoted by religious and cultural traditions will turn out to be incommensurable and that they will continue to be contested. We cannot shy away from these areas of dissonance and ambiguity. Indeed, over time these points of dissonance may provide occasions for deep learning about human needs and desires and may become the basis on which real transformation occurs. James Keenan and Lucas Chan not only make this point but also demonstrate how this can be done in their discussion of the bridging of the distance between Christian ethics and Confucianism.[67]

The nature and tone of conversations through which these engagements are pursued can often be as important as the substance of the dialogue itself. Indeed, when the substantive issues are primarily focused on the protection of human dignity, it behooves the participants to pursue such debate through the language of respect and restraint. There is no doubt that this represents a challenge for many religious and cultural communities as they seek to communicate their views on fundamental ethical issues. The public debate about the rights of those in same-sex relationships is an interesting case in point. Many religious traditions hold that the practice of homosexuality is wrong or sinful, and they regard efforts to advance certain rights to same-sex couples as fundamentally flawed. What is troubling about this debate is the fact that it continues to be conducted along the stereotypical lines that are challenged in this chapter. Particular religious and cultural traditions seek to present a perspective on the issue that admits no recognition of internal dispute or development while the secular society is unwilling to hear these cultural and religious traditions out on their own terms. Even more worrying, however, is the tone of the debate, and in this regard the religions have a serious problem that arises from the language of condemnation through which the practice is evaluated. The European Parliament's Resolution on Homophobia has presented a fundamental challenge for many Christian denominations because, as the then cardinal Ratzinger has noted, "very soon it will not be possible to state that homosexuality, as the Catholic Church teaches, is an objective disorder in the structuring of human existence."[68] In my view, this represents a positive development because it challenges all religions and cultures to be attentive to the manner in which they express their values and defend their practices. Regardless of how deeply held these views are, in a pluralist society each tradition has an obligation to engage in public debate in a manner that upholds rather than corrodes the integrity of the public square. All citizens have a role in ensuring that the public square is a place of civility and respect. Moreover, the values of civility and respect become even more important when individuals believe that certain critical aspects of their community's identity are at stake. In these situations in particular, it is essential that we begin to cultivate the virtues of love and justice in public speech and especially in cross-cultural communication. As I have already argued, shared values will only emerge through a dialogical engagement between multiple situated historical communities, including religious communities, that are open to internally and externally generated social criticism. Thus, one must be prepared to sit lightly on inherited and conventional world views, all the while keeping faith with the ideal of a shared ethical vision. We must be prepared to cultivate a form of virtuous public speech as we debate our deeply held convictions. After all, we are, as the poet Emily Dickinson reminded us, always "just lisping the truth."

Notes

1. Charles Taylor, *A Secular Age* (Cambridge, MA: Belknap Press of Harvard University Press, 2007), 3.

2. Ibid., 21.

3. Ibid., 3.

4. This is the core of Taylor's definition of secularity and is the defining feature of what he calls this "secular age."

5. Edward Burnett Tylor, *Primitive Culture: Researches into the Development of Mythology, Philosophy, Religion, Art, and Custom* (London: John Murray, 1871), quoted in Anne Phillips, *Multiculturalism without Culture* (Princeton, NJ: Princeton University Press, 2007), 42.

6. See Will Kymlicak's *Multicultural Citizenship: A Liberal Theory of Minority Rights* (Oxford: Oxford University Press, 1995), and *Multicultural Odyssey Navigating the New International Politics of Diversity* (Oxford: Oxford University Press, 2007); Charles Taylor's *Dilemmas and Connections: Selected Essays* (Cambridge, MA: Harvard University Press, 2011); and Amy Gutman's *Identity in Democracy* (Princeton, NJ: Princeton University Press, 2004) for a comprehensive overview of these debates.

7. Jacob T. Levy, *The Multiculturalism of Fear* (Oxford: Oxford University Press, 2000), 6.

8. Susan Engle Merry, *Human Rights and Gender Violence* (Chicago: University of Chicago Press, 2006), 12–13.

9. This move reflects the uncertainty surrounding the deployment of the language of race, rather than being the result of a nuanced account of how race, ethnicity, and culture intersect. In short, the language of cultural difference is seen to be a more palatable way of discussing the differences among groups. See David Hollinger's *Postethnic America: Beyond Multiculturalism* (New York: Basic Books, 1995); and Tariq Modood's *Multicultural Politics: Racism, Ethnicity, and Muslims in Britain* (Edinburgh: Edinburgh University Press, 2005), for excellent discussions of this point.

10. Merry, *Human Rights and Gender Violence*, 15.

11. Uma Narayan, "Essence of Culture and a Sense of History: A Feminist Critique of Cultural Essentialism," in *Decentering the Center: Philosophy for a Multicultural, Postcolonial, and Feminist World*, ed. Uma Narayan and Sandra Harding, 80–100 (Bloomington: Indiana University Press, 2000), 86.

12. Ibid., 86.

13. This important issue will be discussed in the sections on community and tradition.

14. Merry, *Human Rights and Gender Violence*, 15.

15. Phillips, *Multiculturalism without Culture*.

16. For this case Phillips uses the work of Gerry Mackie, "Female Genital Cutting: The Beginning of the End," in *Female "Circumcision" in Africa: Culture Controversy and Change*, ed. Bettina Shell-Duncan and Ylva Hernlund, 253–82 (Boulder, CO: Lynne Reiner, 2000). She also draws on the material generated by the nongovernmental organization TOSTAN, *Breakthrough in Senegal: The Process That Ended Female Genital Cutting in 31 Villages* (Washington, DC: US Agency for International Development, 1999). See Phillips, *Multiculturalism without Culture*, 46.

17. Didier Fassin, "Culturalism as Ideology," in *Cultural Perspectives on Reproductive Health,* ed. Carla Makhlouf Obermeyer, 300–307 (Oxford: Oxford University Press, 2001), cited in Phillips, *Multiculturalism without Culture*, 47.

18. Ibid.

19. Ibid.

20. Homi Bhabha, *The Location of Culture* (London: Routledge, 1994).

21. Ibid., 2.

22. Kwok Pui-lan, *Postcolonial Imagination and Feminist Theology* (London: SCM-Canterbury Press, 2005), 43.

23. Bikhu Parek, *Rethinking Multiculturalism: Cultural Diversity and Political Theory* (Hampshire, UK: Palgrave, 2006).

24. Bénézet Bujo, *Foundations of an African Ethic: Beyond the Universal Claims of Western Morality* (Nairobi: Paulines, 2003); and Maria Teresa Davila, "Racialization and Racism in Theological Ethics: History as a Pillar for a Catholic Ethic Grounded on the Preferential Option for the Poor and an Incarnational Anthropology," in *Catholic Theological Ethics, Past, Present, and Future: The Trento Conference*, ed. James Keenan, 307–21 (Maryknoll: Orbis Press, 2012).

25. Rosi Braidotti, *Transpositions: On Nomadic Ethics* (Cambridge, UK: Polity Press, 2006), 78.

26. "Pseudouniversal cosmopolitan bravado" is James Clifford's phrase in "Diasporas," *Cultural Anthropology* 9, no. 3 (2007): 312, quoted in Braidotti, *Transpositions*, 78. See also ibid., 79.

27. See Giorgio Agamben's *State of Exception* (Chicago: University of Chicago Press, 2005) for an excellent discussion of this point as it arises in the European context.

28. Braidotti, *Transpositions*, 44.

29. Claude Geffré, "Double Belonging and the Originality of Christianity as a Religion," in *Many Mansions? Multiple Religious Belonging and Christian Identity*, ed. C. Cornille, 93–105 (New York: Orbis Books, 2002), 93.

30. Catherine Cornille, "Double Religious Belonging: Aspects and Questions," *Buddhist-Christian Studies* 44 (2003):43–49.

31. Peter Phan, "Multiple Religious Belonging: Opportunities and Challenges for Theology and Church," *Theological Studies* 64, no. 3 (September 2003): 495–519, at 507.

32. Paul F. Knitter's *Without Buddha I Could Not Be a Christian* (Oxford: One-World, 2009) provides a fascinating reflection on this phenomenon from a personal perspective.

33. Hans Ucko, "Religious Plurality and Christian Self-Understanding," Preparatory paper no. 13, May 15, 2005. World Council of Churches website. Accessed September 3, 2009. www.oikoumene.org/en/resources/documents/other-meetings/mission-and-evangelism/preparatory-paper-13-religious-plurality-and-christian-self-understanding.

34. Perry Schmidt-Leukel, "Uniqueness: A Pluralistic Reading of John 14:6," in *Ecumenics from the Rim: Explorations in Honour of John D'Arcy May*, ed. John O. Grady and Peter Scherle, 303–14 (Berlin: LIT Verlag, 2007), 304.

35. "The Settle Bed," from *Seeing Things*, 1991, reprinted in Seamus Heaney, *Open Ground: Poems 1966–1996* (London: Faber and Faber, 1998).

36. John T. Noonan Jr., "Development in Moral Doctrine," *Theological Studies* 54 (1993): 662–77, at 669. See also John Noonan, *A Church That Can and Cannot Change: The Development of Catholic Moral Teaching* (Notre Dame, IN: University of Notre Dame Press, 2005).

37. Caleb Foundation, *Proposed Bill of Rights for Northern Ireland: A Response*, Submission 355 (Belfast: Northern Ireland Human Rights Commission, 2001), 1. The Caleb Foundation is an international foundation; in Ireland, it is largely Presbyterian in its makeup.

38. COMECE, Observations of the COMECE Secretariat on the Draft Charter of Fundamental Rights of the European Union, October 18, 2000, accessed December 22, 2014, www.comece.org/site/article_detail.siteswift?so=site_article_detail&do=site_article_detail&c=download&d=article%3A3432%3A2.

39. Pius VI quoted in Bernard Plongeron, "Anathema or Dialogue? Christian Reactions to the Declarations of the Rights of Man in the United States and Europe in the Eighteenth Century," in *The Church and the Rights of Man*, ed. Alois

Muller and Norbert Greinacher, *Concilium* 4, no. 124 (1979): 1–16; and Gregory XVI, *Mirari vos*, in *The Papal Encyclicals 1740–1878*, ed. Claudia Carlen, vol. 1 (Wilmington, NC: Pierian Press, 1990), 198.

40. United Nations Commission on the Status of Women Report on the Fifty-Fourth Session (March 13 and October 14, 2009 and March 1–12, 2010), Economic and Social Council Official Records, 2010 Supplement No. 7, E/2010/27 E /CN.6/2010/11, accessed December 22, 2014, http://www.peacewomen.org/assets /image/Resources/report_csw54_2009_2010.pdf.

41. Haleh Afshar, ed. *Women, State, and Ideology: Studies from Africa and Asia* (Albany: State University of New York Press, 1987); and Afshar, *Islam and Feminism: An Iranian Case-Study* (London: Macmillan 1998); Leila Ahmed, *A Quiet Revolution: The Veil's Resurgence from the Middle East to America* (New Haven, CT: Yale University Press, 2011); and Nira Yuval-Davis, *Gender and Nation* (1997; repr. London: Sage Publications, 2004). See also Fatema Mernissi, *Beyond the Veil: Male-Female Dynamics in Muslim Society* (London: Saqi Books, 1975); Martha Nussbaum, *The New Religious Intolerance: Overcoming the Politics of Fear* (Cambridge, MA: Belknap Press of Harvard University, 2012); Anna Triandafyllidou, Tariq Modood, and Nasar Meer, *European Multiculturalisms: Cultural, Religious and Ethnic Challenges* (Edinburgh, UK: Edinburgh University Press, 2012); Rex Ahdar and Nicholas Aroney, eds., *Shari'a in the West* (Oxford: Oxford University Press, 2010); and Dominic McGoldrick, *Human Rights and Religion: The Islamic Headscarf Debate in Europe* (Oxford, UK: Hart Publishing, 2006).

42. Valentine Moghadam, *Gender and National Identity: Women and Politics in Muslim Societies* (London: Zed Books, 1994), 4.

43. Phillips, *Multiculturalism without Culture*, 9.

44. Ibid., 100.

45. Ibid., 101.

46. See Prabhat Jha, Maya A. Kesler, Rajesh Kumar, Faujdar Ram, Usha Ram, Lukasz Aleksandrowicz, Diego G. Bassani, Shailaja Chandra, and Jayant K. Banthia, "Trends in Selective Abortions of Girls in India: Analysis of Nationally Representative Birth Histories from 1990 to 2005 and Census Data from 1991 to 2011," *Lancet* 377, no. 9781: 1921–28, doi:10.1016/S0140-6736(11)60649-1.

47. Phillips, *Multiculturalism without Culture*, 104; and Chandran Kukathas, *The Liberal Archipelago: A Theory of Diversity and Freedom* (Oxford: Oxford University Press, 2003).

48. Phillips, *Multiculturalism without Culture*, 101.

49. Ibid., 127, citing Gerald Dworkin, *The Theory and Practice of Autonomy* (New York: Cambridge University Press, 1988), 36.

50. Phillips, *Multiculturalism without Culture*, 104.

51. Ibid., 132.

52. This is a central aspect of Martha Nussbaum's discussion of expressed preferences in *Women and Human Development: The Capabilities Approach* (Cambridge: Cambridge University Press, 2000), particularly in chap. 2.

53. Madhavi Sunder, "Cultural Dissent," *Stanford Law Review* 545 (December 2001): 495–567, at 515.

54. Alison Jagger, "Globalizing Feminist Ethics," in *Decentering the Center: Philosophy for a Multicultural, Postcolonial, and Feminist World*, ed. Uma Narayan and Sandra Harding, 1–25 (Bloomington: Indiana University Press, 2000), 10.

55. Ayelet Shachar, *Multicultural Jurisdictions: Cultural Differences and Women's Rights* (Cambridge: Cambridge University Press, 2001), 117.

56. Shachar is particularly interested in groups she describes as *nomoi* groups. She uses the term to refer primarily to religiously defined groups of people who share a comprehensive world view that extends to creating a law for the community. Ibid., 2. Shahar is most interested in the political question of which institutional model is most appropriate to multicultural societies. Her transformative accommodation model proposes a "joint governance" approach, which both enhances the jurisdictional autonomy of religious and cultural minorities and simultaneously challenges rights-violations within these groups. The structural issues are not of specific interest here. Rather more important for our purposes is her sense that it is possible to both "reduce injustice between minority groups and the wider society, while at the same time enhancing justice within them." Ibid., abstract.

57. Kwame Anthony Appiah, *The Honor Code: How Moral Revolutions Happen* (New York: W. W. Norton, 2010) 169.

58. Ibid., 161.

59. Ibid., 170.

60. Michael Walzer, *Thick and Thin: Moral Arguments at Home and Abroad* (Notre Dame, IN: University of Notre Dame Press, 1994), 47. See also his discussion in *The Company of Critics: Social Criticism and Political Commitment in the Twentieth Century* (New York: Basic Books, 2002), in which he looks in detail at the lives and works of eleven public intellectuals and from there draws a number of important insights about the nature of social criticism.

61. Walzer, *Thick and Thin*, 52.

62. "Mutual recognition" is Walzer's term in *Thick and Thin*, 17.

63. EMILIE Project, *A European Approach to Multicultural Citizenship: Legal, Political and Multicultural Challenges* (EMILIE), www.intercultural-europe.org/site/node/1363. This website states that it will shut down in September 2015.

64. Linda Hogan, Introduction to *Religious Voices in Public Places*, ed. Nigel Biggar and Linda Hogan, 1–14 (Oxford: Oxford University Press, 2009).

65. Ibid.

66. See the discussion in Nacira Guénif-Souilamas, "The Other French Exception: Virtuous Racism and the War of the Sexes in Postcolonial France," *French Politics, Culture and Society* 24, no. 3 (2006): 23–41, and a host of essays in Triandafyllidou, Modood, and Meer, *European Multiculturalisms*; and Gavin D'Costa, Malcom Evans, Tariq Modood, and Julian Rivers, *Religion in a Liberal State* (Cambridge: Cambridge University Press, 2013).

67. Yiu Sing Lucas Chan and James Keenan, "Bridging Christian Ethics and Confucianism through Virtue Ethics," *Chinese Cross Currents* 5, no. 2 (July 2008): 74–85.

68. Cardinal Josef Ratzinger, "Cardinal Ratzinger on Europe's Crisis of Culture," *Catholic Education Resource Center*, April 1, 2005, accessed July 27, 2012, http://catholiceducation.org/articles/politics/pg0143.html.

6

Resisting Gravity's Pull

Constructing Human Rights through the Arts

The challenges associated with building a durable culture of human rights are immense. Although the language of human rights now has a global purchase and the legal instruments designed to enforce compliance have been ratified in the majority of countries worldwide, securing respect for human rights appears to be as elusive as ever. As I discuss in the early chapters of this book, the philosophical foundations underpinning human rights continue to be criticized on the basis that they reflect a world view that purports to be universal but that in reality is Western. Throughout this work I have challenged the sweeping nature of this claim and have argued that, whatever its philosophical antecedents, from the late nineteenth century onward human rights thinking has been responsive to a plurality of cultural, philosophical, social, and religious perspectives. I go on to argue that this trajectory of increasing pluralism is not sufficient in itself to stem the criticism. So, even as there is a growing acceptance that human rights categories have ethical and political value, the philosophical basis of their claims is becoming ever more insecure. The central argument of this book is that, notwithstanding this crisis of meaning and legitimacy, human rights categories can and should be defended and that, hand in hand with this defense, there must be a rearticulation of the philosophical basis on which they are constructed. I suggest, in particular, that human rights discourse must be divested of the anthropological essentialism and transcendent rationalism that are legacies of the enlightenment philosophy from which contemporary human rights categories derive. Indeed, since the traces of this enlightenment philosophy are equally evident in theologies of human rights, I argue that this imperative also applies to the theological discourse of rights. Throughout this book I argue that the philosophical and theological bases of human rights claims must be rebuilt, and that nothing less than a fundamental reconsideration of the grounding of human rights is required. I attempt to sketch the contours of a renewed philosophical and theological grounding of human rights by focusing on the three pillars on which human rights discourse has heretofore depended—namely, the nature of the person, the universality of truth claims, and the role of community. I draw on feminist, postcolonial, and communitarian critiques of each of these categories to propose a rearticulation that I believe is more philosophically credible and more theologically resonant.

Human rights discourse is ultimately about individuals and the protections and freedoms to which they can lay claim. The traditional answer to the question about the basis on which individuals can claim these rights has been that all human beings share an essential nature and from this essential nature we can draw certain conclusions about how human flourishing can be secured. Chapter 3 challenges the assumption that it is feasible to speak abstractly about human nature and questions the idea that there are certain marks of the human that are self-evident, that can be read from the nature of persons, and that are universal and transhistorical. In that chapter, which is titled "Ethical Formations: Constructing the Subject of Human Rights," I argue that human rights discourse needs to develop a more dynamic and inclusive understanding of the subject, suggesting that its operative model is premised on an inadequate conceptualization of what is natural for human beings. In particular, I note that the classical account of human nature excludes from its definition many people that it ought to protect and I illustrate this by discussing how feminism has problematized many of our most basic assumptions about what is natural for human beings, including the presumption that gender is binary, that heterosexuality is normative, and that the meaning of embodiment is consistent across all cultures. In that chapter I suggest that a renewed discourse must find ways to capture the obligating features of being human other than the traditional appeal to a universal, transhistorical human nature. Indeed, I proposed that a new paradigm needs to be constructed around the specificity of human life, and must start by considering "the bonds of difference" rather than declaring the existence of a shared human nature abstracted from the particularities of life (i.e., "the bonds of sameness"). In this regard I suggest, for example, that a commitment to solidarity in our shared vulnerability rather than a declaration about the essential autonomy of all human beings may provide a more compelling basis for a human rights ethic. I note that human rights discourse need not eschew all talk about what we hold in common but rather must accept the ethical burden associated with articulating what is held in common. I also note that in so doing one must be vigilant about the itinerary of silence that may be embedded in any such discourse. Undoubtedly we will need to draw upon many different rhetorical devices in order to speak about the obligations that flow from the more dynamic models of subjectivity on which this new paradigm must be based. In this context I suggest that literary and other imaginative devices are likely to be vital in the attempts to articulate a provisional account of what human beings share and from which one can begin to build an ethic that will support human flourishing.

In chapter 4 I address the second "pillar" of traditional human rights discourse—namely, its claim to universality, a claim that I suggest is both the basis of its potency and the condition of its vulnerability. I argue that human rights discourse can no longer be conceived as a set of normative ethical principles to be grasped by the individual independently of the cultural, historical, and religious context she inhabits and from which conclusions that are believed to be objectively and universally true can be drawn. Rather, I propose that a renewed human rights discourse must acknowledge that the norms of rationality are enmeshed in lived traditions of inquiry and that, as a consequence, our understanding of what we are claiming when we assert that human rights are universal needs to be rethought. I ask what kind of universalism is possible in light of what we have come to understand about the nature of moral knowledge. And the answer I give is that the only universalism that is possible is one that is grounded in the recognition that all our knowledge of the world is contextual, one that acknowledges that the universalist convictions we articulate are enmeshed with the cultural values through which they are expressed, and one that accepts that the justifications we marshal are contingent on the conceptual frameworks through which they are intelligible. Indeed, I suggest that if one looks closely at the history of human rights discourse and leaves aside the overblown universalist and essentialist rhetoric that has accompanied it, one can see that it is, in fact, the story of one particular tradition's articulation of the rights to which all human beings should be able to lay claim, which over time, and as a result of the persuasiveness of its appeal, has evolved into a moral discourse that has global resonance.

Human rights discourse is thus redescribed as a form of situated knowledge and as a particularly compelling form of embedded universalism that allows us to think differently about the contested issue of the grounding of human rights. I challenge the traditional assumption that the viability of human rights discourse depends on the articulation of a single universally persuasive account of its foundations and argue that the history of human rights demonstrates that the discourse has endured precisely because it has been receptive to the many different justifications. More importantly, I argue that, from an epistemological perspective, the answer we give to the question of how to explain the foundations of human rights must be a pluralist one. A renewed philosophical and theological grounding of human rights, I suggest, must allow for the presence of a plurality of philosophical, religious, and cultural world views so that the universalism that emerges will be one that is articulated in the midst of multiple, inclusive, tradition-thick, cross-cultural conversations. I argue that a durable culture of human rights will only be attained when we understand more deeply the symbolic, cultural, and ethical worlds of the other, and that meaningful cross-cultural conversations about human dignity can only evolve in the context of such deep learning. Moreover, this deep learning can only occur if we engage with the aesthetic as well as the rational dimensions of the different traditions and world views.

In the preceding chapters of this book I focus on the need to ask the genealogical questions about the foundations of human rights, and particularly about how we conceptualize the critical categories of the person, of truth, and of community. In each case I have attempted to reconceptualize these important categories without recourse to anthropological essentialism or to enlightenment rationalism. I do so by reconceiving human rights discourse in a threefold manner: as ethical assertions about the critical importance of certain values for human flourishing; as an emerging consensus generated by situated communities who are open to internally and externally generated social criticism; and as emancipatory politics whose modus operandi is ultimately that of persuasion. When human rights discourse is reconceptualized in this way, it becomes clear that, although the language of philosophical and theological argument is likely to continue to be important, it will only take one a certain distance in the search for more viable discourse, and that the aesthetic dimensions of the different cultural, moral, and religious traditions will also be vital for this task.

In this chapter, the focus is on the role that aesthetic resources can play in the creation of a durable culture of human rights. First I discuss the contribution that the arts can make to the task of creating an imaginative space in which established parameters of moral concern can be challenged and expanded. I draw on the history of the evolution of human rights claims to demonstrate this point. The chapter then goes on to consider in more detail how the arts can help to expand the moral imagination and can enable a level of understanding that is qualitatively different from other more theoretical forms of discourse and argument. Here I focus on what I regard as some of the more fundamental dimensions of their contribution, but I am aware that there are many others. In particular, I discuss how the arts can provide a compelling account of where the threshold below which human dignity is irrevocably compromised lies (critical in the discussion of the right not to be tortured) and how they can require us to confront more honestly the destructive nature of violence. In drawing out these particular dimensions of the ways in which the arts can expand the moral imagination, it becomes clear that the arts articulate registers of truth beyond the scientific and philosophical and in this way make a unique contribution to the task of building a durable culture of human rights.

Expanding the Moral Imagination: The Role of the Arts

Philosophers and theologians have long since recognized that the imagination plays an important role in moral understanding, although the precise nature of that role has been the subject of debate through the centuries. Building on the idea that human beings have the capacity to think metaphorically and imaginatively, much of the discussion has focused on how the imagination shapes ethical deliberation and decision making. This issue of how the imagination shapes ethical deliberation goes to the heart of the ethical enterprise. As we encounter ethical challenges both traditional and new, the moral imagination enables us to transcend the limitations of inherited norms and explore new ways of thinking and doing. Moreover, its role is multidimensional. Among its many dimensions it allows for an appreciation of unfamiliar perspectives; it enables an emotional identification with positions previously unknown; it allows us to discern the likely harm or benefit that may result if particular actions or choices are undertaken; and it facilitates a fuller understanding of the complex lived realities of others, all of which are vital to the cross-cultural moral deliberation on which a durable culture of human rights depends.[1]

That the arts play a central role in cultivating and expanding the moral imagination is also well understood. Indeed, throughout the history of human rights, the arts have proven to be a particularly rich source of inspiration as traditional assumptions about privilege have ceded to new insights about human worth. In reflecting on the role of the arts in the politics of human rights, the poet Seamus Heaney highlights what he regards as one of the most important contributions that the arts can make, which he calls "the redress of poetry." In using the phrase "the redress of poetry," Heaney is referencing his influential Oxford lectures of the same title.[2] He comments that he first discovered this idea of redress in Simone Weil's *Gravity and Grace*, where Weil observes that "if we know in what way society is unbalanced, we must do what we can to add weight to the lighter scale."[3] In an essay to mark the sixtieth anniversary of the Universal Declaration of Human Rights, Heaney suggests that although the UN Declaration does not have the kind of influence associated with the interventions of a superpower, nonetheless its authority is significant and is akin to the redress of poetry. In particular, it adds the kind of weight of which Weil speaks and "contributes thereby to the maintenance of an equilibrium—never entirely achieved—between the rights and the wrongs."[4] In the context of considering what role the arts can play in promoting a human rights culture, Heaney's concept of the redress of poetry is a rich source of insight. And although Heaney's concern is with the art of poetry, I will pursue this analysis with the conviction that other forms of artistic expression too can effect the redress of which Heaney speaks.[5]

The Glimpsed Alternative

In *The Redress of Poetry* Heaney discusses the complex and manifold ways in which poetry can be understood in terms of redress. At its most fundamental level, the possibility of poetry as redress emerges "from its being a glimpsed alternative, a revelation of potential that is denied or constantly threatened by circumstances."[6] Of course this idea of poetry being "a glimpsed alternative" is deeply embedded in the way poets through the centuries have thought about their work. Heaney draws attention to this through his commentary on particular poems that speak about "crossing from the domain of the matter-of-fact to the imagined" and that allow him to reflect on what he calls "the frontier of writing"—namely, the line that divides "the actual conditions of our daily lives from the imaginative representation of those conditions in literature."[7] In his commentary on Robert Frost's "Directive," in which the remains of a farmhouse (which we learn was the site of lives lived in sorrow and anger) have become a children's playhouse, Heaney insists that poems such as this are "a showing forth of the way poetry brings human existence into a fuller life."[8] Poetry has the potential to transform the familiar into something rich and exotic but can also enable us to absorb and even reexperience loss (what Virgil called *lacrimae rerum*[9]) in such a way as to fill the reader with a momentary sense of freedom and wholeness. The evocation of a sense of what is possible beyond the actual conditions of our daily lives, the transformation of the experience of loss into "a fleeting glimpse of a potential order of things beyond confusion," these are at the heart of Heaney's conviction that poetry can be an important enabler of redress.

Heaney also speaks about his sense of poetry as being "the imagination pressing back against the pressure of reality, quoting Wallace Stevens' phrase about the nobility of poetry being 'a violence from within that protects us from a violence without.'"[10] The poetry of the celebrated English poets of the First World War exemplifies this ability of poetry to press back against the expectations of reality. During that war, as in many wartime situations, there was a tremendous, often unspoken pressure on all citizens to accept and support the government's account of the causes, objectives, and progress of the war. It is clear that many of the war poets themselves went to war without questioning the official view. Yet, through the writing of their poetry, they pressed back against the pressure of reality. They refused to dehumanize the enemy and instead captured the intensity of the suffering of all those on the front, enemy and ally alike. They resisted the ideologies of empire and repudiated the state for exalting the idea of dying for one's country. Instead, and with great effect, they revealed the folly and barbarity of such expectations. Thus, Wilfred Owen tells us that if we could hear, "at every jolt, the blood / Come gargling from the froth-corrupted lungs, / Obscene as cancer, bitter as the cud / Of vile, incurable sores on innocent tongues," then we would not tell "with such high zest / To children ardent for some desperate glory / The old Lie: Dulce et decorum est / Pro patria mori."[11]

The glimpsed alternative that poetry allows is also achieved through its unique ability to give voice to that which has hitherto been unexpressed. Indeed, this has been a fundamental dimension of artistic expression through the ages and has been a key resource for human rights thinking throughout the long history of its development. The history of human rights is essentially a story of the expansion of moral concern, and the gradual recognition that the rights to which a particular group of property-owning white males could lay claim ought to be extended first to other men, then to women, then to indigenous populations, then to those whose sexuality challenged the heteronormativity of the dominant culture.[12] Moreover, it is clear from that history that many of the critical moments in the expansion of human rights would never have happened without the poets and painters whose work gave voice to those who previously had been silent or silenced. One thinks of the extraordinary paintings of Francisco Goya, Pablo Picasso, Fernando Botero, and the poetry of Pablo Neruda and Maya Angelou. In the contemporary context we have become very familiar with this testimonial dimension of art so that its ability to effect redress is both well understood and routinely referenced. For example, Gayatri Spivak promotes this view through her conviction that humanities education can be a vital resource in addressing the itinerary of silence that still besets contemporary life. In this regard, however, Heaney urges us to guard against replacing one simplification with another. Thus, while Heaney acknowledges that it is possible to have a poetry that consciously seeks to promote political or cultural change while retaining its artistic integrity, he insists that the redress of poetry cannot serve any reductive ends and in fact is "at its most exquisite" when "the spirit is called extravagantly beyond the course that the usual life plots for it."[13] Poetry must not simplify. Rather, through the encounter with a work of art, "personal force is being moved through an aesthetic distance, and in a space where anything can happen the longed-for may occur by way of the unforeseen, or may be balked by the limitations of the usual."[14] The glimpsed alternative, therefore, even as it is tracing the itinerary of silence, is inevitably one of heightened complexity rather than of simplification.

An Imaginative Identification

One cannot underestimate the power and resonance of the glimpsed alternative in the work of the moral imagination. It has been and continues to be a critical factor in the expansion of our moral concern and has been vital to the task of building and sustaining a durable culture of human rights. Its transformative effect is particularly evident throughout the history of human rights and is also attested to in contemporary life. Moreover, as has already been discussed, the arts—perhaps more than any other artifact—are the primary means through which this glimpsed alternative is articulated. Equally important in the history of human rights, however, is the formative role that the arts have played in what might be called "the education of the moral sentiments." Over the last three centuries in particular there has been a gradual but unmistakable expansion of moral concern that has been a critical factor in the evolution of human rights and particularly in the articulation of the universality of those rights. Richard Rorty argues that it is this unprecedented growth of moral concern or empathy, more than any other factor, that accounts for the establishment of the contemporary culture of human rights. Rorty's argument about the centrality of empathy is both a philosophical and a historical one. He follows Annette Baier in endorsing David Hume's claim that "corrected sympathy, not law-discerning reason, is the fundamental human capacity."[15] Rorty augments this philosophical point by insisting that, historically, the emergence of the human rights culture seems to owe nothing "to increased moral knowledge and everything to hearing sad and sentimental stories," or what Baier calls "a progress of the sentiments."[16]

moral concern + empathy

In chapter 2, I argue that philosophies of human rights that are anchored in claims about the ahistorical nature of the human being are essentially incoherent and outmoded. I suggest further that, although human rights discourse has traditionally been premised on claims about human nature, there is no reason why this should continue to be the case. Rorty supports this position, suggesting that our growing willingness to neglect the question "what is our nature?" is one of the greatest advances of the last century and can be attributed to the fact that the more we have come to learn about our malleability, the less interested we have become in the question of our nature. As I argue, it is no longer necessary to defend human rights on the basis that human beings have a shared nature, the obligations of which can be understood through moral reasoning. Nor, according to Rorty, do we need to have an "assured knowledge of a truth about what we have in common" in order to promote and defend the idea that all human beings have an inalienable dignity that must be afforded protection.[17] Rather, the durability of human rights claims depends not on the sophistication of our arguments but rather on "an increasing ability to see the similarities between ourselves and people very unlike us as outweighing the differences."[18] It depends on our ability to answer the question about why we should care about a stranger, a person who is no kin to us, a person whose habits we find disgusting, with an answer like "because this is what it is like to be in her situation—to be far from home, among strangers, or because she might become your daughter-in-law, or because her mother would grieve for her."[19] In short Rorty argues, "such stories, repeated and varied over the centuries, have induced us, the rich, safe, powerful people, to tolerate and even cherish powerless people—people whose appearance or habits or beliefs at first seemed an insult to our own moral identity, our sense of the limits of permissible human variation."[20]

Lynne Hunt's *Inventing Human Rights: A History* reinforces Rorty's argument by illustrating the critical role that the literature has played in the evolution of human rights. What her analysis makes clear, however, is that literature's most important contribution to the establishment of human rights lies in the way it made possible the articulation of new kinds of individual experiences which in turn made possible new kinds of social and political concepts.[21] Histories that focus on the concept of human rights have rightly noted that there is a symbiotic relationship between the concept of individual autonomy and the idea of human rights. In addition, philosophical and theological analyses draw attention to the reciprocity implied in the idea of human rights, through the language of obligation or of virtue. Hunt affirms this view that, at least historically, the idea of human rights has depended on the development of concepts of autonomy and reciprocity (empathy), but she insists that the critical turning point came when these concepts became embedded in cultural practices. Hunt's historical analysis demonstrates that, although the concepts of autonomy and empathy had a long gestation in the philosophical and theological traditions of the West, it was not until the second half of the eighteenth century, with the advent of a popular culture of the arts (novels, portraiture, etc.) that these ideas gained a cultural significance that eventually transformed the moral landscape. Since then, most, if not all, of the critical turning points in the history of equality and justice have been accompanied by a flowering of literary and artistic expression that has given voice to those who had previously been marginalized, creating this imaginative identification, "frustrat[ing] common expectations of solidarity" and expanding the circle of moral concern.[22]

For Simone Weil, "obedience to gravity" is the greatest sin. That the arts enable us to resist gravity's pull affirms their importance for the work of the ethical imagination. In this, to paraphrase Heaney, the arts can come to represent "something like the exercise of the virtue of hope" as it is understood by Václav Havel, since for Havel hope "is not the conviction that something will turn out well, but the certainty that something makes sense, regardless of how it turns out."[23] The glimpsed alternative, the imaginative identification, each are essential for the articulation of the creative spaces in which established parameters of moral concern can be challenged and expanded. And it is through the arts more than any other artifact that the "imaginative transformation of human life" is accomplished. As Heaney rightly insists, this "imaginative transformation of human life is the means by which we can most truly grasp and comprehend it."[24]

Resisting Gravity's Pull: Constructing Human Rights through the Arts

Although significant political and legal progress has been made, human rights norms have yet to be fully embedded in the cultures and practices of societies worldwide. In the context of this ongoing challenge, it is suggested that the arts have a unique contribution to make to the establishment of this culture of rights. In this section, I give an account of what the arts uniquely can bring to this task. I do so by focusing on what I regard as two particularly challenging dimensions of human rights politics and by highlighting the particular and unique contribution that the arts can make to the task of addressing these difficult and contested aspects of human rights politics. First, I discuss how the arts can provide a compelling account of why the inalienability of fundamental human rights must never be ceded. Although the inalienability of fundamental human rights is frequently challenged in the context of ethical justifications of torture, I suggest that where rational argument fails, the arts succeed in establishing that there is a threshold below which human dignity is irrevocably compromised. In particular, the arts can capture better than any philosophical argument why we must resist the itinerary of silence that shrouds the politics of torture. I argue that the ethical justification of torture depends, to no small degree, on maintaining the darkness that is at the heart of torture but that it is often through the arts that the unspeakable can eventually be uttered. I move on to discuss a second major challenge and one of the most neglected dimensions of human rights politics today, the way in which violence, even when directed toward just ends, compromises the durability of a culture of rights. Yet again, it is the arts that challenge and undermine the persuasive appeal of reason when the case for the use of violence to establish human rights is made. I show how the arts will not allow us to sanitize or sacralize the use of violence, even for worthy ends, and will require us to confront more honestly its destructive nature. The task of establishing a culture based on respect for human rights is complex and will require all of the resources that we have at our disposal. In what follows, I demonstrate that the language of poetry as well as the language of politics has a central role to play in this process.

Human Dignity: Establishing a Threshold

Arguments justifying torture have grown in the post-9/11 world. Indeed, such is the nature of the global political discussion today that the previously established consensus on the right not to be tortured is, arguably, now under threat. Yet prior to 9/11, the ethical and legal prohibition on torture had been thoroughly embedded in international law. Article 5 of the UN Declaration of Human Rights states that "no one shall be subjected to torture or to cruel, inhuman or degrading treatment" and the International Covenant on Civil and Political Rights, which came into force in 1966, reinforces it. So too does the Convention against Torture and Other Cruel, Inhuman or Degrading Treatment or Punishment, which states categorically that "no exceptional circumstances whatsoever, whether a state of war or a threat of war, internal political instability or any other public emergency, may be invoked as a justification of torture."[25] The laws of war are also unequivocal about the permissibility of torture. Common article 3 of all four of the Geneva Conventions insists that the humanitarian laws of war provide protection against "violence to life and person, in particular

murder of all kinds, mutilation, cruel treatment and torture" and also protect against "outrages upon personal dignity, in particular humiliating and
degrading treatment."[26] Articles in the later conventions elaborate on this
right, as does the Additional Protocol I, which prohibits "torture of all
kinds, whether physical or mental."[27]

This legal consensus was hard won and is a relatively recent achievement. Historically, for example, in Greek and Roman societies and in the
Germanic world, various forms of torture were sanctioned in the different
legal codes. In these contexts, the permissibility of torture was determined
primarily by the nature and seriousness of the crime or by the status of the
accused. Notwithstanding this early rather permissive approach, however,
it was not until the twelfth century, when the new Romano-canonical legal
system was introduced, that torture gained a definitive and central place
in the society in terms of its approach to crime and punishment. An in-
quisitorial procedure replaced the earlier accusatorial one, and within the
new system a confession to a crime was regarded as "the queen of proofs."[28]
Moreover, torture was seen as an instrument to obtain a reliable confession.
Torture, according to Azo of Bologna, is "the inquisition of truth by torment," or according to the *Tractatus de tormentis* it is "an inquisition which
is made to elicit the truth by torment and suffering of the body."[29] Over
time the jurisprudence developed, delineating in great detail when torture
could and could not be used. The regulation of the use of torture was regarded as necessary in order to maintain an important distinction within
this new legal code—namely, that torture was not to be used to force a
guilty plea but rather to force a specific statement that contained details
that none but the criminal could know. Thus, between the thirteenth and
eighteenth centuries, torture was ubiquitous across Europe and the colonies. It had a role in generating a confession and in punishing for serious
crimes. And although there were restrictions on the use of torture (e.g., the
1689 British Bill of Rights prohibited cruel punishment), whipping, brand-
ing, execution by drawing and quartering, and other forms of what we
would now regard as cruel and inhuman punishment were all permitted.

The ethical case against torture was made consistently from the eighteenth century onward by Montesquieu, Voltaire, Beccaria, and others
who began to articulate the view that torture and cruel punishment was
incompatible with the emerging idea of human dignity and of the "rights
of man." Moreover, the ethical arguments were made in a context where

the legal system itself was undergoing a series of reforms that resulted in a diminished role for confession in the attempt to gain a conviction. The campaign against torture was consciously positioned within the context of arguments about the barbarity of the ancien régime ceding to enlightenment. Cesare Beccaria's *Essay on Crimes and Punishment*, first published in 1764, was hugely influential in making the moral case against the use of torture and cruelty in punishment. It was quickly translated into French, English, German, Spanish, Dutch, and Polish and widely disseminated and discussed. Denis Diderot's seminal *Encyclopedia* included an entry that argued against the use of torture by Chevalier Louis de Jaucourt, and in other countries around Europe torture was increasingly being seen as unacceptable. In France, the Jean Calas case was hugely influential in shaping public opinion against torture. In 1792 Calas was convicted of murdering his son to prevent him from converting to Catholicism and was sentenced to death by breaking on the wheel. The extreme barbarity of his death together with the fact that he died protesting his innocence generated a significant debate, led by Voltaire, on the acceptability of the use of torture and cruelty. Rather quickly thereafter, one by one the European powers began to give statutory effect to the abolition of torture so that within a few decades the practice of four centuries of legally sanctioned torture was undone. By the end of the eighteenth century, torture was banned in Prussia (1754), Sweden (1772), and Austria and Bohemia (1776) as well as in Britain and France.[30] The first Geneva Convention (1864) established a minimum threshold for the treatment of combatants, including prisoners and those who were sick and wounded, which almost immediately was accepted by the major powers. Thus the humanitarian laws of war, together with the gradual abolition of judicial torture in states around the world, created within a very short space of time a legal and political consensus in which the use of torture is forbidden.

However, in the post-9/11 world the ethical case against torture is being challenged and, in an assault on fundamental human rights, the legal protections are being dismantled. In the United States, in particular, the legal and moral arguments to support the use of torture and other forms of coercion are being marshaled with increasing force and regularity. When the US government admitted that it was using what it called enhanced interrogation techniques and enforced disappearance against those it defined as high-value detainees, there appeared to be little public outrage. In the words of Mark Danner, "the system of torture has . . . survived its disclosure."[31] The primary ethical argument supporting the use of torture is the "ticking bomb" scenario in which a bomb has been placed in a public place, one of the terrorists has been captured, and there is an opportunity to defuse the bomb if the terrorist can be made to disclose its location. Large numbers of people will be likely to be killed unless interrogators get the terrorist to talk. Of course, in the post-9/11 world the ticking bomb scenario has particular salience and resonance since countries that had previously believed they were relatively secure have suddenly had to contend with terrorist threats. Therefore, the ticking bomb scenario is no longer an abstraction but a real-life dilemma. It asks the question whether it is permissible to use torture for a specific purpose and for a worthy objective. The ticking bomb scenario is not new. It was used by Jeremy Bentham in the nineteenth century and more recently by Michael Walzer when discussing the problem of dirty hands.[32] However, in the post-9/11 world, it is being vigorously debated in public, political, military, and academic fora, and the hard-won consensus that human beings should not torture one another is being challenged by the ticking bomb problem.

The current academic discussion in the United States is characterized by a general willingness to reconsider the absolute prohibition on torture, although a number of philosophers, theologians, and political scientists have argued for the maintenance of the absolute prohibition. Kenneth Himes's work provides one such example.[33] The most robust defense of the use of torture is made by scholars who argue that it is morally defensible on principled grounds and not just permissible on pragmatic or utilitarian grounds. Mirko Bagaric and Julie Clarke, for example, suggest that the self-defense argument can be extended to the ticking bomb scenario. They

insist that it is morally permissible to torture in these circumstances since it is "in fact a manifestation of the right to self-defense, which extends to the right to defend another."[34] By and large, however, the justifications marshaled are consequentialist in nature. The most notable proponent of the use of torture in the post-9/11 world is legal scholar Alan Dershowitz, who has argued that it is morally permissible to use torture in the ticking bomb scenario because "the simple cost-benefit analysis for employing such nonlethal torture seems overwhelming: it is surely better to inflict nonlethal pain on one guilty terrorist who is illegally withholding information needed to prevent an act of terrorism than to permit a large number of innocent victims to die."[35] Dershowitz is concerned about the permissive effect that the ceding of the absolute prohibition may have on the society and so argues for a strict judicial regulation of torture, which he insists should only be used in exceptional circumstances. Daniel Statman and Michael Moore also accept that torture is permissible in the face of catastrophe, with Statman insisting that "the duty not to torture is overridden in a ticking bomb scenario by the duty to prevent negative consequences."[36] Others, like John T. Parry and Oren Gross, moderate this position by suggesting that the categorical ban on the use of torture should be maintained but can be overridden in certain exceptional circumstances and with full accountability.[37]

However, the right not to be tortured or to be subjected to cruel or inhuman punishment has a stronger force than almost any other human right. Within the current framework of international law, the right is absolute; it admits of no exceptions.[38] As David Gushee notes, there are many circumstances in which people can legally be killed but none under which they can legally be tortured. For example, it is perfectly legal (however tragic) to kill an enemy combatant in wartime but not at all legal to take that same person into custody, disarm him, and then torture him.[39] Moreover, the reason why there is no derogation from the obligation not to torture is because of the nature of torture and of its corrosive effects on the individuals involved as well as on the societies wherein it is permitted. Torture involves the deliberate infliction of extreme suffering on a person (usually in custody) in order to break that person's will. It is morally hazardous for the individuals and the society, in part because it has no self-limiting principle, something that even proponents of torture like Dershowitz admit. With utilitarian justification of torture, even when it is to be accompanied by legal oversight and monitoring, there is, in the end, permission to commit the worst atrocity imaginable as long as it is done in order to prevent another. Lord Gerald Austin Gardiner of Kittisford, who worked on an inquiry into techniques of interrogation in Northern Ireland, insists:

> If it is to be made legal to employ methods not now legal against a man whom the police believe to have, but who may not have, information which the police desire to obtain, I, like many of our witnesses, have searched for, but have been unable to find, either in logic or in morals, any limit to the degree of ill-treatment to be legalised. The only logical limit to the degree

of ill-treatment to be legalised would appear to be whatever degree of ill-treatment necessary to get information out of him, which would include, if necessary, extreme torture.[40]

Justifications of torture in the ticking bomb scenario will, in the end, permit any amount of pain to be inflicted and any form of degradation, torment, or humiliation to be meted out. Any conceivable assault on the person can be justified in the name of the benefits that are likely to be gained.[41] Indeed, as the many testimonials of survivors of torture confirm, there seems to be no limit to the horrors that torturers have visited on others. From the human rights perspective, torture represents a fundamental assault on human dignity; it breaches a threshold that should never be breached. Even though most contemporary philosophical and political justifications of torture acknowledge that it represents a fundamental assault on human dignity, nonetheless they are prepared to accept a situation in which human dignity is radically compromised (by representatives of the state and in the name of the society) in order to protect that society from what might be an even greater assault. The absoluteness of the suffering that can be perpetrated and justified is deeply disturbing and brings us to the heart of why a nonderogable prohibition must be upheld. Deliberately inflicted pain, degradation, and humiliation are designed to assault the dignity of the person in a fundamental way. Imprisonment intensifies the vulnerability of these persons whether they are guilty or innocent, whether they are in possession of relevant information or not. As Yuval Ginbar suggests, it is "the totality of the denial of any and every right" that is so disturbing. Torture also degrades and corrupts the perpetrator. Indeed, it is precisely this unlimited power to inflict whatever level and kind of pain and suffering on another human being that also makes torture so corrupting for the torturer. The perpetration of unspeakable acts of violence and depravity thus dehumanizes the torturer as well as the victim—a point that many survivors of torture have made. Aleksandr Solzhenitsyn, reflecting on his time in a Soviet gulag, could conclude that "our torturers have been punished most horribly of all: they are turning into swine, they are departing downward from humanity."[42] So, although one may seek to ignore the reality of what one has done, there is no escape. Thus, X in Willie Doherty's *Secretion* discovered that

as the days darkened and the solitary
winter nights of confinement within the mouldy
walls of the house engulfed him, his condition
worsened and the lesions festered and spread
quickly to cover his entire body.[43]

As many commentators have insisted, any nation that permits or justifies torture is doomed, in the end, to "moral corruption and decay."[44] Thus, in sanctioning the most indescribable acts of torture and cruelty, a society "creates a moral black hole, one that may be small enough in diameter, admitting one or two victims at a time, but the depths of the inhumanity which it allows and justifies are unfathomable—enough to swallow our morality, our humanity whole."[45]

So how can the arts enable us to resist the persuasive appeal of the argument that it is permissible to visit unspeakable acts of cruelty on one person in order to protect many innocents from suffering and death? Can the arts bolster the argument for the maintenance of the absolute prohibition of torture and thereby ensure that this moral black hole does not swallow our humanity whole? The poet Theodore Roethke suggests that "In a dark time, the eye begins to see," and that we meet our shadows "in the deepening shade."[46] Yet it is clear that we need more than philosophical and political argument in order that the eye can see, in order that the shadows are acknowledged, in order that we recognize that accepting the admissibility of torture represents a failure of morality, a failure of humanity.

One of the most common and pernicious features of the contemporary practice of torture relates to the manner in which it is hidden from view. Indeed, even when states seek to normalize the use of torture, albeit in emergency situations, the details of the practice and what it involves remain concealed. Most ethical justifications of torture refuse to confront the barbarity and degradation involved in the practice or the permanence of its destructiveness. The language of enhanced interrogation techniques functions to obscure the totalizing violence visited on fellow human beings so that in the modern state torture is an act of silence rather than an act of spectacle (as it was in earlier times). Thus today torture flourishes only in dark places, and those who seek to maintain regimes of torture depend on this silence being maintained.

However, the personal testimonies of survivors of torture—whether expressed through documentary or fictionalized narratives, through the visual or literary arts, or through music—make no such concessions and insist that those who tolerate torture need to acknowledge the full reality of what it involves.[47] Indeed, it is here that the arts, perhaps more than any other forms of expression, come into their own since it is through the arts that the trauma of abjection and the disorientation of liminality can be best expressed. At a certain level, all that can be uttered is a cry of desolation and lament, as is evoked, for example in Henryk Górecki's *Symphony of Sorrowful Songs*. At another level, it is through the arts that the unspeakable nature of radical human suffering can be conveyed and the corrupting influence of absolute power can be revealed. Artists from Goya to Botero have helped us to understand the shocking brutality of torture through the graphic nature of their works. Thus, in both Francisco Goya's *Disasters of War* and Fernando Botero's *Abu Ghraib Paintings* the viewer is confronted with the bodies of the victims so that we cannot abstract the political "necessity" of torture from the bodies that suffer.[48] And although Chilean artist Guillermo Núñez uses nonfigurative representations of the tortured body, nonetheless his paintings evoke a similar response. For example, in *Only the Mountain Dew on Your Face Only Your Scream in the Wild*, the sheer physicality of torture is evoked symbolically through the flesh and blood of body parts. The sinewy flesh, the eviscerated organs, and the spilled blood remind the viewer of the thousands of tortured bodies hidden from view.[49] The frankness of these visual portrayals of torture, whether figurative or abstract, challenges the evasions and hypocrisies that have characterized political discussions about the acceptability of torture. The broken and bloodied bodies, the torn and tormented flesh resist abstraction and shock the viewer into seeing the singularity and particularity of each act of torture. These images also capture the sexualized brutality and humiliation that has been documented by survivors of torture around the world. No fictions constructed through the language of enhanced interrogation techniques can obscure the truth about the practice of torture. The Botero *Abu Ghraib* sequence is especially interesting since it stands alongside the documentary evidence of the particular acts of torture that it represents. Few can forget the iconic images of soldiers leading a German shepherd dog toward a blindfolded Iraqi prisoner, whose hands were tied behind his back and his genitals exposed, or of naked, bruised, blindfolded, and shackled prisoners in poses designed to humiliate. Botero's extraordinary sequence of paintings mirrors what is captured in the photographs of these acts of torture—photographs, it should be remembered, that were taken by the perpetrators of this torture. His sequence simultaneously reveals the particularity of each assault and the universality of its impact. He thus frames these particular atrocious acts in such a way that forces the viewer beyond the particularity of these shameful events to confront the nature of torture as the most fundamental assault on human dignity. In so doing, he reminds us that

> There are things
> We live among "and to see them
> Is to know ourselves."[50]

The fundamental assault on human dignity that torture represents is reinforced through the permanency of its impact. Holocaust survivor Jean Améry speaks of this, insisting that "whoever was tortured stays tortured. Torture is ineradicably burned into him, even when no clinically objective traces can be found."[51] The traumatization causes an irreparable loss of what Améry calls trust in the world, which stays with the person who has been tortured and becomes a dominating feature of the person's interior life.[52] Writers Elie Wiesel, Primo Levi, Toni Morrison, and Alicia Partnoy each convey a sense of the extreme isolation that the experience of torture imparts to the survivor.[53] This humiliation and abuse functions to sever a fundamental connection between the victim and her fellow human beings since she has to confront what most manage to avoid—namely, the knowledge of what humans are capable of doing to one another. It is no surprise, therefore, that the blindfold figures prominently in artistic renditions of torture and its effects. Núñez's celebrated exhibit *Que hay en el fondo de tus ojos* (What is there in the depth of your eyes) interrogates the significance of the blindfold and asks the viewer to confront what is in the depths of their own eyes having seen the barbarity of which we are capable.[54] The motif of the blindfold appears in much of the Abu Ghraib–inspired art too, including that of Iraqi sculptor Abdul Karim Khalili, whose marble and bronze figures convey the ultimate isolation and desolation of the victim of torture.[55] The hooded figure also reminds us that torture disrupts ordinary human relationships in the most fundamental of ways. The hooded

figure is stripped of her ability to communicate and isolated from her fellow human beings, and her identity and individuality are obliterated. This
assault on the individuality of the one on whom torture has been visited
is also movingly captured in an exhibit in the Holocaust Memorial Museum in Washington, DC. On the third floor of the museum one enters a
space where one is confronted with thousands of worn and battered shoes.
Confiscated from prisoners in the Majdanek concentration camp on the
outskirts of Lublin, Poland, the pitiful sight is a testament to the erasure of
identity and the loss of individuality.[56] When juxtaposed with Ai Weiwei's
Sunflower Seeds, it stands as a powerful reminder of the fundamental threat
to human dignity that torture represents.[57]

In his essay "Ruins and Poetry," Czeslaw Milosz suggests that "death is
not always the greatest menace," something that the art of Goya, Botero,
Núñez, Partnoy, Levi, and others confirm.[58] These extraordinary artistic
works help us to see how deeply torture brutalizes the victim, how utterly
it depraves the victimizer, and how fundamentally it corrupts the society.
They allow us to see why Milosz could suggest that its menace may indeed
be greater than death. Thus we affirm the most recent position taken by
Henry Shue since it articulates exactly why a society should never cross this
threshold. Shue explains:

> So now I take the most moderate position on torture, the position nearest
> to the middle of the road, feasible in the real world: never again. Never, ever,
> exactly as international law indisputably requires. If the perfect time for
> torture comes, and we are not prepared to prevent a terroristic catastrophe,
> we will at least know that we have not sold our souls and we have not bru-
> talized the civilization. These are catastrophes we can actually avoid. Some
> of us may, or may not, as a result of our refusal to tolerate secret torture
> bureaucracies and their gulags, die in some other catastrophe, but civilized
> principles will survive for future generations, who may be grateful for our
> sacrifice so that they may live decent lives.[59]

Overcoming the Logic of Violence

The second area of concern relates to the use of violence in the process
of establishing basic human rights, and specifically in deploying military
force to halt gross violations of human rights. There is no doubt that this

is one of the most difficult issues in political ethics today, notwithstanding the fact that there is a broad consensus among ethicists on the admissibility and necessity of the use of violence in order to achieve humanitarian outcomes. Philosophers Michael Walzer, Brian Orend, and Jean Bethke Elshtain and theologians David Hollenbach, Ken Himes, and Nigel Biggar each defend versions of the just war tradition that allow it to be used to justify military interventions in sovereign states for the purposes of ending gross violations of human rights. Moreover, the Responsibility to Protect doctrine, adopted by the United Nations in 2005, gives the United Nations the ability to intervene militarily in the context of grave abuses of human rights, including genocide, ethnic cleansing, crimes against humanity, and war crimes.[60] It is difficult to argue against the position that holds that in such extreme circumstances, the only ethical course of action is to deploy violence to resist evil. In these situations, the political, economic, historical, humanitarian, and ethical imperatives all converge to make violence seem compelling, necessary, valuable, even inevitable. Rwanda 1994 serves as a caution against any diminution of the commitment to wage war to achieve humanitarian ends. However, even when it is directed toward just ends, the use of violence radically compromises the durability of a culture of human rights. As I have argued elsewhere, the ethical appeal of violence is only compelling because of a fundamental failure of politics, a failure to prioritize nonviolent conflict resolution, a failure to address grievances (real or imagined), a failure to build a culture of respect for human rights.[61]

As we seek to build a durable culture of human rights, we must push back against the weight of this reality and challenge the dominance of the just war paradigm in the ethical responses of these limit situations. In particular, we must consider why human rights advocates have accepted violence as a means of effecting justice and why violence has captured our ethical and political imaginations to such an extent that those who promote nonviolence seem at best naive and at worst irresponsible. Even if the conclusion remains that, as a last resort, violence should be used to achieve humanitarian ends, the fundamental questions about the nature of violence and its impact should not be bypassed. It is vital that we are  clear-sighted about the nature of the violence through which humanitarian interventions are pursued and that we attend to the particularity of the brutality of violence, even when pursued to secure basic human rights. And it is essential that we can understand as fully as possible the multiple meanings that this violence carries. No doubt it is difficult for those of us who have never endured physical violence to understand the havoc that violence creates. Yet those of us who are concerned about the ethical questions raised by the use of violence, particularly in situations of grave humanitarian crisis, do need to gain some proximity to the perspectives of those who have both experienced and perpetrated violence, and it is here, I suggest, that the arts can help.

This consideration is to the fore in my teaching and in the attempt to gain better proximity to the ethical issues at stake. In that context I bring my students to The Hague, to the International Criminal Tribunal for the Former Yugoslavia. Over the years we have observed a number of cases, all involving charges of war crimes and crimes against humanity. In 2007 the case we observed involved the supposed evacuation of a hospital in Vukovar.[62] Before we take our places in Trial Chamber II, we read over the indictment against the individuals whose case we were about to observe. It makes for chilling reading. The accused are charged on the basis of individual criminal responsibility and superior criminal responsibility, with five counts of crimes against humanity and three counts of violations of the laws or customs of war.[63] The indictment relates to an incident that occurred on November 19, "at eleven o' clock in the morning, as Vukovar's crisis headquarters tried, unsuccessfully, to make contact with the outside world." The JNA (Yugoslav People's Army) "entered the hospital complex. To the terror of those inside, they arrived ahead of the international monitors" who, it had been agreed the day before, were to supervise the evacuation. In fact, "the International Committee of the Red Cross truck, carrying medicine for the sick, arrived at six in the evening. By then the JNA had begun to evacuate the sick" and wounded, "without international supervision, and in contravention of the previous day's agreement. . . . The JNA began to separate the men from the women and children . . . and loaded the men onto buses."[64] The buses left the hospital and proceeded to the JNA barracks from whence some of the detainees were then transported to a farm building in Ovčara, where soldiers beat them. Soldiers then transported their non-Serb captives in groups of about 10 to 20 to a ravine in the direction of Grabovo where they killed at least 264 Croats and other non-Serbs from Vukovar Hospital. After the killings the bodies of the victims were buried by bulldozer in a mass grave at the same location.[65] The indictment we hear alleges that the three individuals before us in Trial Chamber II were present in the Vukovar Hospital and were involved in the commission of murder, torture, cruel treatment, extermination, and inhumane acts. It further alleges that two of the individuals (Miroslav Radić and Veselin Šljivančanin) personally participated in the selection of detainees who were to be loaded on buses.

On this particular day of testimony, the then mayor of Vukovar justified his decision to allow the so-called evacuation prior to the arrival of the international monitors, and we struggle to comprehend how the three men before us have come to be charged with such heinous crimes. The historical and political texts we have consulted in advance of our trip help to explain the context. Tim Judah explains how different historical narratives impact on the current political situation and Slavenka Drakulić, though she expresses her incomprehension at the speed and ferocity of the killing, illuminates for us the political culture that helps explain the collective passivity in the face of rising threats.[66] Psychological studies, too, form part of our picture as we contemplate what it might mean to have committed these crimes. And yet, notwithstanding the cumulative weight of this analysis, our questions persist. As the human faces of this atrocity appear before us, our conversation turns to whether one can ever really understand the nature of violence and, more particularly, whether the difficulties of understanding and communication are properly appreciated among those who discuss the ethics of employing violent force to halt gross violations of human rights.

Perhaps it is because violence is so pervasively and persistently represented and because we effectively live in a "society of spectacle" that we assume we know what we are talking about when we come to assess the violence that is at the heart of war.[67] Yet ethical assessments of war rarely pause to ask what violence requires of the person, what being a perpetrator of acts of violence does to the person, how violence impacts on the victim, to what extent the nature of violence can be communicated, how legitimizations of violence function, and how the hazards of idolatry and self-legitimization in the creation of justifications for war can be mitigated.[68] Even when these questions are aired, the focus of the inquiry tends to be a rather narrow and truncated one that is primarily concerned with its intellectual aspects. In fact, we need to adopt many modes of engagement if we are to begin to understand more fully the nature of violence. Over the years, however, I have come to believe that, irrespective of the sophistication of our analysis, reason alone will not deliver an understanding of the nature of violence and its impact on victim and victimizer alike. It is precisely here that we confront the limits of reason. Our questioning needs to leave room for us—indeed, needs to enable, to encourage, and even to prompt us—to cast ourselves (however imperfectly) in the place of the other in the hope that we can begin to comprehend the nature of the ethical questions that recourse to violence raises.

Yet how can one imaginatively inhabit the world of another who has lived through a genocide and seen family and friends tortured and killed? Can one ever begin to understand the mind of one who has committed atrocious acts, one who has rounded up the non-Serb male patients in a hospital, led them onto buses, and arranged for the disposal of their bodies after they had been murdered? In these contexts, there are only partial faltering answers to such questions. In my teaching, I have found that the visual and literary arts are invaluable as I attempt to capture the texture of the ethical questions that are at stake. I have concluded that it is the works of the photographers and the poets even more than the political theorists and theologians that best illuminate the ethical sensibilities in question. In particular, I mention some visual pieces that I use in part because they are so rarely reflected on by ethicists but more importantly because they attempt to represent the unrepresentable; they create a climate in which the emotional, intellectual, and ultimately the ethical aspects of the enactment of violence can be more fully captured.

Representing the Unrepresentable

In a world where visual representations of violence abound and in which the sheer volume of these images can lead to the desensitization of our critical and emotional capacities, it is easy to dismiss the moral power of such representations. Susan Sontag is correct to insist that the viewer ought to be aware of the limits of what can be expressed and communicated with respect to the enactment of violence. And yet, as *Regarding the Pain of Others* recognizes, particular photographs and video installations can indeed capture those aspects of violence that are not amenable to easy representation and as a result can create a context in which the moral questions can be raised in a different register. Moreover, this is the case regardless of how graphic or otherwise the representation may be. Of course, constantly in one's mind are questions about how the line between voyeurism and glamorization, on the one hand, and truthful communication, on the other, can be drawn. Despite the ambivalence of many visual images, they often prompt us to ask questions that rarely surface in discussions about the ethics of war, most especially when they force us to think about the enactment of violence in its totality and in the context of the impact it has on victim-survivors and on victimizers.

Warning SHOTS!, an exhibition of contemporary art that explored conflict and violence and that toured a number of cities in Great Britain in 2000, included an array of visual pieces that, without resorting to melodrama or sentimentality, conveyed an understanding of some aspects of the nature of violence that are unusually difficult to represent. The pieces by Monica Oechsler, Willie Doherty, and Christine Borland were especially striking in terms of challenging the viewer to connect with particular aspects of violence. With her four-and-a-half-minute video titled *Strip* playing in continuous loop, Monica Oechsler creates in the viewer an escalating sense of foreboding and terror as girls as young as eight strip down and reassemble handguns, singing nursery rhymes as they do so. The girls belonged to the only British gun club licensed to have members as young as eight years old. We only see the girls from the neck down as they expertly strip their guns and put them back together again. Our foreboding arises because, having initially been soothed and somewhat mesmerized by their rhythmic singing of nursery rhymes, it gradually begins to dawn on us that they do not understand the power they have with the loaded weapons in their hands. We wonder what they intend to do, who they are, whether they can be trusted not to shoot, whether they are damaged or traumatized in some way. Of course, their youth and the juxtaposition of the nursery rhymes with lethal weapons accentuates the sense of foreboding, yet it is the fluency with which they handle these weapons, the fascination that their power holds and most of all the sheer arbitrariness of the "decision" to use them that creates the sense of menace. In another exhibit Willie Doherty's photograph *At the Border V (Isolated Incident)* presents us with an image of a stained and torn mattress dumped by the roadside somewhere in Northern Ireland. The context imbues this not-uncommon sight of a discarded mattress on the roadside with a particular significance since we know that the holes in the mattress are most likely bullet holes. In this image the pitiless isolation of both victim and victimizer is vividly and unbearably on show. The viewer is immediately prompted to ask what it would mean to have this as one's last encounter in life, one's final experience and memory. One is forced to ask what it would mean to be the one who walked away from this scene, having inflicted lethal violence on another person who was most likely a neighbor, a colleague, or even a friend. The shocking finality and absurdity of violence is expertly evoked in Christine Borland's installation *The Quickening, the Lightening, the Crowning*. The viewer enters a dark walled space (a womb?) in which is displayed anatomical models of childbirth while one listens to a soundtrack of a fetal heartbeat running continuously. Overlaying this is another soundtrack, this time of gunfire created with the guns that were handed over to the police during the amnesty that followed the Dunblane killings.[69] The juxtaposition of the protective space and the strong, rhythmic fetal heartbeat with the roar of the gun expresses better than the most subtle of arguments the beauty and preciousness of the individual life and brings us face to face with the radical destructiveness that such weapons bring.

Sontag may well be correct that those of us who have not experienced the violence of war "can't imagine how dreadful, how terrifying war is; and how normal it becomes. Can't understand, can't imagine." Yet Oechsler, Doherty, and Borland in their respective ways hold our gaze and require us to look again at the practice that is war. The arts, both visual and literary, enable the viewer to raise the ethical questions in a different way. They help us think about what it means to participate in acts of brutality; they prompt us to think about the lure of violence, about the nature of accountability, about the vulnerabilities of ordinary people, about complicity, and about the abdication of responsibility. Most of all, perhaps, they issue a summons to abandon the fictional realities about war that we have created and ultimately a summons to acknowledge head-on the horror that is war. In her magisterial *Foundations of Violence* the late Grace Jantzen argues that we will only be able to resist what she calls the "necrophilic *habitus* of modernity" once we have begun to construct alternative political, ethical, and religious discourses—that is, discourses that no longer valorize, sacralize, or justify violence.[70]

There is no doubt that the arts can make a distinctive and unique contribution to the construction of alternative discourses, not least in what they teach us about the nature of violence. They can force us to look again at the destructiveness of violence even when it is pursued for noble ends. They

can challenge the dominance of the prevailing consensus about the acceptability of the use of violence to secure human rights. They can help us to
restore our faith in politics. They can insist on the imagined identification,
can articulate the glimpsed alternative, can allow us to resist gravity's pull,
and can call the spirit beyond the course that the usual life plots for it. In
this imagined transformation, the hope and the promise of just peacemak-
ing becomes possible and with it our best chance of creating a durable
culture of human rights.

Notes

1. There is an extensive literature in this field. Of particular note are Martha Nussbaum's *Love's Knowledge: Essays on Philosophy and Literature* (New York:
Oxford University Press, 1990) and Mark Johnson's *Moral Imagination: The Importance of Cognitive Science for Ethics* (Chicago: University of Chicago Press,
1994).

2. Seamus Heaney, *The Redress of Poetry* (London: Faber & Faber 1995).

3. Ibid., 3, quoting Simone Weil, *Gravity and Grace*, with an introduction and
postscript by Gustave Thubon, trans. Emma Crawford and Mario von der Ruhr
(London: Routledge, 2002), 117.

4. Seamus Heaney, "The Poetic Redress," in *From the Republic of Conscience:
Stories Inspired by the Universal Declaration of Human Rights*, commissioning editor Sean Love, 15–21 (Dublin: Liberties Press, 2009), at 18. This essay was written
to mark the sixtieth anniversary of the Universal Declaration of Human Rights.

5. Heaney, "The Poetic Redress," 18.

6. Heaney, *Redress of Poetry*, 4.

7. Ibid., xii, xvi.

8. Ibid., xvii.

9. Ibid., xv.

10. Ibid., 1, quoting the Wallace Stevens essay, "The Nobel Rider and the
Sound of the Words," published in 1942.

11. Wilfred Owen, "Dulce et decorum est," in *Collected Poems of Wilfred Owen*,
edited with an introduction and notes by C. Day Lewis, and with a memoir by
Edmund Blunden (London: Chatto & Windus, 1963), 55.

12. This account of the broadening scope of human rights norms represents
the pattern in most parts of the world, although in some places the pattern is
slightly different; for example, in some countries women achieved recognition
before certain men.

13. Heaney, *Redress of Poetry*, 16.

14. Ibid., 11.

15. Annette Baier, "Hume the Women's Moral Theorist?" in *Women and Moral Theory*, ed. Eva Kittay and Diana Meyers, 37–55 (Totowa, NJ: Rowman & Littlefield, 1987), 40.

16. Christopher J. Voparil and Richard J. Bernstein, eds. "Human Rights Rationality and Sentimentality," in *The Rorty Reader* (Oxford: Wylie-Blackwell, 2012), 355, 362, referring to Annette Baier's *A Progress of Sentiments: Reflections on Hume's Treatise* (Cambridge, MA: Harvard University Press, 1991).

17. Voparil and Bernstein, *Rorty Reader*, 363.

18. Ibid., 362.

19. Ibid., quoting Baier, *Progress of Sentiments*, 312.

20. Ibid., 365.

21. Lynne Hunt, *Inventing Human Rights: A History* (New York: W. W. Norton, 2007), 34.

22. Heaney, *Redress of Poetry*, 3.

23. Ibid., 4, quoting Václav Havel, *Disturbing the Peace*, translated from Czech and with an introduction by Paul Wilson (London: Faber & Faber, 1990), 181.

24. Heaney, *Redress of Poetry*, xv.

25. Convention against Torture and Other Cruel, Inhuman or Degrading Treatment or Punishment, article 2, December 10, 1984, 1465, UNTS 85, www.ohchr.org/EN/ProfessionalInterest/Pages/CAT.aspx.

26. The full texts of the Geneva Conventions are available on the International Committee of the Red Cross website, https://www.icrc.org/eng/war-and-law/treaties-customary-law/geneva-conventions/overview-geneva-conventions.htm.

27. Protocol Additional to the Geneva Conventions of August 12, 1949, and Relating to the Protection of Victims of International Armed Conflicts (Protocol I), art. 75, June 8 1977.

28. Edward Peters, *Torture* (Oxford: Blackwell, 1985), 44.

29. Ibid., 55.

30. Hunt, *Inventing Human Rights*, 76.

31. Mark Danner, "We Are All Torturers Now," *New York Times*, January 6, 2005.

32. See the excellent discussion of Bentham's view on torture in W. L. Twining and P. E. Twining, "Bentham on Torture," *Northern Ireland Legal Quarterly* 24, no. 3 (1973): 305–56. See also Michael Walzer, "Political Action: The Problem of Dirty Hands," *Philosophy and Public Affairs* 2 (1973): 160–67.

33. Kenneth Himes, "Why Is Torture Wrong," *Journal of Peace and Justice Studies* 21, no. 2 (2011): 42–55.

34. Mirko Bagaric and Julie Clarke, "Not Enough Official Torture in the World? The Circumstances in Which Torture Is Morally Justifiable," *University of San Francisco Law Review* 39 (2005): 143.

35. Alan M. Dershowitz, *Why Terrorism Works: Understanding the Threat, Responding to the Challenge* (New Haven, CT: Yale University Press, 2002), 143.

36. Daniel Statman, "The Absoluteness of the Prohibition against Torture" [Hebrew], 4 *Mishpat u-Mimshal* 161, (1997): 172.

37. See John T. Parry, "Escalation and Necessity: Defining Torture at Home and Abroad," in *Torture: A Collection*, ed. Sanford Levinson, 145–64 (Oxford: Oxford University Press, 2004), 158; and Oren Gross, "The Prohibition of Torture and the Limits of the Law," in *Torture: A Collection*, edited by Sanford Levinson, 229–53 (Oxford: Oxford University Press, 2004), 240–41.

38. This is why the Bush administration's sanction of torture and coercion as legitimate tools of interrogation is of such concern.

39. David P. Gushee, "Against Torture: An Evangelical Perspective," *Theology Today* 63 (2006): 354, commenting on Lisa Hajjar's "Torture and the Future," *Middle East Research and Information Project*, May 2004, www.merip.org/mero/interventions/torture-future.

40. Report of the Committee of the Privy Counsellors Appointed to Consider Authorized Procedures for the Interrogation of Persons Suspected of Terrorism, Cmmd No, 4901 (Lord Parker of Waddington, Chairman, 1972), para. 20 (2) of the minority report, quoted in Yuval Ginbar, *Why Not Torture Terrorists? Moral, Practical and Legal Aspects of the "Ticking Bomb" Justification for Torture* (Oxford: Oxford University Press, 2008), 66.

41. There is an extensive discussion about whether torture generates reliable information. See John Ip, "Two Narratives of Torture," *Northwestern Journal of International Human Rights* 7, no. 1 (Spring 2009): 35–77, especially 49–64 for the most recent analysis of the debate on this matter.

42. Aleksandr Solzhenitsyn, *The Gulag Archipelago 1918–1956: An Experiment in Literary Imagination*, translated from the Russian by Thomas O. Whitney (Parts I–IV) and Harry Willets (Parts V–VII), edited from the original three-volume edition by Edward E. Ericson Jr., (London: The Folio Society, 2005); part 4, "The Soul and Barbed Wire: The Ascent," 304.

43. Willie Doherty, *Secretion*, Film and Text (Dublin: Irish Museum of Modern Art, 2012).

44. George Hunssinger, "Torture, Common Morality and the Golden Rule: A Conversation with Michael Perry," *Theology Today* 63 (2006): 375–79, at 375.

45. Ginbar, *Why Not Torture Terrorists?*, 91.

46. Theodore Roethke, "In a Dark Time," in *Collected Poems of Theodore Roethke* (New York: Doubleday, 1961).

47. Many organizations worldwide document and validate the reliability of claims about the use of torture. Human Rights Watch is one of the most reliable of such organizations. Its report *Torture Archipelago: Arbitrary Arrests, Torture*

and Enforced Disappearances in Syria's Underground Prisons since March 2011 (www
.hrw.org/sites/default/files/reports/syria0712webwcover_0.pdf) details the torture
methods in use in Syria, but these reports are similar to reports from other parts
of the world. They include "prolonged and severe beating, punching and kick-
ing; beating with objects (cables whips sticks batons pipes); *falaqa* (beating the
victim with sticks, batons or whips on the soles of the feet); *shabeh* (hanging the
victim from the ceiling by the wrists so that his toes barely touch the ground or
he is completely suspended in the air with his entire weight on his wrists, causing
extreme swelling and discomfort); *balanco* (hanging the victim by the wrists tied
behind the back); *basat al-reeh* tying the victim down to a flat board, the head
suspended in the air so that the victim cannot defend himself. One variation of
this torture involves stretching the limbs while the victim lies on the board (as on a
rack); . . . electrocution; mock execution; . . . sexual violence; . . . pulling out fin-
gernails; . . . use of acid to burn skin; burning; and prolonged nudity." Other survivor accounts from Chile, Argentina, and elsewhere recount experiences of rape,
including with objects and animals as well as the extreme mutilation of body parts.

48. Goya, *Disasters of War.* These plates were first produced between 1810 and
1820 and have been reproduced individually and collectively many times. The
plates are currently available in many editions, including *Disasters of War* (Dover:
Dover Fine Art, History of Art, 1967); and G. Roger Denson, "Torture and Terror
in Art History and the Healing Power of Revelation," *Huffington Post*, February 1, 2013,
accessed July 22, 2013, www.huffingtonpost.com/g-roger-denson/torture-and-terror
-in-art_b_2600028.html. Botero produced eighty-seven drawings and paintings,
many of which he donated to the University of California Berkeley Art Museum.

49. See Macarena Gómez-Barris's discussion in "Torture Sees and Speaks:
Guillermo Núñez's Art in Chile's Transition," *Journal on Social History and Literature in Latin America* 5, no. 1 (Fall 2007): 86–107, at 94.

50. George Oppen, "Of Being Numerous (1–22)," *New Collected Poems* (New
York: New Directions Publishing Corporation 2008).

51. Jean Améry, *At the Mind's Limit: Contemplation by a Survivor of Auschwitz
and Its Realities* (New York: Schocken, 1986), 34.

52. Ibid., 28.

53. See, for example, Elie Wiesel, *Night* (London: MacGibbon & Kee, 1960);
Primo Levi, *If This Is a Man* (London: New England Library, 1962); Toni Morri-
son, *Beloved* (London: Vintage 1997); and Alicia Partnoy, *The Little School Tales of
Disappearance and Survival in Argentina* (London: Virago Press, 1988).

54. Gómez-Barris, "Torture Sees and Speaks," 101.

55. Discussed in Denson, "Torture and Terror."

56. United States Holocaust Memorial Museum, photo 19 of 93, accessed January 16, 2015, http://www.ushmm.org/information/exhibitions/permanent/shoes.

57. "Ai Weiwei's *Sunflower Seeds* Opens at Mary Boone Gallery in New York," *Huffington Post*, January 3, 2012, www.huffingtonpost.com/2010/01/03/ai-weiweis-sunflower-seeds-nyc_n_1182019.html.

58. Czeslaw Milosz, "Ruins and Poetry," *New York Review of Books*, March 17, 1983, accessed July 22, 2013, www.nybooks.com/articles/archives/1983/mar/17/ruins-and-poetry/?pagination.

59. Henry Shue, "Torture in Dreamland: Disposing of the Ticking Bomb," *Case Western Reserve Journal of International Law* 37 (2005): 231–39, at 238–39.

60. International Development Research Centre, *The Responsibility to Protect: Report of the International Commission on Intervention and State Sovereignty* (Ottowa, ON, Canada: International Development Research Centre, 2001) was adopted at the Sixtieth Session of the UN General Assembly 2005 as the World Summit Outcome Document.

61. Stanley Hauerwas, Linda Hogan, and Enda McDonagh, "The Case for the Abolition of War in the Twenty-First Century," *Journal of the Society of Christian Ethics* 25, no. 2 (2005): 17–35.

62. Laura Silber and Allan Little describe this event in detail in *The Death of Yugoslavia* (Harmondsworth, UK: Penguin Books, 1996), 179–80.

63. See the Case Information Sheet "Vukovar Hospital" (IT-95-13/1), *The Prosecutor v. Mile Mrkšić, Miroslav Radić & Veselin Šljivančanin*, prepared by the Communications Service of the International Criminal Tribunal for the former Yugoslavia, and available at www.icty.org, accessed July 23, 2013. According to the indictment, the accused held the following positions during the relevant period:

- Mile Mrkšić was a colonel in the JNA and commander of the 1st Guards Motorized Brigade and Operational Group South. After the fall of Vukovar, he was promoted to general rank in the JNA [Yugoslav People's Army] and became the commander of the 8th JNA Operational Group in the Kordun area in Croatia. Following the withdrawal of the JNA from Croatia in 1992, he returned to the Federal Republic of Yugoslavia and occupied several posts in the VJ General Staff. He became the commanding officer of the army of the so-called Republic of Serb Krajina (RSK) in May 1995.
- Miroslav Radić was a captain in the JNA. He commanded an infantry company in the 1st Battalion of the 1st Guards Motorized Brigade.
- Veselin Šljivančanin was a major in the JNA. He was the security officer of the 1st Guards Motorized Brigade and Operational Group South and as such was de facto in charge of a military police battalion subordinated to the 1st Guards Motorized Brigade. After the fall of Vukovar, Šljivančanin was promoted to the rank of lieutenant colonel and was placed in command of the VJ brigade in Podgorica, Montenegro.

Mile Mrkšić was convicted of murder, torture and cruel treatment, Miroslav Radić was found not guilty, and Veselin Šljivančanin was convicted of torture. Article 7(1) of the Statute of the International Criminal tribunal for the Former Yugoslavia describes "individual criminal responsibility" as pertaining to a person who planned, instigated, ordered, committed, or otherwise aided and abetted in the planning or preparation or execution of a crime referred to in articles 2-5 of the statute. Article 2 refers to grave breaches of the Geneva Conventions of 1949, article 3 refers to violations of the laws or customs of war, article 4 refers to genocide, and article 5 refers to crimes against humanity. On superior criminal responsibility, see article 7(3) of the statute. Article 5 of the statute refers to crimes against humanity including persecutions on political, racial, and religious grounds; extermination; murder; torture; and inhumane acts. Article 3 of the statute refers to violations of the laws of war and includes murder, torture, and cruel treatment.

64. This account is from Silber and Little, *Death of Yugoslavia*.

65. MRKSIC et al. Case IT-95-13/1, available at the ICTY website, www.un .org/icty.

66. Tim Judah, *The Serbs: History, Myth and the Destruction of Yugoslavia* (New Haven, CT: Yale University Press, 1997); and Slavenka Drakulić, *They Would Never Hurt a Fly: War Criminals on Trial in The Hague* (London: Abacus, 2004).

67. Susan Sontag, *Regarding the Pain of Others* (New York: Farrar, Straus and Giroux, 2003), 109. "These dead are supremely uninterested in the living: in those who took their lives; in witnesses—and in us. Why should they seek our gaze? What would they have to say to us? 'We'—this 'we' is everyone who has never experienced anything like they went through—don't understand. We don't get it. We truly can't imagine what it was like. We can't imagine how dreadful, how terrifying war is; and how normal it becomes. Can't understand, can't imagine. That's what every soldier, and every journalist and aid worker and independent observer who has put in time under fire, and had the luck to elude the death that struck down others nearby, stubbornly feels. And they are right."

68. Gerhard Beestermöller, "Eurocentricity in the Perception of Wars," *Concilium*, no. 2 (2001): 33–42; and Irina Novikova, "Lessons from the Anatomy of War: Svetlana Alexievich's Zinky Boys," 99–116; and Rada Drezgić, "Demographic Nationalism in the Gender Perspective," 211–35, both in Svetlana Slapšak, ed. *War Discourse, Women's Discourse Essays and Case-Studies from Yugoslavia and Russia* (Ljubljana: TOPOS, 2000).

69. In 1996 Thomas Hamilton entered a primary school in Dunblane, Scotland, and killed sixteen children and a schoolteacher. In the aftermath the police declared an amnesty for those who held illegal handguns.

70. Grace Jantzen, *Foundations of Violence* (London: Routledge, 2004), 10.

Conclusion

Ethical pluralism defines the context within which human rights discourse and politics function, and although ethical pluralism has long been a complicating factor for the articulation of universal human rights, it has acquired a heightened significance in the contemporary context in part because of our increased awareness of its reach. Coupled with this, human rights discourse has itself experienced a crisis of legitimacy, engendered particularly by the widespread distrust of enlightenment rationalism and a consequent loss of confidence in the philosophical assumptions on which the claims of human rights have been built. This work considers the nature and extent of this crisis of legitimacy in its political, philosophical, and theological manifestations and argues that the combined force of the criticisms poses a fundamental challenge for traditional conceptualizations of human rights. I acknowledge that there is a temptation to ignore these criticisms. However, I argue that we ignore them at our peril, and I note Gearty's caution that as postmodern uncertainty embeds itself more deeply in our culture, there is a risk that human rights will be seen as a benign relic of an earlier age and will ultimately lose its political appeal.[1] I suggest that this is indeed likely to happen unless advocates begin to deal with the implications of this major philosophical and cultural shift head on.

This work insists that human rights discourse can be defended in the midst of these challenges and argues that it does not need the false security of enlightenment metaphysics in order for it to be philosophically credible or politically effective. Indeed, not only can human rights survive the end of metaphysics but it can actually flourish in its wake. I suggest, however, that it will only flourish if there is a fundamental reconsideration of the manner in which human rights categories are grounded. I focus on the three pillars on which human rights discourse depend—the nature of the person, the universality of truth claims, and the role of community—and I argue that each needs to be recalibrated in a manner that takes account of feminist, postcolonial, communitarian, and postmodern criticisms.

The central concern of this work is to reconstruct a human rights discourse that has philosophical credibility, theological resonance, and political efficacy. I suggest that this can be accomplished if we recognize that human rights language articulates an ethical project to be accomplished rather than a philosophical claim to be defended. When we build our support for human rights in terms of an ethical project rather than in terms of a philosophical system, then the pillars of traditional human rights discourse will need to be rethought. Chapters 3, 4, and 5 focus on these pillars, and, noting that the legitimacy of each of these categories has been significantly undermined, I propose an alternative reading of each that can serve as the basis for a revised understanding of human rights.

These alternative readings of personhood, moral knowledge, and community lead us to a space in which we must be prepared to think about our shared vulnerability and the bonds of difference; about situated knowledge, plural foundations, and embedded universalism; about hybrid belonging, porous communities, and constructed traditions. It is a place wherein no final conclusions can be drawn but rather is a place of interrogation and self-critique, of creativity and learning. Of course, we come to this ethical project with all the baggage of belonging, which can range from the belief that a purely rational justification for universal human rights can be articulated to the conviction that universal values are revealed in and through a particular religious world view. Yet no matter how deeply held the beliefs associated with cultural or religious belonging may be, they can have—indeed, they must have—a place in the multireligious and intercultural global conversation about what we owe to one another. This work seeks to affirm this important dimension of argument through its engagement with the Christian tradition, by demonstrating how the Christian world view has shaped many of the seminal ethical commitments that are central to human rights, and by showing how, alongside other situated traditions, the Christian tradition continues to have a key role in the ongoing constructive ethical project. There is no doubt that in portraying the vindication of human rights thus, we are moving quite a distance from the traditional liberal philosophical defense. However, it is a route we must travel if human rights discourse is to survive and flourish. This is not a purely pragmatic stance. Rather, as my historical analysis has demonstrated, when we view it in this way, we describe more accurately the trajectory of human rights practice over the last century since this history has shown that it is not the persuasive appeal to abstract rationality but rather the incremental work of intercultural dialogue that has allowed us to insist that all human beings are born free and equal in dignity and rights. In this way one might say that human rights theory is finally catching up with human rights practice.

For many centuries the potency of human rights discourse has rested on the unequivocal nature of its claim to a form of universality that is underpinned by an objective moral order. The genealogical approach pursued in this work recommends an alternative grounding for human rights theory and politics, one that is not fazed by the lack of certitude but rather can keep faith with this profoundly ethical project even while its moorings are insecure. In a similar vein Hans Joas speaks about the genesis of universal values in terms of their being "equally distant from the concept of 'construction' and that of 'discovery.'"[2] The implication of this is that while there can be no purely rational justification for universal values (nor for human rights claims), neither can they be simply deemed to be constructed. Joas positions the genesis of values in such a way that history and justification are interwoven in specific ways. He believes the history of human rights to be essentially the story of the sacralization of the person, with the United Nations Declaration being a highly successful process of value generalization.[3] Joas's approach, while different, complements the position taken in this work. It also supports my argument that once we accept that human rights discourse is a form of situated knowledge, an embedded universalism, then we can acknowledge its contingent character while also resisting relativism. Joas uses the term "affirmative genealogy" to describe such an approach. He explains, "This genealogical, that is, contingency-conscious reconstruction of the past, is described as 'affirmative' because recourse to the process of ideal formation, the genesis of values, rather than negating our commitment to them or endowing us with the sovereignty to assess our value commitments, opens [sic] our minds to the way in which historically embodied meaning calls upon us."[4] Nor is this merely a matter of gaining a better understanding of the historical trajectory of human rights discourse. Rather, since human rights is a discourse that continues to have significant traction globally, the "affirmative genealogy" functions in the contemporary context too so that we can both acknowledge the contingency of its origins while also recognizing the universality of its appeal.

The deep cultural and religious pluralism that characterizes human life must be engaged if a durable global politics of human rights is to be achieved. This pluralism presents itself to us through manifold world views, ethical frameworks, cultural practices, and religious rituals, some of which are familiar, others of which unfamiliar and therefore often experienced as challenging. It accounts for the many ways in which the contours of human flourishing are drawn and also impacts on the manner in which the nature of human dignity is structured within different social and political systems. Throughout this work I have sought to demonstrate that this pluralism, which heretofore has been thought of as a threat to human rights, can in fact be a challenge to complacency, a catalyst for future development, an occasion for innovation, and thereby become a source of its strength. As has already been suggested, it is possible to allow the "surety of our epistemological and ontological anchors" to go and yet to keep faith with the ethical demands of the other, and it is possible to reconstruct a commitment to human rights from this place of uncertainty and creativity.[5]

As we attempt to reinvision human rights in this way, we become aware of how profoundly unsettling it is. Indeed, the dynamic embedded in such a process will inevitably force us to rethink some of our deepest assumptions and confront some of our most enduring vulnerabilities. It will require what Jonathan Lear calls radical hope. What makes such hope radical is "that it is directed toward a future goodness that transcends [our] current ability to understand what it is. Radical hope anticipates a good for which those who have the hope as yet lack the appropriate concepts with which to understand it."[6] The journey I have sketched throughout this work will ultimately require such a radical hope since the traditional ways of structuring significance have been undermined and cannot simply be replicated for a new context. Rather, as I argue, human rights must be radically rethought as ethical assertions about the critical importance of certain values for human flourishing, as an emerging consensus generated by situated communities who are open to internally and externally generated social criticism, and as emancipatory politics whose modus operandi is ultimately that of persuasion. Only in this way will its transformative potential be realized.

Notes

1. Conor Gearty, *Can Human Rights Survive?* (Cambridge: Cambridge University Press, 2006), 20.

2. Hans Joas, *The Sacredness of the Person: A New Genealogy of Human Rights* (Washington, DC: Georgetown University Press, 2013), 3. Joas's approach here complements the arguments that I have been making in terms of both his insistence that the issue of the genesis of values must be decoupled from the question of their validity and his allied conviction that this does not lead to moral relativism but rather can be seen as an affirmative genealogy.

3. Ibid., 8.

4. Ibid., 126.

5. The phrase "the surety of our epistemological and ontological anchors" is Judith Butler's, in *Undoing Gender*, 35.

6. Jonathan Lear, *Radical Hope: Ethics in the Face of Cultural Devastation* (Cambridge, MA: Harvard University Press, 2006), 103. In this remarkable book Lear analyzes the demise of the Crow Nation and suggests that its last traditional Chief Plenty Coup witnesses to the legitimacy of what he calls radical hope.

Bibliography

Afshar, Haleh. *Islam and Feminism: An Iranian Case-Study*. London: Macmillan 1998.

———, ed. *Women, State, and Ideology: Studies from Africa and Asia*. Albany: State University of New York Press, 1987.

Agamben, Giorgio. *State of Exception*. Chicago: University of Chicago Press, 2005.

Ahdar, Rex, and Nicholas Aroney, eds. *Shari'a in the West*. Oxford: Oxford University Press, 2010.

Ahmadu, Fuambai. "Rites and Wrongs: An Insider/Outsider Reflects on Power and Excision." In *Female "Circumcision" in Africa: Culture, Controversy and Change*, edited by Bettina Shell-Duncan and Ylva Hernlund, 305–7. Boulder CO: Lynne Reiner, 2000.

Ahmed, Leila. *A Quiet Revolution: The Veil's Resurgence from the Middle East to America*. New Haven, CT: Yale University Press, 2011.

Allen, Anne Dondapati. "No Garlic Please, We Are Indian: Reconstructing the De-eroticized Indian Woman." In *Off the Menu: Asian and Asian North American Women's Religion and Theology*, edited by Rita Nakashima Brock, Jing Ha Kim, Kwok Pui-lan, and Seung Ai Yang, 183–96. Knoxville, KY: Westminster John Knox Press, 2007.

Alston, Philip. "The UN's Human Rights Record: From San Francisco to Vienna and Beyond." *Human Rights Quarterly* 16, no. 2 (1994): 375–90.

American Anthropological Association. "Statement on Human Rights." *American Anthropologist* 49, no. 2 (1947): 539–43.

Améry, Jean. *At the Mind's Limit: Contemplation by a Survivor of Auschwitz and Its Realities*. New York: Schocken, 1986.

Angle, Stephen C. *Human Rights and Chinese Thought: A Cross-Cultural Inquiry*. New York: Cambridge University Press, 2002.

An-Na'im, Abdullahi Ahmed, ed. *Human Rights in Cross-Cultural Perspectives: A Quest for Consensus*. Philadelphia: University of Pennsylvania Press, 1992.

Appiah, K. Anthony. "Grounding Human Rights." In *Human Rights as Politics and Idolatry*, edited by Michael Ignatieff, 101–16. Princeton, NJ: Princeton University Press, 2001.

———. *The Honor Code: How Moral Revolutions Happen*. New York: W. W. Norton, 2010.

Bagaric, Mirko, and Julie Clarke. "Not Enough Official Torture in the World? The Circumstances in Which Torture Is Morally Justifiable." *University of San Francisco Law Review* 39, no. 3 (2005): 581–616.

Baier, Annette. "Hume the Women's Moral Theorist?" In *Women and Moral Theory*, edited by Eva Kittay and Diana Meyers, 37–55. Totowa, NJ: Rowman & Littlefield, 1987.

———. *A Progress of Sentiments: Reflections on Hume's Treatise*. Cambridge, MA: Harvard University Press, 1991.

Baxi, Upendra. *The Future of Human Rights*, 3rd ed. Oxford: Oxford University Press, 2008.

———. *Human Rights in a Posthuman World: Critical Essays*. Oxford: Oxford University Press, 2007.

Beestermöller, Gerhard. "Eurocentricity in the Perception of Wars." *Concilium*, no. 2 (2001): 33–42.

Bernauer, James. "The Prisons of Man: Foucault's Negative Theology." *International Philosophical Quarterly* 27 (1987): 365–80.

Bhabha, Homi K. *The Location of Culture*. London: Routledge, 1994.

Birla, Rita. "Postcolonial Studies: Now That's History." In *Can the Subaltern Speak? Reflections on the History of an Idea*, edited by Rosalind C. Morris, 87–99. New York: Columbia University Press, 2010.

Bourdieu, Pierre. *Distinction: A Social Critique of the Judgment of Taste*. Cambridge, MA: Harvard University Press, 1984.

Boutros-Ghali, Boutros. "The Common Language of Humanity." *United Nations World Conference on Human Rights: The Vienna Declaration and the Programme of Action*. New York: United Nations, 1993.

Braidotti, Rosi. *Transpositions: On Nomadic Ethics*. Cambridge, UK: Polity Press, 2006.

Brandom, Robert. *Making It Explicit: Reasoning, Representing and Discursive Commitment*. Cambridge, MA: Harvard University Press, 1994.

Bujo, Bénézet. *Foundations of an African Ethic: Beyond the Universal Claims of Western Morality*. Nairobi: Paulines, 2003.

Burke, Roland. *Decolonization and the Evolution of International Human Rights*. Philadelphia: University of Pennsylvania Press, 2010.

Butler, Judith. *Bodies That Matter: On the Discursive Limits of Sex*. London: Routledge, 1993.

———. *Gender Trouble: Feminism and the Subversion of Identity*. New York: Routledge, 1990.

———. *Undoing Gender*. London: Routledge, 2004.

Caleb Foundation. *Proposed Bill of Rights for Northern Ireland: A Response*. Belfast: Northern Ireland Human Rights Commission, 2001.

Cavanaugh, William T. *Theopolitical Imagination*. London: Continuum, 2002.

Cavarero, Adriana. *Relating Narratives: Storytelling and Selfhood*. London: Routledge, 2000.

Chan, Yiu Sing Lucas, and James Keenan, "Bridging Christian Ethics and Confucianism through Virtue Ethics," *Chinese Cross Currents* 5, no. 2 (July 2008): 74–85.

Chatterjee, Partha "Reflections on 'Can the Subaltern Speak?'" In *Can the Subaltern Speak? Reflections on the History of an Idea*, edited by Rosalind C. Morris, 81–86. New York: Columbia University Press, 2010.

Chesterman, Simon. "Human Rights as Subjectivity." *Millennium: Journal of International Studies* 27, no. 1 (1998): 97–118.

Cisneros, Ariane Hentsch, and Shanta Premawardhana, eds. *Sharing Values: A Hermeneutics for Global Ethics*. Geneva: Globethics.net, Series No. 4, 2011. www.globethics.net/documents/4289936/13403236/GlobalSeries_4_Sharing Values_text.pdf/6162b4a5-5cd2-4af6-bdc5-70699b69d923.

Clifford, James. "Diasporas." *Cultural Anthropology* 9, no. 3 (2007): 302–38.

Clooney, Francis. *Comparative Theology: Deep Learning across Religious Borders*. Malden, MA: Wiley-Blackwell, 2010.

Cornell, Drucilla. "The Ethical Affirmation of Human Rights: Gayatri Spivak's Intervention." In *Can the Subaltern Speak? Reflections on the History of an Idea*, edited by Rosalind C. Morris, 100–116. New York: Columbia University Press, 2010.

Cornille, Catherine. "Double Religious Belonging: Aspects and Questions." *Buddhist-Christian Studies* 44 (2003): 43–49.

Cranston, Maurice. *Human Rights Today*. London: Ampersand Books, 1962.

Croce, Benedetto. "The Rights of Man and the Present Historical Situation." In *Human Rights: Comments and Interpretations*. A UNESCO Symposium edited with an introduction by Jacques Maritain, 93–96. London: Allan Wingate, 1949.

Dann, G. Elijah. "Philosophy, Religion and Religious Belief after Rorty." In *An Ethics for Today: Finding Common Ground between Philosophy and Religion*, by Richard Rorty, 27–76. New York: Columbia University Press, 2008.

Danner, Mark. "We Are All Torturers Now." *New York Times*, January 6, 2005.

Davila, Maria Teresa. "Racialization and Racism in Theological Ethics: History as a Pillar for a Catholic Ethic Grounded on the Preferential Option for the Poor and an Incarnational Anthropology." In *Catholic Theological Ethics, Past, Present, and Future: The Trento Conference*, edited by James Keenan, 307–21. Maryknoll, NY: Orbis Press, 2012.

Davis, Charles. *Religion and the Making of Society: Essays in Social Theology*. Cambridge: Cambridge University Press, 1994.

D'Costa, Gavin, Malcolm Evans, Tariq Modood, and Julian Rivers. *Religion in a Liberal State*. Cambridge: Cambridge University Press, 2013.

"Declaration of the Rights of Man and of the Citizen," printed in *The Ethics of World Religions and Human Rights*, ed., Hans Küng and Jurgen Moltmann, *Concilium*, no. 2 (1990): 3–5.

de la Chapelle, Philippe. *La Déclaration universelle des droits de l'homme et le Catholicisme*. Paris: Pinchon et Durand-Auzias, Librarie Générale de Droit et de Jurisprudence, 1967.

Denson, G. Roger. "Torture and Terror in Art History and the Healing Power of Revelation." *Huffington Post*, February 1, 2013. Accessed July 22, 2013. www.huff ingtonpost.com/g-roger-denson/torture-and-terror-in-art_b_2600028.html.

Dershowitz, Alan M. *Why Terrorism Works: Understanding the Threat, Responding to the Challenge*. New Haven, CT: Yale University Press, 2002.

Dewey, John. *Reconstruction in Philosophy*. New York: New American Library, 1950.

Dillon, E. J. *The Inside Story of the Peace Conference*. New York: Harper & Brothers, 1920.

Dobbernack, Jan, and Tariq Modood, eds. *Tolerance, Intolerance and Respect: Hard to Accept?* Basingstoke, UK: Palgrave MacMillan, 2013.

Doherty, Willie. *Secretion*. Film and Text. Dublin: Irish Museum of Modern Art, 2012.

Donnelly, Jack. *Universal Human Rights in Theory and Practice*. Ithaca, NY: Cornell University Press, 1989.

Drakulić, Slavenka. *They Would Never Hurt a Fly: War Criminals on Trial in The Hague*. London: Abacus, 2004.

Drezgić, Rada. "Demographic Nationalism in the Gender Perspective." In *War Discourse: Women's Discourse Essays and Case-Studies from Yugoslavia and Russia*, edited by Svetlana Slapšak, 211–35. Ljubljana, Slovenia: TOPOS, 2000.

Dworkin, Gerald. *The Theory and Practice of Autonomy*. New York: Cambridge University Press, 1988.

Dworkin, Ronald. *Religion without God*. Cambridge, MA: Harvard University Press, 2013.

———. *Taking Rights Seriously*. London: Duckworth Press, 1977.

El Fadl, Khaled Abou. "Islam and the Challenge of Democratic Commitment." In *Does Human Rights Need God?*, edited by Elizabeth M. Bucar and Barbra Barnett, 58–103. Grand Rapids, MI: Eerdmans, 2005.

Éla, Jean-Marc. *My Faith as an African*. Maryknoll, NY: Orbis, 1988.

Fanon, Frantz. *A Dying Colonialism*. Translated by Haakon Chevalier. New York: Grove Weidenfeld, 1965.

Farley, Margaret. "A Feminist Version of Respect for Persons." *Journal of Feminist Studies in Religion* 9, no. 1–2 (Spring–Fall 1993): 183–98.

Fassin, Didier. "Culturalism as Ideology." In *Cultural Perspectives on Reproductive Health*, edited by Carla Makhlouf Obermeyer, 300–307. Oxford: Oxford University Press, 2001.

Fergusson, David. *Community, Liberalism and Christian Ethics*. Cambridge: Cambridge University Press, 1998.

Feyissa, Abebe, with Rebecca Horn. "There Is More Than One Way of Dying: An Ethiopian Perspective on the Effects of Long-Term Stays in Refugee Camps." In *Refugee Rights, Ethics, Advocacy and Africa*, edited by David Hollenbach, 13–26. Washington, DC: Georgetown University Press, 2008.

Foucault, Michel. "Afterword: The Subject and Power." In *Michel Foucault: Beyond Structuralism and Hermeneutics*, edited by Hubert Dreyfus and Paul Rabinow, 208–28. New York: Harvester Wheatsheaf, 1982.

———. *The Archaeology of Knowledge*. London: Tavistock, 1972.

———. *Discipline and Punish: The Birth of the Prison*, 2nd ed. New York: Vintage, 1995.

———. *Madness and Civilization: A History of Insanity in the Age of Reason*. New York: Pantheon, 1965.

———. *The Order of Things: An Archaeology of the Human Sciences*. New York: Vintage, 1994.

———. *Power: Essential Works of Foucault 1954–1984*, vol. 3, edited by James D. Faubion. New York: New Press, 2002.

Freeman, Michael. *Human Rights: An Interdisciplinary Approach*. Cambridge, UK: Polity Press, 2002.

Fricker, Miranda. "Feminism in Epistemology: Pluralism without Postmodernism." In *The Cambridge Companion to Feminism in Philosophy*, edited by Miranda Fricker and Jennifer Hornsby, 146–65. Cambridge: Cambridge University Press, 2000.

Gay, Peter. *The Enlightenment: An Interpretation*. Vol. 2, *The Science of Freedom*. London: Weidenfeld & Nicolson, 1969.

Gearty, Conor. *Can Human Rights Survive?* Cambridge: Cambridge University Press, 2006.

Geffré, Claude. "Double Belonging and the Originality of Christianity as a Religion." In *Many Mansions? Multiple Religious Belonging and Christian Identity*, edited by Catherine Cornille, 93–105. New York: Orbis Books, 2002.

Gewith, Alan. *The Community of Rights*. Chicago: University of Chicago Press, 1996.

———. "The Golden Rule Rationalized." In *Human Rights: Essays on Justification and Applications*. Chicago: University of Chicago Press, 1992.

Ginbar, Yuval. *Why Not Torture Terrorists? Moral, Practical and Legal Aspects of the "Ticking Bomb" Justification for Torture*. Oxford: Oxford University Press, 2008.

Glendon, Mary Ann. *A World Made New: Eleanor Roosevelt and the United Nations Declaration of Human Rights*. New York: Random House, 2001.

Glover, Jonathan. *Humanity: A Moral History*. New Haven, CT: Yale University Press, 2001.

Gómez-Barris, Macarena. "Torture Sees and Speaks: Guillermo Núñez's Art in Chile's Transition." *Journal on Social History and Literature in Latin America* 5, no. 1 (Fall 2007): 86–107.

Goya, Francisco de. *Disasters of War*. Dover: Dover Fine Art, History of Art, 1967.

Gray, John. *Enlightenment's Wake*. London: Routledge, 1995.

Gregory XVI. *Mirari vos*. In *The Papal Encyclicals 1740–1878*, vol. 1, edited by Claudia Carlen. Pasadena, CA: Pierian Press, 1990.

Gross, Oren. "The Prohibition of Torture and the Limits of the Law." In *Torture: A Collection*, edited by Sanford Levinson, 229–53. Oxford: Oxford University Press, 2004.

Guénif-Souilamas, Nacira. "The Other French Exception: Virtuous Racism and the War of the Sexes in Postcolonial France." *French Politics, Culture and Society* 24, no. 3 (2006): 23–41.

Gushee, David P. "Against Torture: An Evangelical Perspective." *Theology Today* 63 (2006): 349–64.

Gutman, Amy. *Identity in Democracy*. Princeton, NJ: Princeton University Press, 2004.

Habermas, Jürgen. *Theory of Communicative Action*, vol. 1, translated by Thomas McCarthy. Cambridge, UK: Polity Press, 1984.

Hall, Stuart. "The West and the Rest: Discourse and Power." In *Formations of Modernity*, edited by Stuart Hall & Bram Gieben, 275–320. Cambridge, UK: Polity Press, 1992.

Hauerwas, Stanley. *After Christendom*. Nashville: Abingdon Press, 1991.

———. *A Community of Character*. Notre Dame, IN: University of Notre Dame Press, 1981.

———. *Performing the Faith: Bonhoeffer and the Practice of Non-Violence*. Ada, MI: Brazos Press, 2004.

Hauerwas, Stanley, and Romand Coles. *Christianity, Democracy, and the Radical Ordinary Conversations between a Radical Democrat and a Christian*. Eugene OR: Cascade Books, 2008.

Hauerwas, Stanley, Linda Hogan, and Enda McDonagh. "The Case for the Abolition of War in the Twenty-First Century." *Journal of the Society of Christian Ethics* 25, no. 2 (2005): 17–35.

Havel, Václav. *Disturbing the Peace*. Translated from Czech and with an introduction by Paul Wilson. London: Faber & Faber, 1990.

Heaney, Seamus. *Opened Ground: Poems, 1966–1996*. London: Faber & Faber, 1998.

———. "The Poetic Redress." In *From the Republic of Conscience: Stories Inspired by the Universal Declaration of Human Rights*, commissioning editor Sean Love, 15–21. Dublin: Liberties Press, 2009.

———. *The Redress of Poetry*. London: Faber & Faber 1995.

Himes, Kenneth. "Why Is Torture Wrong." *Journal of Peace and Justice Studies* 21, no. 2 (2011): 42–55.

Hogan, Linda. Introduction to *Religious Voices in Public Places*, edited by Nigel Biggar and Linda Hogan, 1–14. Oxford: Oxford University Press, 2009.

———. "Religion and Public Reason in the Global Politics of Human Rights." In *Religious Voices in Public Places*, edited by Nigel Biggar and Linda Hogan, 216–31. Oxford: Oxford University Press, 2009.

Hogan, Linda, and John D'Arcy May. "Gender and Culture as Dimensions of Bodiliness." In *Bodiliness and Human Dignity: An Intercultural Approach*, edited by Harm Goris, 45–61. Münster: LIT, 2006.

Hollenbach, David. "A Communitarian Reconstruction of Human Rights: Contributions from the Catholic Tradition." In *Catholicism and Liberalism: Contributions to American Public Philosophy*, edited by Bruce Douglass and David Hollenbach, 127–50. Cambridge: Cambridge University Press, 1994.

———. *The Global Face of Public Faith: Politics, Human Rights, and Christian Ethics*. Washington, DC: Georgetown University Press, 2003.

Hollinger, David. *Postethnic America: Beyond Multiculturalism*. New York: Basic Books, 1995.

Honneth, Axel. *The I in We: Studies in the Theory of Recognition*. Cambridge, UK: Polity Press, 2012.

Humphrey, John. *Human Rights and the United Nations: A Great Adventure*. London: Transnational, 1984.

Hunsinger, George. "Torture, Common Morality and the Golden Rule: A Conversation with Michael Perry." *Theology Today* 63 (2006): 375–79.

Hunt, Lynne. *Inventing Human Rights: A History*. New York: W. W. Norton, 2007.

Hurrell, Andrew. "Power, Principles and Prudence: Protecting Human Rights in a Deeply Divided World." In *Human Rights in Global Politics*, edited by Tim Dunne and Nicholas Wheeler, 277–302. Cambridge: Cambridge University Press, 1999.

Ignatieff, Michael. "The End of Human Rights." *New York Times*, February 5, 2002.

———. *Human Rights as Politics and Idolatry*. Princeton, NJ: Princeton University Press, 2001.

International Development Research Centre. *The Responsibility to Protect: Report of the International Commission on Intervention and State Sovereignty*. Ottawa, ON: International Development Research Centre, 2001.

Ip, John. "Two Narratives of Torture." *Northwestern Journal of International Human Rights* 7, no. 1 (Spring 2009): 35–77.

Jagger, Alison. "Globalizing Feminist Ethics." In *Decentering the Center: Philosophy for a Multicultural, Postcolonial, and Feminist World*, edited by Uma Narayan and Sandra Harding, 1–25. Bloomington: Indiana University Press, 2000.

Jantzen, Grace. *Foundations of Violence*. London: Routledge, 2004.

Jha, Prabhat, Maya A. Kesler, Rajesh Kumar, Faujdar Ram, Usha Ram, Lukasz Aleksandrowicz, Diego G. Bassani, Shailaja Chandra, and Jayant K. Banthia. "Trends in Selective Abortions of Girls in India: Analysis of Nationally Representative Birth Histories from 1990 to 2005 and Census Data from 1991 to 2011." *Lancet* 377, no. 9781: 1921–28. doi:10.1016/S0140-6736(11)60649-1.

Joas, Hans. *The Sacredness of the Person: A New Genealogy of Human Rights*. Washington, DC: Georgetown University Press, 2013.

Johnson, Mark. *Moral Imagination: The Importance of Cognitive Science for Ethics*. Chicago: University of Chicago Press, 1994.

Judah, Tim. *The Serbs: History, Myth and the Destruction of Yugoslavia*. New Haven, CT: Yale University Press, 1997.

Jung, Patricia Beattie, and Aana Marie Vigen, with John Anderson, eds. *God, Science, Sex, Gender: An Interdisciplinary Approach to Christian Ethics*. Urbana: University of Illinois Press, 2010.

Kamenka, Eugene. "The Anatomy of an Idea." In *Human Rights*, edited by Eugene Kamenka and Alice Erh-Soon Tay, 1–12. Port Melbourne: Edward Arnold, 1978.

Kao, Grace. *Grounding Human Rights in a Pluralist World*. Washington, DC: Georgetown University Press, 2011.

Keenan, James. "Impasse and Solidarity in Theological Ethics." *Catholic Theological Society of America Proceedings* 64 (2009): 1–14.

Klug, Francesca. "Religious Pluralism and Human Rights: Problems and Opportunities." In *Rights and Righteousness: Perspectives on Religious Pluralism and Human Rights*, edited by David Tombs, 31–40. Belfast: Northern Ireland Human Rights Commission, with Irish School of Ecumenics, Trinity College Dublin, 2010.

———. *Values for a Godless Age*. London: Penguin, 2000.

Knitter, Paul. F. *Without Buddha I Could Not Be a Christian*. Oxford: OneWorld, 2009.

Korey, William. *NGOs and the Universal Declaration of Human Rights: A Curious Grapevine*. New York: St. Martin's, 1998.

Kukathas, Chandran. *The Liberal Archipelago: A Theory of Diversity and Freedom*. Oxford: Oxford University Press, 2003.

Kwok, Pui-lan. *Postcolonial Imagination and Feminist Theology*. London: SCM-Canterbury Press, 2005.

———. "Unbinding Our Feet: Saving Brown Women and Feminist Religious Discourse." In *Postcolonialism, Feminism and Religious Discourse*, edited by Laura Donaldson and Kwok Pui-lan, 62–81. New York: Routledge, 2001.

Kymlicak, Will. *Multicultural Citizenship: A Liberal Theory of Minority Rights*. Oxford: Oxford University Press, 1995.

————. *Multicultural Odyssey: Navigating the New International Politics of Diversity.* Oxford: Oxford University Press, 2007.

Laclau, Ernesto, and Chantal Mouffe. *Hegemony and Socialist Strategy: Towards a Radical Democratic Politics.* London: Verso, 2001.

Langlois, Anthony. *The Politics and Justice of Human Rights: Southeast Asia and Universalist Theory.* Cambridge: Cambridge University Press, 2001.

Lauren, Paul Gordon. *The Evolution of International Human Rights: Visions Seen.* Philadelphia: University of Pennsylvania Press, 1998.

Lear, Jonathan. *Radical Hope: Ethics in the Face of Cultural Devastation.* Cambridge, MA: Harvard University Press, 2006.

Lerner, Michael. "Jesus the Jew." *Tikkun,* May–June 2004, 33–37.

Levi, Primo. *If This Is a Man.* London: New England Library, 1962.

Levy, Jacob T. *The Multiculturalism of Fear.* Oxford: Oxford University Press, 2000.

Lotringer, Silvere, ed. *The Politics of Truth: Michel Foucault.* Los Angeles: Semiotext(e), 2007.

Luard, Evan. *A History of the United Nations.* Vol. 2, *The Age of Decolonization 1955–65.* London: Palgrave MacMillan, 1989.

MacDonald, Margaret. "Natural Rights." In *Theories of Rights,* edited by Jeremy Waldron, 21–40. Oxford: Oxford University Press, 1984.

MacIntyre, Alasdair. *After Virtue: A Study in Moral Theory.* London: Duckworth, 1981.

————. "A Partial Response to My Critics." In *After MacIntyre: Critical Perspectives on the Work of Alasdair MacIntyre,* edited by John Horton and Susan Mendus, 283–304. Cambridge, UK: Polity Press, 1996.

————. *Whose Justice? Which Rationality?* Notre Dame, IN: University of Notre Dame Press, 1989.

Mackie, Gerry. "Female Genital Cutting: The Beginning of the End." In *Female "Circumcision" in Africa: Culture Controversy and Change,* edited by Bettina Shell-Duncan and Ylva Hernlund, 253–82. Boulder, CO: Lynne Reiner, 2000.

Mahoney, John. *The Challenge of Human Rights: Origin, Development and Significance.* Oxford: Blackwell, 2006.

Maoz, Asher. "Can Judaism Serve as a Source of Human Rights?" *Heidelberg Journal of International Law* 64 (2004): 677–721.

Maritain, Jacques. *The Rights of Man and Natural Law.* New York: Charles Scribner's Sons, 1944.

May, John D'Arcy. *After Pluralism: Towards an Interreligious Ethic.* Münster: LIT Verlag, 2000.

————. *Transcendence and Violence: The Encounter of Buddhist, Christian, and Primal Traditions.* New York: Continuum, 2003.

May, John D'Arcy, and Linda Hogan. "Visioning Ecumenics as Intercultural, Interreligious and Public Theology." In *From World Mission to Interreligious Witness*, edited by Felix Wilfred, Solange Lefebvre, Norbert Hintersteiner, and Linda Hogan, 70–84. *Concilium* Special Issue, no. 1 (2011).

Mayer, Elisabeth Ann. "Universal versus Islamic Human Rights: A Clash of Cultures or a Clash with a Construct?" *Michigan Journal of International Law* 15, no. 2: 307–404.

McGoldrick, Dominic. *Human Rights and Religion: The Islamic Headscarf Debate in Europe*. Oxford, UK: Hart Publishing, 2006.

McNay, Lois. *Foucault and Feminism*. Oxford, UK: Polity Press, 1992.

Mernissi, Fatema, *Beyond the Veil: Male–Female Dynamics in Muslim Society*. London: Saqi Books, 1975.

Merry, Sally Engle. "Changing Rights, Changing Culture." In *Culture and Rights: Anthropological Perspectives*, edited by Jane K. Cowan, Marie-Benedicte Dembour, and Richard Wilson, 31–55. Cambridge: Cambridge University Press, 2001.

———. *Human Rights and Gender Violence*. Chicago: University of Chicago Press, 2006.

Mies, Maria. *The Lacemakers of Narsapur: Indian Housewives Produce for the World Market*. London: Zed Books, 1982.

Mikhail, John. "Islamic Rationalism and the Foundation of Human Rights." *Pluralism and Law*. Proceedings of the 20th IVR Congress, edited by Arend Soeteman, *Global Problems* 3 (March 2005): 61–70; Georgetown Public Law Research Paper No. 777026. Available at SSRN: http://ssrn.com/abstract=777026.

Milbank, John. *Theology and Social Theory: Beyond Secular Reason*. Cambridge, MA: Blackwell, 1990.

Milosz, Czeslaw. "Ruins and Poetry." *New York Review of Books*, March 17, 1983. Accessed July 22, 2013, www.nybooks.com/articles/archives/1983/mar/17/ruins-and-poetry/?pagination.

Modood, Tariq. *Multicultural Politics: Racism, Ethnicity, and Muslims in Britain*. Edinburgh: Edinburgh University Press, 2005.

Modood, Tariq, and Jan Dobbernack. "Accepting Multiple Differences: The Challenge of Double Accommodation." In *Tolerance, Intolerance and Respect: Hard to Accept?* edited by Jan Dobbernack and Tariq Modood, 186–207. Basingstoke, UK: Palgrave MacMillan, 2013.

Moghadam, Valentine. *Gender and National Identity: Women and Politics in Muslim Societies*. London: Zed Books, 1994.

Mohanty, Chandra Talpade. "Feminist Encounters: Locating the Politics of Experience." In *Feminist Theory Reader: Local and Global Perspectives*, edited by Carole McCann and Seung-Kyung Kim, 460–71. London: Routledge, 2003.

Morrison, Toni. *Beloved.* London: Vintage 1997.

Morsink, Johannes. *Inherent Human Rights: Philosophical Roots of the Universal Declaration.* Philadelphia: University of Pennsylvania Press, 2009.

———. *The United Nations Declaration of Human Rights: Origins, Drafting, and Intent.* Philadelphia: University of Pennsylvania Press, 1999.

Moyn, Samuel. *The Last Utopia: Human Rights in History.* Cambridge, MA: Harvard University Press, 2010.

Narayan, Uma. "Essence of Culture and a Sense of History: A Feminist Critique of Cultural Essentialism." In *Decentering the Center: Philosophy for a Multicultural, Postcolonial, and Feminist World,* edited by Uma Narayan and Sandra Harding, 80–100. Bloomington: Indiana University Press, 2000.

Newlands, George. *Christ and Human Rights: The Transformative Engagement.* Aldershot, UK: Ashgate, 1988.

Noonan, John T. *A Church That Can and Cannot Change: The Development of Catholic Moral Teaching.* Notre Dame, IN: University of Notre Dame Press, 2005.

———. "Development in Moral Doctrine." *Theological Studies* 54 (1993): 662–77.

Normand, Roger, and Sarah Zaidi. *Human Rights at the UN.* Bloomington: University of Indiana Press, 2008.

Novak, David. "God and Human Rights in a Secular Society: A Biblical-Talmudic Perspective." In *Does Human Rights Need God?,* edited by Elizabeth M. Bucar and Barbra Barnett, 48–57. Grand Rapids, MI: Eerdmans, 2005.

Novikova, Irina. "Lessons from the Anatomy of War: Svetlana Alexievich's Zinky Boys." In *War Discourse: Women's Discourse Essays and Case-Studies from Yugoslavia and Russia,* edited by Svetlana Slapšak, 99–116. Ljubljana: TOPOS, 2000.

Nozick, Robert. *Anarchy, State, and Utopia.* New York: Basic Books, 1974.

Nurser, John. *For All Nations and Peoples: The Ecumenical Church and Human Rights.* Washington, DC: Georgetown University Press, 2005.

Nussbaum, Martha. "Compassion: The Basic Social Emotion." *Social Philosophy and Policy* 13, no. 1 (Winter 1996): 27–58.

———. *Creating Capabilities: The Human Development Approach.* Cambridge, MA: Harvard University Press, 2011.

———. *Love's Knowledge: Essays on Philosophy and Literature.* New York: Oxford University Press, 1990.

———. *The New Religious Intolerance: Overcoming the Politics of Fear.* Cambridge, MA. Belknap Press of Harvard University, 2012.

———. *Women and Human Development: The Capabilities Approach.* Cambridge: Cambridge University Press, 2000.

Obiora, L. Amede. "Bridges and Barricades: Rethinking Polemics and Intransigence in the Campaign against Female Circumcision." *Case Western Reserve Law Review* 47, no. 2 (Winter 1997): 277–387.

O'Donovan, Joan Lockwood. "Historical Prolegomena to a Theological Review of 'Human Rights.'" *Studies in Christian Ethics* 9, no. 2 (1996): 52–65. doi:10.1177/095394689600900205.

O'Donovan, Oliver. *The Desire of the Nations: Rediscovering the Roots of Political Theology.* Cambridge: Cambridge University Press, 1996.

Oduyoye, Mercy Amba. "Christianity and African Culture." *International Review of Mission* 84 (1995): 86–87.

———. *Daughters of Anowa: African Women and Patriarchy.* Maryknoll, NY: Orbis, 1995.

Oppen, George. "Of Being Numerous (1–22)." *New Collected Poems.* New York: New Directions, 2008.

Orobator, Agbonkhiameghe. *Theology Brewed in an African Pot.* Maryknoll, NY: Orbis, 2008.

Owen, Wilfred. *Collected Poems of Wilfred Owen,* edited with an introduction and notes by C. Day Lewis, and with a memoir by Edmund Blunden. London: Chatto & Windus, 1963.

Parekh, Bhikhu. "Non-Ethnocentric Universalism." In *Human Rights in Global Politics,* edited by Tim Dunne and Nicholas Wheeler, 128–59. Cambridge: Cambridge University Press, 1999.

———. *Rethinking Multiculturalism: Cultural Diversity and Political Theory.* Hampshire, UK: Palgrave, 2006.

Parsons, Susan. *The Ethics of Gender.* Oxford: Blackwell, 2002.

Parry, John T. "Escalation and Necessity: Defining Torture at Home and Abroad." In *Torture: A Collection,* edited by Sanford Levinson, 145–64. Oxford: Oxford University Press, 2004.

Partnoy, Alicia. *The Little School Tales of Disappearance and Survival in Argentina.* London: Virago Press, 1988.

Perry, Michael. *Toward a Theory of Human Rights: Religion, Law, Courts.* Cambridge: Cambridge University Press, 2007.

Peters, Edward. *Torture.* Oxford: Blackwell, 1985.

Phan, Peter. "Multiple Religious Belonging: Opportunities and Challenges for Theology and Church." *Theological Studies* 64, no. 3 (September 2003): 495–519.

Phillips, Anne. *Multiculturalism without Culture.* Princeton, NJ: Princeton University Press, 2007.

Phiri, Isabel Apawo. "HIV/AIDS: An African Theological Response in Mission." In *Hope Abundant: Third World and Indigenous Women's Theology,* edited by Kwok Pui-lan, 219–28. Maryknoll, NY: Orbis, 2010.

Plongeron, Bernard. "Anathema or Dialogue? Christian Reactions to the Declarations of the Rights of Man in the United States and Europe in the Eighteenth

Century." In *The Church and the Rights of Man*, edited by Alois Muller and Norbert Greinacher. *Concilium* 4, no. 124 (1979): 1–16.

Pogge, Thomas W. *World Poverty and Human Rights*. Malden, MA: Blackwell, 2002.

Pollis, Adamantia. "Human Rights: A Western Construct with Limited Applicability." In *Human Rights: Cultural and Ideological Perspectives*, edited by Adamantia Pollis and Peter Schwab, 1–18. New York: Praeger, 1979.

Porter, Jean. "The Search for a Global Ethic." *Theological Studies* 62 (2001): 105–22.

Ratzinger, Cardinal Josef. "Cardinal Ratzinger on Europe's Crisis of Culture." *Catholic Education Resource Center*, April 1, 2005. Accessed July 27, 2012. http://catholiceducation.org/articles/politics/pg0143.html.

Raz, Joseph. *Ethics in the Public Domain: Essays in the Morality of Law and Politics*. Oxford, UK: Clarendon Press, 1994.

Reed, Esther. *The Ethics of Human Rights: Contested Doctrinal and Moral Issues*. Waco, TX: Baylor University Press, 2007.

Regan, Ethne. *Theology and the Boundary Discourse of Human Rights*. Washington, DC: Georgetown University Press, 2010.

Rich, Adrienne. *Blood, Bread, and Poetry: Selected Prose 1979–1985*. New York: W. W. Norton, 1986.

Richter, Cornelia. "The Productive Power of Reason." In *Faith in the Enlightenment? The Critique of the Enlightenment Revisited*, edited by Lieven Boeve, Joeri Schrijvers, Wessel Stoker, and Hendrik M. Vroom, 23–38. New York: Rodopi, 2006.

Roethke, Theodore. "In a Dark Time." In *Collected Poems of Theodore Roethke*. New York: Doubleday, 1961.

Rorty, Richard. "Human Rights, Rationality, and Sentimentality." In *On Human Rights: The Oxford Amnesty Lectures*, edited by Stephen Shute and Susan Hurley, 112–34. Oxford: Basic Books, 1993.

———. *Objectivity, Relativism, and Truth: Philosophical Papers*. Cambridge: Cambridge University Press, 1991.

———. *Philosophy and the Mirror of Nature*. Princeton, NJ: Princeton University Press, 1979.

———. *Philosophy and Social Hope*. London: Penguin, 1999.

———. "Response to Appiah." In *Globalising Rights: The Oxford Amnesty Lectures, 1999*, edited by Matthew Gibney, 233–37. Oxford: Oxford University Press, 2003.

———. *Truth and Progress: Philosophical Papers*. New York: Cambridge University Press, 1998.

Rowland, Tracy. *Culture and the Thomist Tradition after Vatican II*. London: Routledge, 2003.

Rudy, Kate. *Sex and the Church: Gender Homosexuality and the Transformation of Christian Ethics.* Boston: Beacon Press, 1997.

Ruston, Roger. *Human Rights and the Image of God.* London: SCM Press, 2004.

Ryan, Maura, and Brian Linnane. *A Just and True Love: Feminism at the Frontiers of Theological Ethics; Essays in Honor of Margaret A. Farley.* Notre Dame, IN: University of Notre Dame Press, 2007.

Said, Edward. *Culture and Imperialism.* London: Chatto & Windus, 1993.

Sandel, Michael. "The Procedural Republic and the Unencumbered Self." In *Communitarianism and Individualism*, edited by Shlomo Avineri and Avner de-Shalit, 12–28. Oxford: Oxford University Press, 1992.

Schmidt-Leukel, Perry. "Uniqueness: A Pluralistic Reading of John 14:6." In *Ecumenics from the Rim: Explorations in Honour of John D'Arcy May*, edited by John O'Grady and Peter Scherle, 303–14. Berlin: LIT Verlag, 2007.

Schwab, Peter. *Cuba: Confronting the US Embargo.* London: Macmillan, 1998.

Shachar, Aylelt. *Multicultural Jurisdictions: Cultural Differences and Women's Rights.* Cambridge: Cambridge University Press, 2001.

Shivji, Issa. *The Concept of Human Rights in Africa.* London: Codesria Book Series, 1989.

Shue, Henry. "Torture in Dreamland: Disposing of the Ticking Bomb." *Case Western Reserve Journal of International Law* 37 (2005): 231–39.

Silber, Laura, and Allan Little. *The Death of Yugoslavia.* Harmondsworth, UK: Penguin Books, 1996.

Simpson, A. W. B. *Human Rights and the End of Empire: Britain and the Genesis of the European Convention.* Oxford: Oxford University Press, 2001.

Solzhenitsyn, Aleksandr. *The Gulag Archipelago 1918–1956: An Experiment in Literary Imagination.* Translated from Russian by Thomas O. Whitney (Parts I–IV) and Harry Willets (Parts V–VII), edited from the original three-volume edition by Edward E. Ericson Jr. London: Folio Society, 2005.

Sontag, Susan. *Regarding the Pain of Others.* New York: Farrar, Straus and Giroux, 2003.

Spelman, Elizabeth. *Inessential Woman: Problems of Exclusion in Feminist Thought.* Boston: Beacon Press, 1988.

Spivak, Gayatri Chakravorty. "Can the Subaltern Speak?" In *Can the Subaltern Speak? Reflections on the History of an Idea*, edited by Rosalind C. Morris, 237–91. New York: Columbia University Press, 2010.

———. "In Response: Looking Back, Looking Forward." In *Can the Subaltern Speak? Reflections on the History of an Idea*, edited by Rosalind C. Morris, 227–36. New York: Columbia University Press, 2010.

———. "A Moral Dilemma." In *What Happens to History: The Renewal of Ethics in Contemporary Thought*, edited by Howard Marchitello, 215–36. New York: Routledge, 2001.

———. "Righting Wrongs." in *Human Rights, Human Wrongs*, edited by Nicholas Owen, 164–227. Oxford: Oxford University Press, 2002.

Stackhouse, Max. "Why Human Rights Needs God: A Christian Perspective." In *Does Human Rights Need God?*, edited by Elizabeth M. Bucar and Barbra Barnett, 25–40. Grand Rapids, MI: Eerdmans, 2005.

Statman, Daniel. "The Absoluteness of the Prohibition against Torture" [Hebrew]. 4 *Mishpat u-Mimshal*, 161 (1997), 161–98.

Steiner, George. *Real Presences: Is There Anything in What We Say?* London: Faber & Faber, 1989.

Steward, Julian. "Comments on the Statement on Human Rights." *American Anthropologist* 50, no. 2 (1948): 351–52.

Stout, Jeffrey. *Blessed Are the Organized: Grassroots Democracy in America*. Princeton, NJ: Princeton University Press, 2010.

———. *Democracy and Tradition*. Princeton, NJ: Princeton University Press, 2004.

Strauss, Leo. *Natural Right and History*. Chicago: University of Chicago Press, 1953.

———. *The Political Philosophy of Hobbes: Its Basis and Its Genesis*. Chicago: University of Chicago Press, 1952.

Sunder, Madhavi. "Cultural Dissent." *Stanford Law Review* 545 (December 2001): 495–567.

Taylor, Charles. *Dilemmas and Connections: Selected Essays*. Cambridge, MA: Harvard University Press, 2011.

———. *A Secular Age*. Cambridge, MA: Belknap Press of Harvard University Press, 2007.

———. *Sources of the Self: The Making of the Modern Identity*. Cambridge: Cambridge University Press, 1989.

Tierney, Brian. *The Idea of Natural Rights: Studies in Natural Rights, Natural Law, and Church Law, 1150–1625*. Atlanta: Scholars Press, 1997.

TOSTAN. *Breakthrough in Senegal: The Process That Ended Female Genital Cutting in 31 Villages*. Washington, DC: US Agency for International Development, 1999.

Triandafyllidou, Anna, Tariq Modood, and Nasar Meer. *European Multiculturalisms: Cultural, Religious and Ethnic Challenges*. Edinburgh, UK: Edinburgh University Press, 2012.

Twining, W. L., and P. E. Twining. "Bentham on Torture." *Northern Ireland Legal Quarterly* 24, no. 3 (1973): 305–56.

Twiss, Sumner, and Bruce Grelle. "Human Rights and Comparative Religious Ethics: A New Venue." *Annual of the Society of Christian Ethics* 33 (1995): 21–48.

Tylor, Edward Burnett. *Primitive Culture: Researches into the Development of Mythology, Philosophy, Religion, Art, and Custom*. London: John Murray, 1871.

Ucko, Hans. "Religious Plurality and Christian Self-Understanding." Preparatory paper no. 13, May 15, 2005. World Council of Churches website. Accessed September 3, 2009. www.oikoumene.org/en/resources/documents/other-meetings/mission-and-evangelismpreparatory-paper-13-religious-plurality-and-christian-self-understanding.

Vattimo, Gianni. Introduction to *An Ethics for Today: Finding Common Ground between Philosophy and Religion*, by Richard Rorty, 1–6. New York: Columbia University Press, 2008.

Villey, Michel. "La genèse du droit subjectif chez Guillaume d'Occam." *Archives de philospphie du droit* 9 (1964): 97–127.

Voparil, Christopher J., and Richard J. Bernstein, eds. *The Rorty Reader.* Oxford: Wylie-Blackwell, 2010.

Waldron, Jeremy, ed. *"Nonsense upon Stilts": Bentham, Burke and Marx on the Rights of Man.* London: Metheun Books, 1987.

Waltz, Susan. "Reclaiming and Rebuilding the History of the Universal Declaration of Human Rights." *Third World Quarterly* 23, no. 3 (2002): 437–48.

———. "Universal Human Rights: The Contribution of Muslim States." *Human Rights Quarterly* 26, no. 4 (2004): 799–844.

———. "Universalizing Human Rights: The Role of Small States in the Construction of the Universal Declaration of Human Rights." *Human Rights Quarterly* 23, no. 1 (2001): 44–72.

Walzer, Michael. *The Company of Critics: Social Criticism and Political Commitment in the Twentieth Century.* New York: Basic Books, 2002.

———. "Political Action: The Problem of Dirty Hands." *Philosophy and Public Affairs* 2 (1973): 160–67.

———. *Politics and Passion: Towards a More Egalitarian Liberalism.* New Haven, CT: Yale University Press, 2004.

———. *Thick and Thin: Moral Arguments at Home and Abroad.* Notre Dame, IN: University of Notre Dame Press, 1994.

Weil, Simone. *Gravity and Grace*, with an introduction and postscript by Gustave Thubon, translated by Emma Crawford and Mario von der Ruhr. London: Routledge, 2002.

Wiesel, Elie. *Night.* London: MacGibbon & Kee, 1960.

Wilfred, Felix. *Asian Public Theology: Critical Concerns in Challenging Times.* Dehli: ISPCK, 2010.

Witt, Charlotte. "Feminist Metaphysics." In *A Mind of One's Own: Feminist Essays on Reason and Objectivity*, edited by Louise M. Anthony and Charlotte Witt, 273–87. Boulder, CO: Westview Press, 1993.

Witt, John. *The Reformation of Rights: Law, Religion and Human Rights in Early Modern Calvinism.* Cambridge: Cambridge University Press, 2007.

Wolterstorff, Nicholas. *Justice: Rights and Wrongs*. Princeton NJ: Princeton University Press, 2008.

Wu, Rose. "A Story of Its Own Name: Hong Kong's *Tongzhi* Culture and Movement." In *Off the Menu: Asian and Asian North American Women's Religion and Theology*, edited by Rita Nakashima Brock, Jing Ha Kim, Kwok Pui-lan, and Seung Ai Yang, 275–92. Louisville, KY: Westminster John Knox Press, 2007.

Yanling, Meng. "Women, Faith and Marriage: A Feminist Look at the Challenges for Women." In *Hope Abundant: Third World and Indigenous Women's Theology*, edited by Kwok Pui-lan, 229–40. Maryknoll, NY: Orbis, 2010.

Yearley, Lee. *Mencius and Aquinas: Theories of Virtue and Conceptions of Courage*. Albany: State University of New York, 1990.

Yeğenoğlu, Meyda. "Sartorial Fabric-ations Enlightenment and Western Feminism." In *Postcolonialism, Feminism and Religious Discourse*, edited by Laura E Donaldson and Kwok Pui-lan, 82–99. New York: Routledge, 2002.

Yoder, John. *For the Nations: Essays Evangelical and Public*. Eugene, OR: Wipf and Stock, 2002.

———. *The Priestly Kingdom*. Notre Dame, IN: University of Notre Dame Press, 1984.

Yuval-Davis, Nira. *Gender and Nation*. 1997. Reprint, London: Sage, 2004.

Yuval-Davis, Nira, and Floya Anthias, eds. *Woman, Nation, State*. London: Macmillan, 1989.

Index

Abu Ghraib Paintings (Botero), 190–91
accommodation: cultural/religious values
  and gender norms, 151–56; Shachar's
  transformative accommodation model
  for cultural change, 159–60, 170n56;
  term, 65; and theological suspicions of
  liberalism, 57–65, 149
Adams, John, 60
Afnan, Bedia, 22, 23
Afshar, Haleh, 151
After Virtue (MacIntyre), 39
agency: agent-centered approaches to
  belonging and cultural membership,
  157–58; feminist critics on autonomy/
  cultural constraint and, 153–56
Ahmadu, Fuambai, 78
Ahmed, Leila, 151
Ai Weiwei, 192
Alanus, 59
Alatas, Ali, 27
Ali Khan, Begum Ra'ana Liaquat, 22
Allen, Anne Dondapati, 79
Althusius, Johannes, 60
American Anthropological Association
  (AAA), 16–18
Améry, Jean, 191
Amzi, Mahund, 22
Anabaptists, 65
Angelou, Maya, 179
Angle, Stephen, 56
An-Na'im, Abdullahi Ahmed, 18
Apel, Karl-Otto, 126
Appiah, Kwame Anthony, 7, 121, 160–62
Aquinas, Thomas, 65, 130
arts: and construction of a durable culture

of human rights, 9, 172–204; conveying
  the unspeakable and hidden, 189–90; expanding the moral imagination, 176–82;
  Heaney and "the redress of poetry,"
  177–79; and issue of humanitarian
  military uses of violence to halt human
  rights violations, 192–93; and issue of
  the nature of violence in war, 193–96,
  198, 203–4n63, 204n67; and issue of
  torture and its fundamental assault
  on human dignity, 183–92; literature,
  181–82; role of the arts in the expansion
  of human rights, 179, 180–82, 198–99;
  and "the education of the moral sentiments," 180–82; visual representations
  of violence and torture (representing the
  unrepresentable), 190–92, 196–99
Ashraf, Princess (Iran), 25–26
Asian Public Theology (Wilfred), 90
Asian values debate (1990s), 26–29, 37
At the Border V (Isolated Incident)
  (Doherty), 197–98
autonomy: and empathy (reciprocity),
  181–82; feminist and communitarian
  critiques, 92; feminists on questions of
  agency and cultural constraint, 153–56;
  postcolonial theologians on subjectivity
  and, 91–93
Azo of Bologna, 184

Bagaric, Mirko, 186
Baier, Annette, 41–42, 180
Baker, Ella, 65
Baroody, Jamil, 25
Barth, Karl, 65

Bauman, Zygmunt, 42
Baxi, Upendra, 13, 36, 39
Beauvoir, Simone de, 73
Beccaria, Cesare, 184–85
Beijing Fourth World Conference on Women (1995), 151
belonging: and agent-centered approaches to cultural membership, 157–58; community and the shape of, 145–47, 206
Benhabib, Seyla, 7
Bentham, Jeremy, 1, 186
Bernauer, James, 35
Beza, Theodore, 60
Bhabha, Homi, 143–44, 145, 147
Biggar, Nigel, 193
Birla, Rita, 83
Boas, Franz, 17
body. See embodiment
Borland, Christine, 197, 198
Botero, Fernando, 179, 190–91, 192
Bourdieu, Pierre, 125
Boutros-Ghali, Boutros, 12–13
Braidotti, Rosi, 92, 145–47
Buddhism, 55, 150
Bujo, Bénézet, 145
Burke, Roland, 20–24, 44n9
Burlamaqui, Jean-Jacques, 62–
Butler, Judith, 6; on the concept of the human, 36; postmodern challenge to gender essentialism, 74–76, 97n7; on the violent/nonviolent response to living the ambiguity of difference, 96

Cairo Declaration of Human Rights in Islam, 28, 47n48
Calas, Jean, 185
Caleb Foundation, 148
Calvinism, 60, 62
"Can the Subaltern Speak?" (Spivak), 82–83, 99n29
Care and Compassion: Methodologies in Sharing Values across Cultures and Religions (Nairobi, 2009), 126–27

Cassin, René, 19, 21–22
Catholic Commission of Bishops' Conferences of the European Community (COMECE), 148–49
Cavanaugh, William, 52, 63–64
Chan, Lucas, 164
Chang, Peng Chung, 18, 19, 22
Chatterjee, Partha, 82
Chesterman, Simon, 42
Clarke, Julie, 186
Clooney, Francis, 124
Coles, Romand, 65
colonialism: "colonial clause" in the UN Declaration draft covenant, 20–24; neocolonialism, 25, 29; postcolonial deconstruction of the concept of community, 145; postcolonial political self-determination and idea of human rights, 118; and unlearning historic entitlements to speak for the marginalized, 86–87. See also postcolonial theological critiques of human rights discourse
communitarian critique of human rights discourse, 6–7, 30–43; and the Asian values debate, 27; and autonomy, 92; concept of community, 144; and liberalism's normative conception of the unencumbered self, 31–33, 48n58; philosophical critique of human rights, 30–43, 48n58, 50n84; on the processes of social embodiment, 32
community, concept of, 144–47; agent-centered approaches to belonging and cultural membership, 157–58; postcolonial deconstruction of, 145–47; and the shape of belonging, 145–47, 206; as site of pluralism in the articulation of a renewed human rights ethic, 144–47; stereotype of unitary, 144–47; theological critique of, 146. See also culture, category of; tradition, category of
Confucianism, 55, 57, 164
constructivist political philosophy, 3, 5;

Dworkin's foundationless approach to human rights foundations, 115–16; feminist challenge to conceptualizations of embodiment, 76. *See also* personhood (constructing the subject of human rights: the human person)

Convention against Torture and Other Cruel, Inhuman or Degrading Treatment or Punishment, 183–84

Convention on the Political Rights of Women, 21, 22–23

Cornell, Drucilla, 83

Cornille, Catherine, 146

correspondence theories of truth, 40–41, 107–8

Cranston, Maurice, 59

Croce, Benedetto, 56

cultural change, 157–64; Appiah on moral revolutions/the code of honor and, 160–61; and dialogue in the multireligious pluralist public square, 122, 162–66; and established hierarchies and cultural gatekeepers, 159; the role of immanent cultural critiques, 161–62; Shachar's transformative accommodation model for promoting, 159–60, 170n56

cultural rights, 110–12

culture, category of, 139–44, 156–66; and agent-centered approaches to belonging, 157–58; the anatomy of cultural change, 157–64; cultural interpretations of embodiment, 77–80, 129; cultural/ moral relativism and the universality of human rights claims, 16–18, 20–29, 104–13; debates about multiculturalism, 140, 152–56; and dialogue in the multireligious pluralist public square, 122, 162–66; and the exit option (right to exit), 156–57; feminist critics' deconstructions of the stereotype of, 141–44, 153; feminist critics on question of agency/autonomy and cultural constraint, 153–56; issue of gender norms and extent to which cultural values can be accommodated, 151–56; postcolonial critique of, 143–44; reimagining as a site of emancipatory politics, 156–66; as site of pluralism in the articulation of a renewed human rights ethic, 139–44, 156–66; stereotype of essentialism and, 139–44

Danner, Mark, 186

Davila, Maria Teresa, 145

Day, Dorothy, 65

Declaration of the Rights of Man and of the Citizen (1789), 58, 149

Decolonization and the Evolution of International Human Rights (Burke), 20–21, 44n9

de la Chapelle, Philippe, 44n9

Deleuze, Gilles, 83

Dershowitz, Alan, 186–87

Descartes, René, 42

Dewey, John, 41

dialogue, multireligious and cross-cultural, 9, 103, 120–31, 162–66, 175, 206–7; discourse that attends to the politics of power, 125–29; discourse that proceeds from an acknowledgment of the depth of difference, 129–31; learning from comparative theology and interreligious dialogue, 123–25; as multidimensional, multimethodological, and multidisciplinary discourse, 124–25

Diderot, Denis, 185

dignity, human: Morsink on human rights and shared belief in, 117; and plural foundations of human rights discourse drawing on diverse moral frameworks, 103, 117–20; torture and the fundamental assault on, 183–92

Disasters of War (Goya), 190, 202n48

Discipline and Punish (Foucault), 34, 42, 49n68

Dobbernack, Jan, 113

Doherty, Willie, 188–89, 197–98

Donnelly, Jack, 114–15, 132n21
Drakulić, Slavenka, 195
Dukes, Charles, Lord Dukeston, 110
Dworkin, Gerald, 55, 154–55
Dworkin, Ronald, 115–16
A Dying Colonialism (Fanon), 79

economic and social rights, 19, 91, 100n40, 110–12, 132n13
economic lives: and global capitalism, 90, 92; postcolonial critics on the economic dimension of experience and the construction of subjectivity, 89–93, 100n40; UN Declaration's inclusion of economic and social rights, 19, 91, 100n40
Ecuador, maternal health clinics in, 13
Éla, Jean-Marc, 90
Elshtain, Jean Bethke, 193
embodiment: communitarian theory on the processes of social, 32; debate over female genital cutting in Africa, 77–78; diversity of cultural interpretations of, 77–80, 129; feminist conceptualizations of, 76–80; the issue of Muslim women's veiling, 79
EMILIE Project (*A European Approach to Multicultural Citizenship: Legal, Political and Multicultural Challenges*), 162
empathy: and autonomy, 181–82; and role of the arts in expansion of the moral imagination, 180–82; Rorty's argument for grounding human rights in, 57, 116, 133n25, 180–81
Encyclopedia (Diderot), 185
Enlightenment: critiques of enlightenment rationalism, 3, 30, 38, 42, 175, 205; ethical case against torture, 184–85; Foucault on, 42; grand narrative and legacies of, 14–15, 38, 118, 173; voluntarism, 60–62
epistemological assumptions of human rights discourse, 6–7, 101–35, 174–75, 206. *See also* foundationalism, human

rights; universality of human rights truth claims
Essay on Crimes and Punishment (Beccaria), 185
essentialism: cultural, 139–44; feminist and postmodern challenges to binary gender essentialism, 73–76; feminist critiques of the cultural, 141–44, 153; liberal feminism and gender essentialism, 73–74, 97n5; Spivak on adopting "practices of strategic essentialism," 95
ethical pluralism, 7–9, 15–18, 28, 112–13, 136–71, 205; the AAA and the UN Declaration debates, 16–18; the category of culture, 139–44; the category of tradition, 147–50; the concept of community, 144–47; deconstructing stereotypes of culture, community, and tradition, 139–50; and dialogue of voices in the multireligious pluralist public square, 9, 103, 120–31, 162–66, 175, 206–7; feminist scholars and, 141–44, 151–56; and the limits of accommodation, 151–56; plural foundations for human rights drawing on diverse moral frameworks, 103, 117–20; postcolonial critiques, 145–47; reimagining culture as a site of emancipatory politics, 156–66; and the universality of human rights, 15–18, 112–20
European Parliament's Resolution on Homophobia, 165
European Union Draft Charter of Fundamental Rights, 148–49

Fanon, Frantz, 79
Farley, Margaret, 91–92
Fassin, Didier, 143
female genital cutting, 77–78, 142–43, 153
feminist critics of human rights discourse, 1–3, 38–39; on agency/autonomy and cultural constraint, 153–56; and alternative conceptualizations of personhood, 71, 72–80; challenges to binary gender

essentialism, 73–76; conceptualizations of embodiment, 76–80; deconstructions of culture, 141–44, 153; gender equality/norms and the limits of accommodation to religious values, 151–56; on paradoxes of women's positions in religious communities, 151–52; and reason, 42–43; rethinking assumptions about what is natural for human beings ("troubling the natural"), 71, 72–80; tensions between feminism and multiculturalism, 152–56

Feyissa, Abebe, 88–89

Finnis, John, 55

Foucault, Michel, 6; and the burden of representing the subaltern, 83; on the Enlightenment project, 42; philosophical critique of human rights, 33–37, 42–43; politics of the self (and cultural context), 33–37, 49n67, 49n68, 71; on production of knowledge enmeshed in power regimes, 42–43; on sexuality and the self, 34, 77; "subjugated knowledges," 36, 43

foundationalism, human rights: alternative of plural foundations drawing on diverse moral frameworks, 103, 117–20; critiques and debate over, 40–42, 52, 103, 113–20, 180–81; Donnelly on, 114–15; Dworkin's foundationless constructivist approach, 115–16; Ignatieff on, 114, 132n19; Morsink on necessity of metaphysical foundations and epistemic universality, 116–19; recommendations to abandon discussion of metaphysical foundations, 114–16, 132n19, 132n21, 180–81; Rorty's argument for grounding human rights in empathy and compassion, 57, 116, 133n25, 180–81; Rorty's pragmatist critique and rejection of, 40–42, 52, 116, 180–81. *See also* universality of human rights truth claims

Foundations of Violence (Jantzen), 198

Fox, George, 65

French revolution, 15, 57–58

Frost, Robert, 178

Gardiner, Lord Gerald Austin, 187–88

Gearty, Conor: on future of human rights discourse, 2, 4–5, 13, 43–44, 205; on postmodern uncertainty, 30, 205

Geffré, Claude, 146

gender norms: and cultural interpretations of embodiment, 77–80, 129; feminist and postmodern challenges to binary gender essentialism, 73–76; feminist conceptualizations of embodiment, 76–80; and homosexuality, 165; liberal feminism and gender essentialism, 73–74, 97n5; and the limits of accommodation to cultural/religious values, 151–56; non-Western examples of ambivalent constructions of gender, 74–75. *See also* women's human rights

Geneva Conventions, 183–84, 185, 203–4n63; Additional Protocol I, 184

Gewith, Alan, 38, 55

Ginbar, Yuval, 188

Glendon, Mary Ann, 18

"global ethic" project, 134n38

globalization, 4, 12, 90, 92, 145

Glover, Jonathan, 63–64

God, Science, Sex, Gender: An Interdisciplinary Approach to Christian Ethics (Jung and Vigen, eds.), 75

Godfrey of Fontaines, 59

Górecki, Henryk, 190

Goya, Francisco, 179, 190, 192, 202n48

Gratian, 59

Gravity and Grace (Weil), 177

Gray, John, 14

Gregory XVI, Pope, 149

Gross, Oren, 187

Guattari, Félix, 83

Guha, Ranajit, 98n23

Gunewardene, Ratnakirti, 25

Gushee, David, 187
Gutman, Amy, 119

Habermas, Jürgen, 126, 134n44
Hall, Stuart, 14–15
Hauerwas, Stanley, 52, 63–65, 104
Havel, Václav, 182
Heaney, Seamus, 94, 147, 177–79, 182
Himes, Kenneth, 186, 193
Hinduism, 85–86, 150
The History of Sexuality (Foucault), 42
Hobbes, Thomas, 68n21
Hollenbach, David, 2, 57, 88, 193
Holocaust Memorial Museum (Washington, DC), 192
homosexuality, 165
Honneth, Axel, 113
The Honor Code (Appiah), 160
humanitarian military interventions, 192–93
Humanity: A Moral History of the Twentieth Century (Glover), 63–64
Human Rights Commission on the Bill of Rights (Northern Ireland), 148–49
human rights discourse, 1–4; contingent character of development of, 5, 11n8, 207–8; evolution and expansion of, 15–16, 56–57, 109–12, 118–19, 172, 179–82, 199n12, 207–8; Gearty on future of, 2, 4–5, 13, 43–44, 205; global appeal of, 4, 113, 118–19, 120–23, 133n32; Joas's "affirmative genealogical" approach to, 207–8, 209n2; reconceptualization and renewed understanding of, 3–4, 172–76, 205–9; three pillars of, 5, 173–76, 206. See also ethical pluralism
Human Rights Watch, 201–2n47
Hume, David, 41–42, 180
Humphrey, John, 19, 22
Hunt, Lynne, 181–82

Ignatieff, Michael, 56, 114, 132n19
Ikramullah, Shaista, 19

incommensurability, language of, 39
India: gender caste, 74–75; Mies's study of lacemakers of Narsapur, 90–91; Spivak's discussion of sati and the itinerary of silence, 85–86; subaltern studies, 98n23
Inessential Woman: Problems of Exclusion in Feminist Thought (Spelman), 97n5
Inherent Human Rights (Morsink), 2, 96n1
International Bill of Rights, 54
International Conference on Human Rights in Tehran (1968), 47n49, 111
International Convention on the Elimination of All Forms of Racial Discrimination (1965), 47n49
International Covenant on Civil and Politics Rights (1966), 111, 183
International Covenant on Economic, Social and Cultural Rights (1966), 100n40, 111
International Criminal Tribunal for the Former Yugoslavia at The Hague, 194–95, 203–4n63
Inventing Human Rights: A History (Hunt), 181
Islam: Cairo Declaration of Human Rights, 28, 47n48; evolutionary nature of the tradition, 150; the issue of women's veiling, 79, 153, 154; the public square and secular/religious conflicts, 163–64; Shar'ia law, 20, 28, 47n47; theological arguments in support of human rights, 54–55, 67n7; women's human rights, 22
"Is Multiculturalism Bad for Women?" (Okin), 152

Jaggar, Alison, 159
Jantzen, Grace, 198
Jefferson, Thomas, 62
Joas, Hans, 207–8, 209n2
Judah, Tim, 195
Judaism: evolutionary nature of the tradition, 150; theological arguments in support of human rights, 54–55, 67n7

Jung, Patricia Beattie, 75
just war tradition, 193

Kant, Immanuel, 38, 55, 91–92
Kao, Grace, 119
Kayala, Abdul Rahman, 18
Keenan, James, 92, 164
Khalili, Abdul Karim, 191–92
King, Martin Luther, Jr., 65
Klug, Francesca, 53–54, 66n3
knowledge, situated, 108–13, 174–75, 206
Kwok, Pui-lan, 6, 7, 72, 96n2, 104; on the challenges associated with conceiving human subjectivity, 90, 93; characterization of the nature of religious pluralism, 132n16; critique of category of cultural difference, 144; critique of concept of community, 145

Laclau, Ernesto, 36
Langlois, Anthony, 29–30
Lauren, Paul Gordon, 18–19
Laurentius, 59
The Law of Peoples (Rawls), 120
Lear, Jonathan, 208, 209n6
Lee Kuan Yew, 27–28
Leenhardt, Maurice, 79, 81
Levi, Primo, 191, 192
Levinas, Emmanuel, 84
Levy, Jacob, 141
liberalism, theological critique of, 57–65, 149. *See also* theological critique of liberal human rights discourse
Liu Huaqiu, 28
The Location of Culture (Bhabha), 143–44
Locke, John, 49–50n76, 62, 68n21, 69n39

MacDonald, Margaret, 31
MacIntyre, Alasdair, 32, 37–40, 49n76, 59, 115
Madness and Civilization (Foucault), 34, 42
Mahathir Mohamad, 27–28
Mahoney, Jack, 2

Malik, Charles, 18
Maritain, Jacques, 31, 56
May, John D'Arcy, 131
Mehta, Hansa, 18
Melanesian culture, 79
Mencius, 130
Mennonites, 65
Menon, Lakshmi, 22
Merry, Susan Engle, 142
Mies, Maria, 90–91
Milbank, John, 52, 63
Milosz, Czeslaw, 192
Milton, John, 60
Mirari vos (Gregory XVI), 58, 149
Modernity and the Holocaust (Bauman), 42
Modood, Tariq, 113
Moore, Michael, 187
Morrison, Toni, 191
Morsink, Johannes, 116–19; on doctrine of simple inherence, 117; on "epistemic universality," 37; on future of human rights discourse, 2; on moral intuitionism, 50n78; on UN Declaration draft debates, 18–19, 96n1, 116–17, 132n13
Mouffe, Chantal, 36
Moyn, Samuel, 11n8, 47–48n49
multiculturalism, 140, 152–56. *See also* culture, category of
Multiculturalism without Culture (Phillips), 152–53

Narayan, Uma, 141–42
National Constituent Assembly of France (1789), 57–58, 149
natural law tradition, 38, 49n76, 59–63; historical antecedents for Christian theological language of rights, 59–63, 68n21; Stoic and Christian concept of human nature, 30–31; the universality claim and Christian language of, 107
neocolonialism, 25, 29
Neruda, Pablo, 179
Newlands, George, 2

The New Religious Intolerance (Nussbaum), 163

Ni Putes Ni Soumises, 163

Noonan, John, 148

Nozick, Robert, 48n56

Núñez, Guillermo, 190, 191–92

Nurser, John, 2

Nussbaum, Martha, 55, 57, 163–64

Obiora, Leslye Amede, 78

O'Donovan, Joan Lockwood, 61–62, 63

O'Donovan, Oliver, 61, 63

Oduyoye, Mercy Amba, 6, 72, 90

Oechsler, Monica, 197–98

Okin, Susan Moller, 152

The Order of Things (Foucault), 49n67

Orend, Brian, 193

Orobator, Agbonkhiameghe, 6, 72, 90

Owen, Wilfred, 178–79

Pacem in Terris (John XXIII), 148

Parekh, Bhikhu, 145

Paris Peace Conference (1919), 118

Parry, John T., 187

Partnoy, Alicia, 191, 192

Perry, Michael, 53, 54–55

personhood, nature of, 6, 70–100, 173–74, 206; and ethical responsibility in human rights discourse, 83–85; the experience of situated individuals, 88, 93–96; feminist challenges to binary gender essentialism, 73–76; feminist conceptualizations of embodiment, 76–80; feminist rethinking of traditional Western assumptions ("troubling the natural"), 71, 72–80; and human rights discourse that starts from the bonds of difference, 72, 87–96; issues of autonomy and subjectivity, 91–93; philosophical objections to concept of human nature (the problem of the unencumbered self), 30–33; postcolonial theologians and alternative conceptualizations of, 72, 87–96; rendering visible the experiences of the unseen and marginalized, 71–72, 80–87; Spivak and "the burden of representation," 71–72, 81–85, 99n29, 99n34; the UN Declaration and concept of human nature, 32–33, 70, 96n1. *See also* subjectivity

Phan, Peter, 146

Phillips, Anne, 142–43, 152–56

philosophical objections to concept of human rights, 13, 29–43; the communitarian critique, 6–7, 30–43, 48n58, 50n84; critique of concept of human nature (the problem of the unencumbered self), 30–33; critique of human rights foundationalism, 40–42, 52, 113–20, 180–81; critique of universal rationality (moral reason), 37–43; feminist critique, 38–39; Foucault, 33–37, 42–43; MacIntyre, 37–39, 40; postcolonial perspective, 36–37; Rorty, 40–42. *See also* foundationalism, human rights; universality of human rights truth claims

Philosophy and the Mirror of Nature (Rorty), 40

Phiri, Isabel Apawo, 79

Picasso, Pablo, 179

Pius VI, Pope, 58, 149

pluralism. *See* ethical pluralism

poetry: First World War, 178–79; the redress of, 177–79

Pogge, Thomas, 116, 119–20

Political Liberalism (Rawls), 120

Politics and Passion (Walzer), 32

Pollis, Adamantia, 15

Porter, Jean, 130

postcolonial theological critiques of human rights discourse, 1–3; and alternative conceptualizations of personhood and subjectivity, 72, 87–96; critique of category of culture, 143–44; critique of the concept of community, 145–47; and the economic dimension of experience, 89–93, 100n40; on issues of subjectivity and autonomy, 91–93; and reason, 42–43; writing from perspective of the marginalized, 88–93

postmodern critique of human rights discourse, 30–43; Butler's challenge to gender essentialism, 74–76, 97n7; and feminist challenges to binary gender essentialism, 73–76; and postmodern uncertainty, 30, 205

poststructuralism, 71–72, 88, 96n2

power, politics of: addressing power relations and differentials, 127–29; Foucault on production of knowledge, 42–43; human rights dialogue that attends to the genealogical issue of, 125–29

public square: ensuring civility and respect in, 165; multireligious, pluralist dialogue in, 9, 103, 120–31, 162–66, 175, 206–7; secularist assumptions of religion in, 122; Wilfred's concept of the public sphere, 129–30

Pufendorf, Samuel von, 62

Que hay en el fondo de tus ojos (What is there in the depth of your eyes) (Núñez), 191–92

The Quickening, the Lightening, the Crowning (Borland), 198

Quod aliquantum (Pius VI), 58

racial categories, language of, 141, 166n9

radical hope, 208, 209n6

rationality, universal, 37–43

Rawls, John, 120, 131n9

Raz, Joseph, 130–31

redress of poetry, 177–79

The Redress of Poetry (Heaney), 177–79

Reed, Esther, 2

Reformed tradition, 58, 148–49

Refugee Rights, Ethics, Advocacy and Africa (Hollenbach, ed.), 88–89

Regan, Eithne, 2

Regarding the Pain of Others (Sontag), 196, 204n67

Reimer, David Peter, 97n7

relativism: and contingent knowledge, 104–13; and the correspondence use of truth, 40–41, 107; Stout on context dependent process of adjudication of ethical claims, 104–7; the UN Declaration debates, 16–18, 20–29; and the universality of human rights, 17–18, 20–29, 104–13

religious traditions: the evolution of, 147–50, 158–59; feminist critics on paradoxes of women's position in context of, 151–52; gender norms and accommodation to, 151–56; role of the Christian tradition in a renewed human rights discourse, 3, 9, 206–7; theological dimensions of the relationship between Christianity and liberalism, 63–65. *See also* Buddhism; Confucianism; dialogue, multireligious and cross-cultural; Hinduism; Islam; Judaism; Roman Catholic Church; theological critique of liberal human rights discourse

Responsibility to Protect doctrine, 193

Richter, Cornelia, 38

The Rights of Man and Natural Law (Maritain), 31

Robespierre, Maximilien de, 62

Roethke, Theodore, 189

Roman Catholic Church: debate about homosexuality and same-sex relationships, 165; the evolution of the moral tradition of, 148–49, 158–59; suspicion of liberalism and the politics of accommodation, 58, 149

Romero, Oscar, 65

Rorty, Richard, 7, 107, 133n25; Amnesty Lecture, 41; argument for grounding human rights in empathy and compassion, 57, 116, 133n25, 180–81; and correspondence use of truth, 40–41, 107; critique of human rights and universal rationality, 40–42; pragmatist argument against

Rorty, Richard (*continued*)
  human rights foundationalism, 40–42,
    52, 116, 180–81
"Ruins and Poetry" (Milosz), 192
Ruston, Roger, 58, 62, 69n39
Rwandan genocide (1994), 193

Said, Edward, 14
Sandel, Michael, 31–32, 34, 48n58
sati, 85–86
Schmidt-Leukel, Perry, 147
Secretion (Doherty film and text), 188–89
A Secular Age (Taylor), 137
Shachar, Ayelet, 159, 170n56
Shar'ia law, 20, 28, 47n47
*Sharing Values: A Hermeneutics for Global
  Ethics* (Cisneros and Premawardhana,
  eds.), 126
Shivji, Issa, 18
Shue, Henry, 192
silence, itinerary of: and the redress of
  poetry, 179; Spivak on humanities
  education as resource in addressing, 179;
  Spivak's discussion of *sati* and, 85–86
situated individuals, 88, 93–96. *See also*
  personhood, nature of
situated knowledge, 108–13, 174–75, 206
Solzhenitsyn, Aleksandr, 188
Sontag, Susan, 196–97, 198, 204n67
Spivak, Gayatri Chakravorty, 6, 81–87;
  on adopting "practices of strategic es-
    sentialism," 95; discussion of *sati* and
  the itinerary of silence, 85–86; on ethical
  responsibility in human rights discourse,
  83–85; on humanities education, 179;
  and postcolonial deconstruction of the
  concept of community and the shape
  of belonging, 145; on the subaltern and
  "the burden of representation," 71–72,
  81–85, 99n29, 99n34
Stackhouse, Max, 55
Statman, Daniel, 187
Steiner, George, 94

Stevens, Wallace, 178
Stout, Jeffrey, 7, 39, 104–7, 131n4
Strauss, Leo, 68n21
Strip (Oechsler), 197
subaltern studies, 82, 98n23. *See also* Spivak, Gayatri Chakravorty
subjectivity, postcolonial theologians on,
  72, 87–96; attention to material conditions, 90–91; and economic dimension
  of experience, 89–93, 100n40; issues of
  autonomy and, 91–93. *See also* personhood, nature of
Suharto, 27–28, 127
Sunder, Madhavi, 158
Sunflower Seeds (Ai Weiwei), 192

Taylor, Charles, 32, 49–50n76, 137, 166n4
Temple, William, 122
theological critique of liberal human rights
  discourse, 2, 52–69; and arguments for
  a secular grounding, 56–57; debate over
  the theological appropriation of human
  rights language in Christian social ethics, 59–65; MacIntyre's indictment of
  liberal moral reasoning, 37–39, 49n76;
  the "new traditionalists," 57–58; and the
  normative conception of the unencumbered self, 32, 34; objections to a secular/
  nonreligious grounding for human
  rights politics, 53–57; and relationship
  between Christianity and liberalism,
  63–65; suspicions of liberalism, 57–65,
  149. *See also* postcolonial theological
  critiques of human rights discourse
Tierney, Brian, 4, 58–59, 62
torture, 183–92; eighteenth-century ethical
  case against, 184–85; as fundamental
  assault on human dignity, 183–92; and
  humanitarian laws of war, 183–84,
  185; international agreements regulating, 183–84, 187; and the language of
  enhanced interrogation techniques,
  185–86, 189–91; post-9/11 legal and

moral arguments justifying, 183, 185–89; reports of human rights organizations, 201–2n47; role of art and visual portrayals of, 190–92; role of art in conveying the unspeakable and hidden, 189–90; survivor testimonies, 190, 191, 202–2n47; the ticking bomb scenario, 186–88

tradition, category of, 147–50; bringing a genealogical perspective to, 7–8, 149–50; the evolution of religious tradition, 147–50, 158–59; as site of ethical pluralism in the articulation of a renewed human rights ethic, 147–50; stereotype of unchanging timelesssness, 147–50. *See also* community, concept of; culture, category of

Twiss, Sumner, 121

Tylor, Edward B., 139

Ucko, Hans, 147

UN Commission on Human Rights, 24; Resolution 1235 (1967), 24–25; Resolution 1503 (1970), 25

UN Committee on Human Rights, 24

UN Declaration on Granting Independence to Colonial Countries and Peoples, 47n49

UN Economic and Social Council (Resolution 75), 24

UNESCO Symposium on Human Rights (1947), 56

UN General Assembly, 1, 16, 29

UN High Commissioner for Human Rights, 24–26

universalism, embedded, 108–13, 174–75, 206

universality of human rights truth claims: and the Asian values debate (1990s), 26–29, 37; and concept of "epistemic universality," 37; and the debate on women's human rights, 21, 22–23; debate over creation of the position of High Commissioner for Human Rights,

24–26; debate over the "colonial clause" in the draft covenant, 20–24; Foucault's politics of the self and critique of, 33–37, 49n67, 49n68; the link to Western political hegemony, 14–16; philosophical critiques of foundationalism, 40–42, 52, 113–20, 180–81; political debates about, 13, 14–29; and relativism, 16–18, 20–29, 104–13; rethinking the claim to, 37–43, 101–13, 174–75, 207; and UN Declaration debates, 16–29, 32–33, 70, 96n1. *See also* foundationalism, human rights

UN Universal Declaration of Human Rights (1948), 1–2, 5, 15, 16–29, 70, 207; Article 2, 22–23, 33; Article 5, 78, 183; Article 21, 18–19, 22–23, 45n19; and concept of human nature, 32–33, 70, 96n1; and cultural relativism, 16–18, 20–29; cultural rights, 110–12; debate over inclusion of a "colonial clause" in the draft covenant, 20–24; debates over adoption, 16–20; economic and social rights, 19, 91, 100n40, 110–12, 132n13; gender norms and women's human rights, 21, 22–23, 151; and Heaney's concept of the redress of poetry, 177; and human nature (the unencumbered self), 32–33; political debates about the universality of human rights, 16–29; the right of the individual to full development, 110; second- and third-generation rights, 110–12; Third Committee debates, 18–19, 22–23, 29, 45n19, 96n1, 110–12

Values for a Godless Age (Klug), 53–54, 66n3

Vattimo, Gianni, 41, 104

Vicentius Hispanus, 59

Vienna Declaration (1993), 26–29, 37

Vigen, Aana Marie, 75

Villey, Michel, 68n21

Vitoria, Francisco de, 65

Voltaire, 184–85

Waltz, Susan, 18–19

Walzer, Michael, 39, 138, 186; critique of liberalism's normative conception of the unencumbered self, 32, 34; on immanent cultural criticism, 161–62; and just war tradition, 193

war: First World War poetry, 178–79; humanitarian laws of, 183–84, 185; humanitarian military interventions, 192–93; just war tradition, 193; violence in, 193–96, 198, 203–4n63, 204n67. *See also* torture

Warning SHOTS! (2000 art exhibition), 197

We Are Church movement, 158

Weil, Simone, 177, 182

Wiesel, Elie, 191

Wilfred, Felix, 7, 90, 129–30

Winthrop, John, 60

Witte, John, Jr., 58, 60–62

Wittgenstein, Ludwig, 40

Wolff, Christian, 62

Wolterstorff, Nicholas, 53, 55, 57, 62

women's human rights: and the Convention on the Political Rights of Women, 21, 22–23; female genital cutting, 77–78, 142–43, 153; and the limits of accommodation to cultural/religious values, 151–56; and multiculturalism, 152–53; Muslim women's veiling, 79, 153, 154; the UN Declaration debate, 21, 22–23, 151. *See also* gender norms

World Conference on Human Rights in Vienna (1993), 26–29, 37

Wu, Rose, 79

Yanling, Meng, 79

Yearley, Lee, 130

Yeğenoğlu, Meyda, 79

Yoder, John, 61, 63–64

Yuval-Davis, Nira, 151